Hippocrene Companion Guide to
BRITAIN

Hippocrene Companion Guide to BRITAIN

England, Scotland & Wales

Henry Weisser

HIPPOCRENE BOOKS
New York

Copyright © 1993 By Henry Weisser

All rights reserved, including the right to reproduce this book or portions thereof in any form.

Photos by the author.

For information, address:
HIPPOCRENE BOOKS, INC.
171 Madison Avenue
New York, NY 10016

Library of Congress Cataloging-in-Publication Data
Weisser, Henry, 1935-
    Hippocrene companion guide to Britain : England, Scotland & Wales / Henry Weisser
        p.   cm.
    Includes index.
    ISBN 0-7818-0147-8 $14.95
    1. Great Britain—Guidebooks. I. Title
DA650.W36   1993
914.104'859—dc20   93-23036
       CIP

Printed in the United States of America

CONTENTS

Introduction	7
CHAPTER ONE: **Travel: Some Practical Advice**	11
Some Basics	11
Accommodations	16
A Few Practical Hints on Luggage and What to Bring	23
Using the Telephone	25
Food	26
The Hapless Pedestrian	37
Driving	38
Travel by Rail	53
Taking the Bus	55
Shopping	56
Getting Along with the British	58
Confronting American Characteristics in Britain	67
CHAPTER TWO: **Travel: What to See in Britain**	75
Working Out a Strategy	75
London	83
Strategies for Scotland	98
Strategies for Wales	103
Castles	104
Cathedrals	110
Stately Homes	120
Colorful Historic Cities, Towns and Villages	125
CHAPTER THREE: **Understanding British Geography, Economics and Sociology**	137
Understanding British Geography	137
Significant Aspects of the British Economy	148
Class and Gender in Britain	157
CHAPTER FOUR: **Understanding Aspects of British Culture**	165
Language	165

Education	184
Television and Radio	195
Religion	197
CHAPTER FIVE: **Understanding British Politics**	207
Understanding the British Parliamentary System	208
Understanding the British Monarchy	216
Understanding British Political Parties	228
Sensitive Areas in Politics	233
CHAPTER SIX: **Understanding British History**	251
Introduction: Why It Is Important to Get a Grip on British History	251
Prehistoric Britain	254
Roman Britain	255
Anglo-Saxon England, 450-1066	256
Medieval Britain, 1066-1485	258
The Age of the Tudors, 1485-1603	263
The Stuart Era, 1603-1714	268
The Georgian Era, 1714-1789	275
Britain in an Age of Revolution	279
The Early Nineteenth Century	283
The Magnificent Victorian Era, 1837-1901	285
The Edwardian Era, 1901-1914	289
The Era of World War I	291
The Interwar Era, 1918-1939	295
The Era of World War II, 1939-1945	298
The Postwar Era, 1945 to the Present	301
Index	311

MAPS

The West End of London: A Simple Diagram	88
The Parts of the Island of Britain	139

INTRODUCTION

THIS is not an ordinary book about Britain. Part of it is about travel and the rest of it is about everything else: culture, politics, geography, economics, and history. It is written for various groups of thoughtful people: prospective travelers, those who have been to Britain and want to understand more about what they have experienced, students and Anglophiles in general. Anyone involved in Anglo-American relationships might get some insights from it. It also ought to be useful for those who plan to spend six months or a year in Britain on sabbatical or for business purposes.

This book does not contain a jumble of blurbs about accommodations and restaurants, nor does it sprinkle historical anecdotes through sets of bewildering itineraries. It is organized to inform the reader of the basics about Britain clearly and succinctly. It is for readers who do not want to be teased by something short and superficial nor exhausted by the task of plowing though several volumes.

This book is an expanded and revised edition of an earlier book, *Understanding the U.K.*, also published by Hippocrene Books, which was successful both in the classroom and as a companion for trips to Britain. It served particularly well in introductory college survey classes in British studies, including British history. It answers many of the typical questions that come up year after year about travel and cultural differences, thereby freeing instructors to get on with their subjects.

These books have grown out of countless experiences with Britain and the British, including over thirty years of studying the subject and over twenty-five years of teaching it, primarily at Colorado State University, where I have been a professor of history directly responsible for explaining British civilization. All during this time, people came to me with all sorts of questions about Britain, such as: Does the Queen have any real power? What is shepherd's pie? What are British universities really like? What are the best places to visit if you only have one or two weeks in Britain? How does their school system work? What do you think of their National Health Service? Why do the British stay in Northern Ireland? How can you get used to driving on the left side? What is a bed sit? These questions and hundreds more are answered in the following pages.

I have crossed the Atlantic to Britain dozens of times and continue to do so. On several occasions I was able to live in Britain for a while. So over the years I have been able to engage in discussions on all kinds of subjects with diverse and varied British people. Yet the most informative insights for some sections of this book came from conducting six student tours to the United Kingdom and Ireland. I was able to share in the excitement of well over a hundred people who were exploring Britain for the first time. *The Hippocrene Companion Guide to Britain* contains the kind of information they needed to know to get the most out of their visit.

The author expects continued criticism for being opinionated, idiosyncratic, for shooting from the hip, creating stereotypes and offering generalizations that are too sweeping. Such must be the price of attempting to present an account of a civilization that stretches back over two thousand years and is represented by over fifty-six million live and diverse inhabitants. What I can say in my defense is that I have tried to be careful and balanced throughout and to rely on a wide variety of sources, living and printed. I hope that the usefulness of this treatment will outweigh criticisms that readers may find.

It is impossible to name and thank all of the people who have contributed to this book through their conversations, thoughts, experiences and suggestions. My daughter, Jeanette Weisser Moscato, who at the time of this writing lives in North Yorkshire, deserves a special word of thanks for her keen criticisms and proofreading assistance over the years. I also wish to specially thank Dr. George Blagowidow, publisher of Hippocrene Books, for his constant encouragement.

CHAPTER ONE

Travel: Some Practical Advice
SOME BASICS

Why Americans Should See Britain First

NEARLY everything in this book is written with the firm conviction that one of the best things any American can do to enhance life is to spend some time in Britain. For history, culture, language, literature, philosophical outlook, and general attitudes, Britain still is and has always been the mother country for America, regardless of the ethnic diversity of Americans and all of the separate development which has taken place since 1776.

Just as a "special relationship" exists in international affairs between Britain and America, whereby each nation can almost always count on the understanding, commitment and support of the other, a special relationship also exists between visiting Americans and British people. We are not "foreigners"; the foreigners live as close as 24 miles away across the English Channel. We are often regarded as more like cousins from the country, a bit raw, a bit naive, amusing in some ways, but energetic and enthusiastic people who are to be indulged in their great interest in Britain and its past.

For Americans who have never been abroad, Britain is always the best place to start for several reasons besides the similar language. Both countries share the conviction that life should be carried on according to rules, many of which are laws, and that all individuals have rights and liberties, including the right to privacy, and that anyone in authority is limited in power by these arrangements. This may sound abstract, but it becomes very concrete when confronting, say, a British policeman or ticket agent compared to someone in a Third World country in a military uniform or a minor functionary who will only "discover" some tickets when plied with a bribe. In short, Britain has a safe, neighborly, gentle, kind environment, where life goes on with a sense of right and wrong. All this makes it easier for an American to enjoy a trip to Britain, whether it is the first or the thirty-first.

What follows are some very practical considerations about travel in Britain. The big question of what to see is postponed until the next chapter.

Dealing with Culture Shock

Since the language, history and culture of Britain and America are so similar, the impact of culture shock will not be as great as in other nations. Nevertheless there will be some. Every American visitor to Britain will be confronted with a plethora of details that are different from the details at home. Culture shock is the cumulative effect of these differences. The details can be material, in the form of plugs with strange prongs, kettles with strange switches, curious heating devices or doors that open inward when they are expected to swing outwards.

Some details take the form of strange words and phrases that need translation, such as "white tea" or "p" or V.A.T. or strange usage, such as references to Europe as some other place than Britain itself. Some details involve the clock: there are odd times to do banking, shopping and drinking. There are odd holidays. Just what closes on a "Bank Holiday"? Then there are behavioral customs and practices that are different. For example, the check-out clerk at a grocery store will not bag purchases gleefully or have anyone else do it. Behind all of these details are larger patterns of social behavior and human interaction that produce a much more subtle and pervasive form of culture shock.

People who have never been to Britain before discover that it takes them much more time to shop, make a telephone call, arrange for a rental, conduct business in a bank or do a hundred other tasks. This is because little perplexing surprises crop up, little adjustments have to be made, and little mysteries have to be solved while doing ordinary tasks. Taken together, the cumulative effect of all of the little differences between life in Britain and life in the United States can, at worst, leave the American visitor frazzled, dazed, frustrated, exhausted and withdrawn all at once. These are the most unfavorable effects of culture shock. It is hoped that the information in this and subsequent chapters will serve to minimize the phenomenon.

Dealing with the Expensiveness of Britain Today

Perhaps the most shocking aspect of culture shock is that Britain in the 90s is extremely expensive for Americans. Due to both the considerable inflation that has gone on in Britain in recent years and to the relative weakness of American currency, the dollar simply commands only a fraction of what it used to in that country a few decades ago. Older Americans become nostalgic over how cheap everything in Britain was compared to American prices in the decades after the Second World War ended. Now it is just the reverse.

This will make travel in Britain a hardship for poorer students and for tourists who must economize like them. In fact, in 1992 I met former students of mine in Edinburgh, Scotland, quite by accident and learned that they were buying and boiling potatoes for meals in order to make ends meet.

At worst, things cost just about twice as much in Britain as they do in the United States. This can be demonstrated easily by looking at prices in pence for ordinary items in grocery stores. They are frequently identical with prices in cents in America. So if it costs 69 pence for, say, a green pepper, $1.38 is closer to its real price.

It is somewhat unnerving to hear British people complaining that they found prices elsewhere in Europe twice as high as prices at home. That means that certain parts of Europe, such as Scandinavia, may be close to Japan on the list of places that are exorbitant for American tourists. So when upset about the cost of something in Britain, be consoled by the fact that it could be twice as costly across the North Sea.

There are other ways of reconciling oneself to the high cost of traveling in Britain. Reflect on the fact that fine wines cost more than cheap wines, and travel in Britain is one of those splendid experiences in life that must be, at least for now, a costly affair. Mature travelers may want to revert back to a time in life when conditions were more stringent economically for them and live that way again for the duration of a trip to Britain. It may turn out to be a refreshing experience. If not, bite the bullet and flash the less painful plastic.

Yet another way of bracing for higher prices was suggested to me on several occasions by my eldest daughter, in particular during those times when I contemplated menus. "Dad," she exhorted, "stop translating prices." It is good advice. Try very hard to think of prices only in pounds. Stop looking for bargains in terms of dollars because it is highly unlikely that there will be any. Look for bargains in pounds only.

A Few Hints About Getting There

The old adage that "getting there is half the fun" certainly does not apply to trips to Britain. Flights from the United States usually depart from the East Coast in the evening and arrive in Britain in the morning of the next day. Flying against the direction of the sun means that the internal clocks of travelers are set at the early hours after midnight when they arrive in England, where it is bright and busy in the early morning of the next day. Travelers coming from the West have a longer ordeal, sometimes with a long wait in an East Coast city. If possible, arrange a direct flight with no change of planes.

Many people who fly to Britain for the first time, particularly students, become so keyed up that they cannot sleep or do not want to sleep. Usually this is a mistake. Even snatching a few minutes of sleep while roaring over the Atlantic can pay big dividends the next day in Britain. People who can go to sleep for a few hours gain big benefits from it after they arrive. It may be wise to bring along ear plugs to help drown out noisy passengers, particularly the screaming babies who almost invariably are seated close by.

Arrival at Heathrow Airport, or any other international airport in Britain, is anti-climactic. After some exciting views from the window of green fields, busy cars on the opposite side of the road, and glimpses of the vast sprawl of London, if that is the destination, what follows is a tiresome and lengthy bureaucratic procedure to get out of the airport. Passports must be examined, questions answered, and luggage gathered and, in some cases, inspected. All of this takes time, and people who have had no sleep or very little sleep, and look it, can become very impatient and annoyed.

After these procedures at Gatwick, most passengers board a train for London which connects with the Underground system. At Heathrow, the terminals are connected to the Underground directly. Just purchase a ticket with the few pounds of British cash that you acquired before arriving or exchanged at the terminal (where the exchange rates are rather poor, incidentally). Traveler's checks will not be cashed at Underground stations. Be sure to snag a pushcart for your luggage at the terminal baggage claim. It can be wheeled almost up to the gates of the Underground station. Taking a taxi from Heathrow or Gatwick to central London is outrageously expensive.

Cures for jet lag, that odd hangover sensation from being

at one time anatomically and another time in reality, are many and varied. Some people go to a hotel room as quickly as possible and sleep as much as they can. Others write off a night's sleep and carry on until the sun goes down, when they may collapse into the sleep of the dead or be red-eyed and alert until far after midnight.

Whatever the procedure, people are far from their best at arrival, so it is a very good idea to have a secure room reservation for at least one night in advance. Scrambling about for a place to stay when dead tired and experiencing some culture shock for the first time is an unpleasant experience. There is consolation in knowing that there is one solid bed in one room somewhere in Britain waiting for the weary passenger.

ACCOMMODATIONS

A Bargain in America but not in Britain

It takes a short time for Americans to realize what a bargain they have in accommodations at home. When it comes to hotels and motels, the dollar simply gets immensely more value in the United States than in Britain. For example, it is not remarkable to find many moderate motels in America offering swimming pools, saunas, play rooms for youngsters and other amenities. In Britain only the most luxurious and therefore the most alarmingly expensive establishments would have such features.

Double occupancy is often charged at twice the single rate rather than on a sliding scale as in America. Be sure that prices quoted contain the Value Added Tax, which can give any price a hefty mark-up if it is not included originally.

Predictability and uniformity are other characteristics of lodgings in the United States, where blind people can book into motels of certain chains and feel perfectly at home in them whether they are located in Maine or New Mexico.

Blind people in Britain will have to explore each and every new modest accommodation, because the size, shape, furnishings and facilities in every room are likely to vary considerably.

Quality can vary considerably also. London has a collection of grim little hotels with dingy rooms without a view that may cost two or three times what a spacious, well-furnished, airy, bright room with a grand view in the provinces goes for. Various people tinker with their houses in order to go into the bed and breakfast business, and the result is a surprising variety of accommodation. The lucky visitors find bed and breakfast in redone buildings dating back several centuries, where it is a treat to wake up to see dark Tudor half timber set off by brilliantly whitewashed walls.

No matter how charming the scene may be upon waking, bitter cold in the room can detract from it very quickly. Some places have space heaters which need to be plugged in or otherwise activated before going to bed. Some places do have central heating, but the British idea of what it is supposed to do may differ from what American visitors expect. It may be wise to chat with the proprietor about what can be expected.

Sometimes only one great stuffed quilt is supplied in place of a blanket, and the sleeper may be too cold or become too warm under it. Do not be shy about asking the proprietor for extra blankets if they are necessary or, if warmth is a problem, thinner ones as a substitute for a quilt. British pillows are huge and come in pairs, so Americans who do not want to prop themselves up are likely to toss one aside.

There are all kinds of rooms to rent in Britain. Some are in old castles, some are in big Victorian railway hotels, some are in quaint cottages and some are in ordinary houses built during the depression and filled with the odors of exotic cooking. What is guaranteed is that at least something about each place will seem awkward or inconvenient, unless they are built on American models. But if this is the case, and the hotel room looks like a Motel 8, the prices are apt to be astronomical. So when dealing with the problems that accommodations present in Britain, traditional sage advice for all travelers is particularly appropriate: Take it as it comes. Put up with inconvenience and less than desirable surroundings and indifferent service because it is all very temporary. The Britain you have come to see is outside of the hotel or the bed and breakfast establishment.

The Dubious Realm of Tub and Toilet

With every passing year more and more locations in Britain have showers, tubs and toilets attached to rooms, a condition dubbed "en suite." Very expensive hotels have had such arrangements for a long time, but ordinary accommodations are just in the process of converting. Sometimes the results are ludicrous, such as a conspicuously standing new shower in a cramped room which emits only a few trickling sprays of water at unpredictable temeratures.

Ordinary hotels and bed and breakfast places have long expected their guests to trudge down a hall to use a toilet, universally called the "w.c.," the initials stemming from a polite euphemism for toilet or "loo," the "water closet." The lucky visitor finds the w.c. just some feet away. The unlucky visitor may discover it tucked far away somewhere, such as underneath a staircase, or somewhere up a staircase. Another unlucky visitor may be right next to it, and therefore be required to listen to the heroic thundering of British plumbing every time it is used.

In America, the bath and the toilet are almost invariably adjoining the sleeping room and together. This is not the case for most of the older accommodations in Britain, where the bath and, if you are lucky, the shower, are in a room down the hall and the toilet is separate from the bath and in another room down the hall. There is an efficiency to this, of course, because guests with one purpose in mind do not have to wait for guests attending to a different need. The separation of the toilet also mean that Americans who declare that they must "go to the bathroom" may be liable to some humorous chiding, such as, "Why? Do you need a bath?"

While using a shower shared by several guests may not put Americans off, sharing a bathtub may. Unfortunately many places have no showers attached to their tubs. In more modest accommodations tubs may come in odd shapes and have questionable supplies of hot water. Courtesy requires that each user leave the tub in a sparkling condition, but not all users are so fastidious. When using either tub or shower down the hall, be sure to take the towels provided in the room with you.

The grim alternative to a bath in a dubious tub is the classic British "wash" at the sink. Sinks and water glasses do come with most of the less expensive rooms. For generations, British people have been used to quick sinkside washes which adroitly apply the washcloth to those parts of the human anatomy most in need of daily attention.

Another complication from the exterior location of tub and toilet is that other guests are likely to be encountered in the halls at all hours, and particularly in the early morning. The worst of all situations is a small queue, or line, waiting for the toilet. Fortunately this is not encountered frequently because most places offering lodging have a fair number of facilities sprinkled about and if one is in use another can be sought out. For these strolls about the premises it is necessary to pack a decent looking bathrobe.

Before deciding to discriminate against all accommodations that do not have bath and toilet "en suite," consider that the trudge down the hall may cut the price of a room in half. Budget conscious travelers have always accepted the fact that they must do without these conveniences because insisting upon them would only result in unacceptably high costs for lodging. The situation is changing rapidly, and more and more places are going American, at least to the extent of having a shower and toilet, no matter how cramped and small, for private use.

The Breakfast Part of the B and B

The "full English breakfast" is highly controversial. First of all, most ordinary British people do not have them at home because it is too much of a fuss to prepare them. They, like Americans, are apt to grab some cereal or other prepared food, perhaps bread and jelly or marmalade, along with coffee or tea and the newspaper before racing off to work. Yet British people regard someone else cooking and serving a full English breakfast for them as one of the fondest aspects of being on vacation, or "on holiday," as they put it. Some Americans gag at these breakfasts, regarding them as unhealthy because of all of the grease, calories and cholesterol. Other Americans recognize these shortcomings but indulge in them nonetheless, regarding them as a sinful delight, a temporary break from a healthy diet at home. Some have even declared that the full English breakfast was the best meal of the day. Besides, all of this shimmering, splattered stuff was paid for as part of the accommodation, and so it should not go to waste. As a practical consideration, an English breakfast eliminates the need to have anything but the lightest of lunches or snacks at midday.

Most places offer the alternative of a Continental breakfast to the more fastidious, health conscious or those who cannot abide the English breakfast because of doctor's orders. But bread and rolls are a paltry substitute for all of the hearty fare that the British have always regarded as the best way to fortify oneself for the day ahead.

Until recently, English breakfasts had more variety. Kippers, a good smoked fish dish, often showed up in the morning. Nowadays, breakfasts can be interchanged from the tip of Scotland to the Cliffs of Dover with dull monotony. Here is what is included: Eggs are featured. There is a choice of scrambled eggs with grease throughout, or fried eggs with the grease shining underneath, or poached eggs with the grease both over and under. Meat is in the form of "bangers," greasy little brown sausages of mysterious composition, and bacon, with full gleaming fat. There are also fried tomatoes or fried mushrooms or both, although mushrooms do not show up very often. Tomatoes can be counted on, however, and will be positioned on the side of the plate, sometimes just in the form of shiny and runny red blobs. The real pièce de résistance is the "fried slice," which is a piece of bread that has sopped up the grease used to fry everything else and is itself fried so that it gains a heaviness and turns brown. Some tend to be wet and some tend to be dry and all can contribute to keeping cardiologists busy.

These items are but the main course at breakfast. There is also juice and a choice of dry cereal beforehand and bread and toast during or afterwards, accompanied by various butter, marmalade, and jelly selections. A heavy tankard of tea or coffee comes with breakfast. Those taking tea have a tankard of hot water also, used to dilute the tea. Nothing can be more British than the solid thunking sounds of these tankards combined with the delicate clanking sounds of china in use.

Booking a Room

One way to book a room is to arrive in a place and walk or drive around looking for signs offering accommodations. If the place is large and no B and Bs or hotels are in sight, a brief inquiry at a local store will usually tell you where the cluster or clusters of such places are.

Obviously, such a technique is chancy, particularly during those peak periods when millions of British people and hundreds of thousands of Continental tourists are also traveling. The peak periods are from June through August, but particularly in August, because schools are out and whole families will be on "holiday," which is what they call vacations in Britain. There is also a busy period from Christmas until two weeks afterwards.

Another method is to make full use of the British Tourist Authority's information offices, which are also booking offices. They are sprinkled all over Britain, even in some of the smaller and more remote places. Their agents are very familiar with Americans and their requirements. For a very modest fee they will try to get you accommodations in your price range with the amenities that you specify as important, such as the existence of a shower or a color television set. By the way, make sure that the color television set is in the room rather than downstairs in the public lounge.

Some people like to make the booking once they arrive at the Tourist Office at their destination, and others like to book ahead. In a busy season, the latter course is wise. The agents will phone ahead and keep on phoning until they locate what the visitor wants. Their lists ordinarily screen out all of the dubious places.

The Vocabulary of Accommodation and Housing

Bathroom — Literally, this is a room where people bathe. Americans curiously use it as a euphemism for toilet, because Americans usually have toilets in the bathrooms. European homes and hotels may not, particularly if they are older structures.

Bed sitter or bed sit — This refers to a room that serves as a living room and a sleeping room. Single people, particularly the young and the poor, are likely to rent them. There is a vast turnover in such rentals, as advertisements in the newspapers clearly indicate.

Council house or flat — This refers to subsidized public housing. In recent years much of it has been sold off to occupiers.

Detached — This means a house standing without being joined to another. Semi-detached is more ordinary, meaning attached on one side but not on the other.

En suite — This term is used to indicate that a bed and breakfast accommodation also has a private toilet and private bathing facilities included, something that one would take for granted at the most modest of American motels.

First floor — In America, the British first floor is the second floor. What Americans call the first floor is the ground floor in Britain.

Flat — This is the ordinary word for apartment.

Ground floor — This is what Americans call the first floor.

Maisonette — This is a duplex apartment, often part of a house.

Mews — This can be an old alley, perhaps originally containing a row of stables which now may be very quaint and fashionable.

Semi-Detached — This is a term referring to a house that is attached to another house on one side but not on the other.

Service flat — This is an apartment which is cleaned and serviced as part of the rental agreement.

Terrace — This refers to a row of houses joined together.

Terrace house — This is one of the houses in a row of houses joined together.

Tower block — This means a high-rise apartment building.

A FEW PRACTICAL HINTS ON LUGGAGE AND WHAT TO BRING

The most important point about luggage is that nearly everyone takes too much of it to Britain. Americans bring too many clothes, too many gadgets and too much stuff. Hauling unnecessary bulk around becomes a drag very quickly. While those who lead tour groups declare this admonition time and time again, it is very difficult to get people to adhere to it.

Another helpful point is to be a loose packer, so that extra space is left in suitcases. This, that and the other thing picked up along the way will take up the extra space very quickly.

Do not take clothes in which to have dinner with the Queen, or to go to famous horse races, regattas or official ceremonies. The tiniest percentage of the population ever dresses for such occasions, and Americans going to Britain cannot expect to be invited to such functions, unless they are famous and important.

American students planning a trip to Britain will be relieved to know that British students frequently dress in attire that can be called super ratty. Old, worn, drab, ill-matched and even ragged clothes are proudly worn by British students, even at the best universities, at least for a good part of the time.

Everyone should remember that Britain is a very civilized country where friendly shopkeepers in well stocked shops all speak English. What this means is that you can buy anything you need easily, and if you are debating how much underwear or how many sweaters to bring, decide to take the minimal number. If you are short of any items in Britain, buy them there.

Many American visitors come from parts of the United States that have much less rain than Britain. They should give special attention to bringing what will keep them dry, particularly their heads and feet. Umbrellas really are needed in Britain any time of the year.

It is also wise to tuck away a roll of wonderfully soft American toilet paper in the luggage. Bring along plugs for the ears in case some accommodations are noisy, although this is much more likely to happen in the United States than in Britain. Bring a wash cloth because many accommodations are not likely to provide them. It is also wise to bring small amounts of soap and shampoo because these too may not be provided at many lodgings, or someone may forget to provide them on a given day. It is helpful to have sets of plastic knives, forks and spoons for the odd meals from store purchases which might be necessary for one reason or another. Since so many trips may have to be made to a toilet or a bath or a shower at some distance from the bedroom, it is important to pack a bathrobe that one would not mind being seen in. Do not lug electrical shaving equipment and adapters from America. It is too much extra weight and chances are that many tricky British electric outlets will preclude operation. Bring along cheap, light, throw away American plastic safety razors instead.

USING THE TELEPHONE

British Telecom, the now private national telephone company, is expensive but polite. Connections may not always be as good or as clear as Americans may have come to expect. Yet it affords only a tiny fraction of the hassles that using the phone systems in most Third World countries or eastern European countries would entail. Even so, some Americans always discover that the simple task of using the telephone in this English speaking country can involve miscommunications, particularly when some of the simple terms presented in the following list are misunderstood.

Here are some other tips: British people are likely to answer the phone by reciting their number. When answering a ring, Americans should avoid their usual "hello" and recite the number of their phone instead. If you borrow someone else's phone, ask the operator for "advice of duration," and the operator will come on after the call and advise you of the charge. If you pick up a phone after it rings and you hear rapid pips, this indicates that your caller is grappling for coins in a phone booth. Do not hang up. When you are calling, ringing will be signaled by a repeated double burr on the line. This sound will carry through to the old style British phones with such a blasting volume that it grates on the nerves. A busy signal is a repetitious single tone. A continuous tone means that the number is either out of order or that it does not exist.

One way to minimize the task of phoning is to buy a green Phonecard, which is sold in various denominations at newsvendors and post offices. Telephone booths, called "boxes" in Britain, are decorated in red or green. The green ones, which are now almost everywhere, take phone cards. Upon insertion, a little window on the phone tells the user how many units he or she has left, a unit being a specific amount of time calculated with reference to distance. Phonecards certainly do eliminate the trouble of gathering and lugging odd amounts of that characteristically heavy British change around in order to make phone calls.

Vocabulary for Using the Phone

999 — This is the all purpose emergency number for fire, police or ambulance.

Directory enquiries — This is the phrase for telephone information.

Engaged — This is the British word for busy.

Ring off — This means to end a telephone conversation.

Ring up — This means to telephone or to "call" in America.

Telephone box — This is used instead of telephone booth.

Through — In a phone conversation, this means connected, not finished. When the operator asks, "Are you through?" this means "Are you connected?"

Triple plus a number — Operators will rattle out "double four, treble six" for 44666. American operators are likely to say "four, four, six, six, six." Sometimes it takes a bit of concentration to get all the numbers of a British operator giving numbers fast when they include doubles and triples.

Trunk Call — This means a long-distance phone call.

FOOD

Some Contentious Generalizations

Ordinary British food tends to be like British weather. It is mostly unexciting but there are a few bright spots amid the general dreariness. Unlike Germany or France, Britain does not have a celebrated cuisine redolent with special sauces and delectable combinations. At best, British food is similar to good American food. At worst, it is greasy and overcooked. At least it is better, on average, than eastern European food, which does not really say all that much for it.

Remarks such as these can provoke a storm of protest from Britons who point out that since World War II and the surge of affluence following it, food has become infinitely better in Britain. It has also become highly cosmopolitan. The arrival of many foreign chefs and the examples they set in a great variety of restaurants are cited as a cause of the improvement of British cuisine. So is the time and effort that so many British people can now afford to put into food preparation. Also, affluence has made a greater variety of quality meats and vegetables a part of the British diet.

Even before these developments, the British did cook a few traditional items quite well: simple, plain, unspiced roasts, particularly roast beef, for instance, or various kinds of fresh fish, also prepared simply. Dover sole and plaice, a fish like a flounder, have always been reliable selections. In addition, many pubs are noted for serving good and inexpensive food at midday. A good example of this "pub grub," as it is called, is "shepherd's pie," a simple concoction of ground meat and onions covered with mashed potatoes. It may be wise to avoid sandwiches in pubs and other places because they are apt to be thin and not very good.

Despite all of the improvements in British cuisine and the continuation of good traditional fare, the chamber of horrors of British food is still there. One of the most reliable ways to encounter bad British food is to go to a cheap short order restaurant. Many of them are called cafes, and they all tend to bask in the glare of fluorescent light and have a deafening level of noise from the roar of the cooking grease, the semi-intelligible shouts of the staff and the endless clatter of heavy dishes. Here one can sample the family of meat pies. The British love to bake pies around concoctions of meat. Pork pies deserve their notoriety. They have the specific gravity of lead, and they can be thrown just like hand grenades or baseballs. One can remove the pie crust and expect to find a layer of shiny green gelatinous scum. Inside this layer is a core of pinkish, grayish pork that looks as if it is composed of ground snouts or tails. Steak and kidney pies are another British culinary wonder. British people insist that the dish is very fine when it is cooked just right, but they seem to complain that their particular steak and kidney pie is overdone, or, something worse, underdone, when the kidneys do, alas, remind one of their essential function when they were embedded in a living animal. Yorkshire pudding, although widely celebrated, seems to be only pastry made in the grease that comes from the roasting.

None of these pie dishes do much for the calorie or blood cholesterol count, but concern for a healthier diet does not manifest itself among British people to the extent that it does among Americans. This can be said more emphatically for the poorer British people. In the more affluent neighborhoods, particularly in the southern part of the country, better diets are consciously achieved by utilizing health foods and low fat products. In working class districts, particularly in the north, poor diets, combined with heavy smoking and drinking, pose serious health problems and dictate a shorter life span. American dietary concerns will in all likelihood make at least some inroads in these neighborhoods also in the future. American fast foods certainly have. The golden arches of McDonald's can be seen all over, although the food at such places tends to be more expensive and its arrival slower than in the United States.

Britain's old, original fast food was fish and chips. Nowadays, there are several kinds of fast food fish and chips establishments in Britain as well as in the United States, all resplendent in gleaming aluminum and plastic under ever present fluorescent lights. These newer places do not serve the traditional proletarian fish and chips, which consisted of a hunk of unspecified fish in a puff of fried batter accompanied by a mass of greasy fried potatoes. All of this used to be served up in a cone of ordinary newspaper that rapidly became translucent with grease. Rough looking characters used to be seen propped up in doorways clawing into their greasy cones for this old staple of the British diet. Today, with fish much more expensive, the cheap hamburger seems to have become something of a replacement. Nevertheless, just recently the author was able to purchase a translucent cone of chips in northern England that were so rich in grease that each individual chip would drip profusely when held suspended over the pavement. The chips, by the way, are what we call French fried potatoes. The British word for what we call potato chips is "crisps." These are essential vocabulary words for all Americans in Britain, particularly younger Americans.

An old fashioned fast food that is still seen here and there are the famous cockles, mussels and winkles. The last are jellied eels. Piers at seaside amusement parks and open air pushcarts in London still sell such seafood, which was once very cheap and enjoyed by the poor but is now somewhat expensive. Just as oyster eaters have their own elaborate rituals in America, those who eat cockles and mussels have their peculiar procedures in Britain. Given the degree of pollution in the oceans these days, eating anything raw from them is risking hepatitis and perhaps much else besides.

In Britain, vegetables can suffer a fate as horrible as that of the coagulated meat pie. "Veg" usually means peas, but on poorer menus Brussels sprouts can be substituted. Peas can plop onto plates cooked to death, all concave and grayish green. Brussels sprouts can be so overcooked that a simple thrust with a fork can cause them to explode like a green caterpillar under foot.

A critique of that quite controversial and quite traditional British meal, the "full English breakfast," is included in the section under accommodations, since it comes with the room.

Some Curiosities of British Dining

Fast food and exotic takeaways have to a considerable extent eroded the generalization that the British are much more rigid than Americans when it comes to serving food at prescribed hours. Nevertheless, there are many restaurants and hotels and other places that follow a strict regimen. Lunch will begin and end promptly at prescribed hours. Dinner might not begin until 7 or 7:30 p.m., and when it does it may have a first course of an appetizer, called a "starter," a fish course, perhaps, an entreé with vegetables and a "sweet" or a variety of cheeses for dessert.

"Tea" is a word that can mean several things, including, of course, simply a cup of that often ceremoniously made liquid which sustains the British throughout life. Afternoon tea, especially "cream tea" means an opportunity to indulge in a conscientious cardiologist's nightmare of baked goods smeared with thick cream, jam and butter. "High Tea," which is served in many restaurants and hotels, means a light supper served around 5 or 5:30 p.m.

Britain's traditional class structure adds a further confusion to the meaning of "tea." Traditional working class Britons eat a light meal in the evening that they call "tea." At lunchtime, workers have a big meal that they call "dinner," and so they call the mid-day meal instead of the evening meal "dinnertime." The more conventional middle and upper class use of "lunch" and "dinner" seem to be replacing the working class designations rapidly.

Frequently the liquid tea comes in one of a group of three pots. One will have the tea, another hot water to dilute the tea and a third will have hot milk. Often the tea comes already mixed with milk. British tea is really very good, which is something that cannot be said about much of the coffee served in the country. English coffee comes with brown sugar, as well as white sugar. Brown sugar, dumped in liberally, is supposed to make it much better. Sometimes coffee comes already mixed with milk, so if black coffee is desired, it is important to specify this when ordering.

There are other customs worth noting. Many places will not serve water automatically because the proprietors happily anticipate that the diners will quench their thirst with wine and beer instead. Water has to be asked for specifically in many establishments, and a request for "ice water" is wise if the usual American restaurant's glass of water is desired. If there are vacant seats at a table, total strangers may be placed at them or arrive at them in a self-seating restaurant. In crowded Britain, unlike America, the single person is never seen commanding and holding a booth or table that will seat six.

British Imperial Food: The Best Bargain in Britain

Britain's imperial past lives in its food. London and all of the major towns and cities have numerous Indian and Chinese restaurants which offer tasty meals that tend to be less pricey than regular fare.

Since Americans are ordinarily well acquainted with Chinese food, there is no point in describing it here. Britain has had a long connection with China through extensive trading activity and the acquisition of Hong Kong. Chinese people also migrated to British Malaya and Singapore and took jobs in the worldwide British maritime navy. It is therefore no wonder that substantial numbers of Chinese came to Britain, bringing their wonderful ways of cooking with them.

Nearly every British town of any size has at least one Chinese restaurant. They can range from a fast takeaway outlet to gracious and expensive dining in lovely surroundings. The greatest concentration of Chinese restaurants is in London, naturally, both in an intensely busy Chinatown and scattered throughout the metropolis. The location of London's Chinatown is worth noting. It is just behind Trafalgar Square, a few blocks to the northwest along Gerrard and Lisle streets. An amazing number of restaurants are crammed into this rather small area, offering the usual Cantonese style plus seafood specialties, Peking style and Szechwan style.

The cuisine of the Indian subcontinent is a special glory in Britain, and something with which most Americans are not yet very familiar. It is rather unfair to call the cuisine simply "Indian" because Bangladesh and Pakistan have contributed their share of people and restaurants to the British scene, the Bangladeshis in particular. Nevertheless, when the British were in India it was altogether in one political entity. On that basis, the name Indian will be used to refer to the restaurants of Pakistan and Bangladesh as well.

Anglo-Indian relations have a long history. The British

were active in India as traders and administrators long before the American Revolution. In India, British influence can still be seen everywhere, and in Britain, Indian influence can be found in art and architecture, but above all, in the presence of people from the Indian subcontinent and their descendants. They and their aromatic restaurants are ubiquitous.

Just recently the number of Indian restaurants in Britain surpassed the number of Chinese restaurants. There were only a handful of them after World War II, but now there are thousands and a new one opens just about every day.

Few locations have them in the United States, but their number is growing. Even so, many Americans in Britain hesitate to patronize Indian restaurants either because they are unfamiliar with them, or they are reluctant to try new things, or they have negative images of a starving, dirty, impoverished Indian subcontinent. India, Pakistan and particularly Bangladesh do share the problems of the Third World: high death rates, terrible slums and massive malnutrition. But this does not preclude the existence of wealthy, healthy and prosperous groups in the same region, and these people are very well nourished on very delicately and richly spiced foods.

American visitors should not be daunted by the exotic aromas and sights of good Indian food, nor should they be afraid of being seared by hot dishes because Indian fare ranges from mild to medium to hot to very hot. Waiters are very helpful to newcomers who ponder what might seem to be a strange menu, and they are usually very willing to make recommendations to help customers steer away from the hot dishes. Sometimes language problems do intrude when an American accent and an Indian accent mutually lower the level of intelligibility.

Americans from the Southwest who regularly enjoy hot Mexican food should not become overconfident in an Indian restaurant. The very hot dishes, such as Vindaloo curry and Madras meat, can numb mouth and tongue totally and put the sinus system out of commission for a day or more. These dishes come from the hottest regions of India, and some chefs have never been there and liberally use their imaginations when adding the spices. Visitors should always try dishes from the cooler, mountain regions and the milder, wetter regions along the coasts of the Indian Ocean because foods from these places are milder and feature gentle amounts of spices.

Besides offering a great variety of curries of meat and vegetables, Indian cuisine features rice dishes, many of them called Biriani, various appetizers and carefully roasted items, many in the Tandoori fashion. For some people, Indian food seems almost addictive. In the most extreme cases, a real craving for curry can develop. British people struck with it can satisfy themselves at thousands of Indian restaurants but Americans may suffer curry withdrawal pangs when they return to the United States. Mexican food can help somewhat in overcoming this condition. The danger of withdrawal symptoms notwithstanding, no American visitor to Britain should pass up the opportunity to try a variety of Indian foods.

The British Vocabulary for Food and Drink

Most of the terms on British menus are the same as they are on American menus, but the following terms do require translation or explanation:

Food:

Aubergine — This means eggplant.

Banger — This is a small, bland, brown sausage. "Bangers and mash" is a dish of them and mashed potatoes.

Biscuit — In Britain this means cookie or cracker.

Black pudding — This is a sausage made from oatmeal, herbs and blood.

Braising steak — This is what Americans call a pot roast.

Bubble and squeak — This is an odd name for an odd concoction, a mixture of Brussels sprouts or cabbage mixed with onions and potatoes and rolled into balls which are covered with bread crumbs. The name refers to what they are supposed to do externally, while in preparation, rather than the internal activities that they may produce.

Cornet — This is the British word for cone, such as an ice cream cone.

Clotted cream — This is a super thick cream, a specialty of Devon and Cornwall, places that probably produce the richest and thickest ice cream in all the world.

Cold — Cold does not mean ice cold, as it does in America. It means cool.

Cold supper — This often means cold meat and green salad served late, usually between 9 and 11 p.m.

Corn — This is a word for all grains. The American word "corn" is translated as "maize" or "Indian corn". It does not grow well in most of Britain. Europeans use it for animal food.

Chips — These are French fried potatoes in America.

Cornish pasties — This is pastry filled with minced meat, onions and potatoes.

Courgettes — These are zucchini in the United States.

Crisps — These are potato chips. Note the translation of chips just above.

Crumpet — These are flat yeast breads that are quite close to what Americans call "English muffins."

Flan — This is a pie that has no top on it.

Gateau — This French word for cake really means a rich, fancy cake, but the word has come to be applied to cakes in general.

Greens — This is the term for green vegetables, but it usually means peas.

Haggis — This is a pudding made from the heart, liver and sometimes the entrails of sheep, with suet, onions and oatmeal; the mixture is packed into the stomach of a sheep, and boiled. Haggis was a basic food for poor people in Scotland for a long time. Now it is often touted to get a rise out of tourists.

Ice — This can mean ice or ice cream.

Joint — This means a large piece of meat for roasting.

Lancashire hot pot — This is a kind of lamb stew with a rich sauce and numerous ingredients.

Minced meat or Mince — This is what Americans call chopped beef or hamburger meat.

Mixed grill — This is a main dish consisting of several diverse kinds of grilled meat with some vegetables.

Mulligatawny soup — This is an Indian soup which was concocted much in the same way that chop suey was concocted by Chinese cooks. Since the British began their meals with a soup course, Indian cooks invented this peppery brown soup. It varies immensely from restaurant to restaurant in thickness and flavoring.

Pancake — In Britain this means crepe instead of the classic American pancake.

Plaice — A plaice is a flat European fish that resembles and tastes like flounder.

Pudding — In Britain this is a general term for dessert, but in America the word means a very specific custard kind of dessert.

Salt beef — In America this is called corned beef.

Scone — This is a baked item made from a soft, raised flour-and-egg mixture. It is very popular at afternoon teas where it is smeared with super high calorie spreads.

Scotch egg — This is a hard boiled egg covered with fried sausage meat that is served cold.

Shepherd's pie — This is ground meat and onions covered with mashed potatoes. It can usually be relied upon to be good.

Sorbet — Americans would call this fruity ice dessert sherbet.

Starters — These are the items that Americans would call appetizers or the first course.

Sultana — This is a white raisin which is used to decorate many baked goods.

Sweet — This can mean either a dessert or a piece of candy. The plural form, sweets, means candy.

Treacle — This is a very sweet liquid, like molasses, which is poured over a dessert.

Tin — This means "can," so *tinned* is the British word for canned.

Underdone — This is the British word for rare.

Drink:

Bitter — This is the most widely consumed beer. It is literally more bitter than American beer, as well as darker and heavier. It is often mixed with other kinds of beer, such as brown ales, stout, and light ales.

Cider — English cider is strong hard cider, meaning it has a notable content of alcohol.

Cream tea — This is not just tea. It includes thick cream that is supposed to be spread on scones or other baked delicacies, along with jam and butter.

Cuppa — This is slang for a cup of tea and is a very colloquial expression. Cups of tea are downed at regular intervals by British people during the workday as well as before and after it.

High tea — When served in hotels or restaurants, it means a light dinner served from 5 to 5:30 p.m.

Jar — This is slang for a pint of beer.

Lager — This brew is similar to light ale in America.

Lager and lime — This is a mild drink, traditionally a favorite of ladies.

Pale ale — This is light in color and body.

Pint — A pint means a pint of beer, filling a glass that is just a little larger than an American pint.

Shandy — This is a light drink of beer mixed with lemonade or ginger beer. It is the drink that genteel ladies used to be expected to sip.

Stout — This is a heavy, dark, sweet beer. The most devastating variety is imported by tanker from Ireland and looks like heavy motor oil capped with foam.

Tea — This can mean a cup of tea, usually with milk already added, or an afternoon snack where various baked items are consumed. See also *High Tea, Cream Tea,* and *White Tea* in this section and above.

White tea — This means tea with milk in it. Also, white coffee is coffee with milk in it.

Whiskey — This means Scotch.

THE HAPLESS PEDESTRIAN

The survival of nearly all pedestrians in Britain is nothing short of an ongoing miracle. Hazards are worst in London, of course, but everywhere in Britain cars are driven with a controlled fury that places the pedestrian's life at risk. While British drivers are polite and skilled, they are nonetheless the pedestrian's antagonists because they compete constantly for space and the right of way in that crowded country.

One sanctuary for pedestrians is the safe and sacred road crossing known as the "zebra crossing." Zebra, by the way, is pronounced with a flat short *e* (as the *e* in bed) instead of the long, sharp double *e* that Americans use for that animal's name. These crossings have large white stripes across them, and hence their name. Motorists are warned by large, flashing orange beacons on poles that flank these crossings. Cars must stop at these zones when pedestrians enter, and, amazingly, it seems that 99.8% of them do, which is yet another tribute to the law-abiding nature of the British.

Pedestrians should be bold on a zebra because it is his or her clear right of way at all times. Enter one and be amazed at how ferocious columns of vehicles shudder to a halt in your honor. But keep a wary eye out for the driver who might belong to that .02% that will have trouble stopping.

Sometimes extremely busy streets appear to be without zebras, making crossing an extremely risky business. Pedestrians should look around for a "subway" at such places. These are not subways in the American sense of the term. The "underground" is the equivalent term for an American "subway." A British subway is a convenient pedestrian underpass, found rather frequently in British cities. Foreign pedestrians often miss them and then become frustrated at the numerous iron fences that seem to thwart access to intersections but actually function to channel the flow of pedestrians away from tempting but dangerous crossings.

The Ultimate and Most Important Survival Rule for Americans in Britain

The rule is: Look *both* ways *every* time you want to cross a street. If this rule is not followed, a time will inevitably come when a visitor will suddenly find ferocious traffic hurtling from an unexpected direction. Injury or death might thereby become the end result of what was supposed to have been a wonderful trip to Britain. The author remembers one occasion in particular in London when survival was a matter of an inch or two after a quick turn of the head revealed a gigantic, red double-decker bus rapidly approaching from an unexpected quarter.

Since Americans and Continental Europeans have been conditioned all of their lives to look only in one direction for traffic, a habit has to be instilled to look *both* ways every time a street is crossed. In Britain vehicles will surprise visitors time and again by suddenly appearing from unexpected directions because traffic moves on the left-hand side of the road. In London and other cities signs to look to the right are actually embedded in the pavement for the benefit of visitors.

British children receive vigorous basic pedestrian survival training from their earliest years. It is equally important for Americans who bring their children to Britain to drill them on pedestrian safety.

DRIVING

The Joys and Hazards of Multi-Lane Motorways

In recent years a remarkable development of the highway system has taken place, enabling drivers to cover vast distances at high speeds on unimpeded multi-lane highways, much as they do in the United States. The difference is that excessive speeds are tolerated to a much greater extent. It is quite possible to sail along at 85 m.p.h. and have cars cruise by at speeds sometimes exceeding 100 m.p.h. What makes it rather harrowing is the tendency for high speed cars to follow one another more closely than what is usual in the United States. Many highways are often too crowded to allow such speeds, but when there is open space available many British drivers seem to behave as if they are Spitfire pilots out of the heroic past.

The slowest traffic is required to stay in the leftmost lane in Britain and faster traffic passes to the right, which is just the opposite from the way it is done in the United States. Lane changes are a precise art in Britain. Vehicles do not wallow from one lane to another the way they do in most of the United States. The American admonition to "keep to the right unless passing" is rigidly practiced by British drivers who insist on "keeping to the left unless passing." In Britain cars tend to pull out to pass very precisely, usually with turn signals blinking, and they pull back into the original lane at the first good opportunity. It is regarded as extremely bad form to stay in a passing lane when not passing. To be passed from a slower lane, to the right in America and to the left in Britain, is regarded as indicative of bad driving. Many British drivers, particularly those in big, expensive cars, will encourage a slower car to move to the proper lane by flashing lights, blowing horns and tailgating in a most imposing manner.

The ancient Romans are partly responsible for these conditions because the roads they built often went straight as arrows for long distances. Eighteenth-century turnpikes were built right over them, and later the multi-laned motorways. The most famous of them all is the M-1, which shoots north from London to Yorkshire.

Work on transforming old fashioned roads into multi-laned motorways continues, as well as efforts to build new straight routes right across the green fields. Consequently, up-to-date road maps are a necessity. The fastest and best roads will almost invariably have an "M" for motorway designation and a number and show up as a thick blue line on road maps.

Some Britons are quite proud of the engineering complexity of the intersections of their modern roads. One such complex of intersections, near Birmingham, has gained the popular name of "Spaghetti Junction." Those who marvel at the complex of roads and ramps coming and going at this particular place ought to be invited for a day of freeway fun around Los Angeles!

The Vocabulary of the Road

Articulated lorry — This is what Americans call a tractor trailer truck.

Bonnet — This is the term for the hood of the car.

Boot — This is the term for what Americans call the trunk of the car.

Caravan — This word is used for a trailer or recreational vehicle. In America, it means a procession of vehicles or objects.

Car park — This is the very literal phrase used in Britain for parking lot.

Cat's Eyes — These are the small reflectors on the road. One odd roadworks sign in Britain reads: "Cat's eyes removed ahead!"

Divider — This is the line or strip in the middle of the road dividing traffic.

Dual carriageway — This is the term used in Britain for divided highway.

Dynamo — This is the word for generator.

Estate car — This is the word used in Britain for station wagon.

Fender — This is what Americans call a bumper. What Americans call fenders are wings in Britain.

Gallon — A gallon in Britain is larger than a gallon in America. Britain's imperial gallon holds 277.42 cubic inches of liquid; the American gallon holds 231 cubic inches.

Gear lever — These are the words for gear shift.

Give way — Signs reading "give way" on British roads are direct equivalents of yield signs in the United States.

Goods lorry — This means a truck carrying freight.

Junction — Americans prefer to use the term "intersection" when roads meet and "junction" for the places where railroads meet. In Britain, junction is used for both roads and railroads.

Lamp — This word is used in place of the American word 'light.' So headlamps mean headlights, parking lamps mean parking lights, etc.

Litre — This is the British spelling for "liter," the metric unit of measurement in which petrol (gas) is sold in Britain. A liter is slightly larger than a quart, so a rough calculation of four liters comes close to an American gallon, and five liters comes close to an Imperial (British) gallon.

Lorry — The word means truck in Britain.

Manual gears — Cars with a stick shift are said to have manual gears as opposed to an automatic.

M.O.T. — This is the abbreviation for Ministry of Transport. Applied to cars, especially in classified sales ads, M.O.T. means that the car has passed the ministry's rather stringent inspection requirements. A M.O.T. sticker on the windshield, called a windscreen in Britain, permits the vehicle to operate.

Motor — To motor means to drive a vehicle.

Nearside — This is the word used in Britain for the part of the road that is near the sidewalk.

Number Plate — This means license plate in Britain.

Offside — This word is used in Britain for the part of the road that is away from the sidewalk.

Overtaking — This is the word for passing. "No overtaking" means no passing.

Pavement — This is the word for sidewalk.

Petrol — This is the term always used in Britain for gas or gasoline.

Silencer — This is the word for muffler.

Spanner — This is the term for wrench.

Sump — This is the word for oil pan.

Torch — This is the word for flashlight.

Verge — This is the word used to denote the strip of grass on the edge of a road. Americans would call it a shoulder and ordinarily expect it to be paved.

Wing — This means fender.

Wing Mirrors — These are what Americans would call side mirrors.

Windscreen — This is the British term for windshield.

Is Driving Worth It?

Since buses and trains go almost everywhere, long walks promote health and taxis are abundant when a short car ride is unavoidable, why should Americans rent cars? Long before great masses of Britons began to buy their own cars, an extensive grid of relatively low-cost public rail and bus transportation had been laid out. Much like the inhabitant of Manhattan, the visitor to Britain can do without a car and still enjoy it immensely.

Most Americans, however, are wedded to their cars and find it difficult to spend time without having their own wheels available. America is a nation on wheels, particularly in places like Los Angeles or Cheyenne or Reno, where it is impossible to get around without one. So many will find it difficult to break the driving habit in Britain and use alternative transportation instead. For these visitors, car rentals will be readily available, but quite expensive, particularly in times of a weak dollar. A passport and a valid driver's license from any state and a major credit card are all that are needed. The major American car rental chains are all there, along with some British and European firms.

Renters should make a point of checking with their insurance companies before departing, because ordinarily American insurance stops at the border. Proper coverage is easy to pick up with car rental, but beware of deductibles and the extra insurance that may not be necessary, such as health coverage in case of an accident. It also may be wise to ask about the question of theft coverage before contracting. Americans who belong to auto clubs should check to see that there are collaborating branches of their clubs in Britain also.

Despite the warnings about all of the difficulties and hazards pertaining to driving in Britain that appear in the following sections, there are some decided advantages to getting around by car. Train travel may involve long waits at stations to make awkward connections. Many stately homes and other attractions are off the rail and bus lines, or, if they can be reached by bus, the trip may tie up too much time because of infrequent buses. In some parts of the country traffic is not as bad as in others. With luck, the traveler can zip around far more efficiently in many places with a car than on public transportation.

A Hazard of Driving in Britain: Heavy Traffic

The percentage of Britons who own and drive cars has been creeping upwards steadily since World War II. It has not reached the world-leading percentage of Americans, but the gap is being closed. The problem is that Britain is so small and so densely populated that most of the roads are terribly crowded with cars that drive as quickly as possible under the circumstances. Outside of the major motorways, Britain's roads are for the most part old, narrow and inadequate to handle the streams of traffic that sail along most of them. The most daunting statistic about British traffic is simply this: Nowhere in the world are there more cars per mile of paved surface.

British people who have experienced driving in America tend to remark on how open and wide the roads are and how steadily and conservatively the traffic moves. An American may make such a remark about driving in the emptier parts of the interior of the country, but British visitors make these remarks about the most congested routes in America.

Driving in London can be a nightmare. It is best to rent outside of London or at Heathrow airport and drive away from London. Then again, any British town or city can become a nightmare at rush hours, when gridlock becomes a plague. Motorists can sit in seemingly endless queues, or creep along in low gear for little advances before stopping again. In many instances Americans may think that there must be an accident up ahead, but nearly all of the time it is the simple mathematical fact that too many metal boxes are trying to occupy too little space.

Planning helps. Try to be off the road as much as possible during morning and evening rush hours and on Bank Holidays and weekends if possible. It is said that the traffic congestion headed towards the West Country beaches at the start of a summer Bank Holiday becomes backed up just like the traffic for the D-Day invasion of France.

Exercises in Spatial Relations: Trying to Park in Britain

Crowded roads mean difficult parking conditions. Towns try to cope by setting aside as many parking lots, or, as they simply say, car parks, as possible. The hitch is that they are not free. It costs some pence or a pound to get a little piece of paper out of a machine to affix to the windscreen. This enables an hour or two of sightseeing, but it may require a return to put more money into the machines.

Many people cannot abide paying out sums, however small, when the same opportunity may be had up some street for free. A double yellow line along the curb means no parking at any time, but in many locations cars are parked in these areas, sometimes with one wheel on the double lines and one wheel on the sidewalk. A single yellow line means limited parking for and at limited times. A wise thing to do is to ask local people about what restrictions exist and how energetic the local traffic wardens are. In some places they are veritable zealots and in other places benign neglect prevails for one reason or another.

What is most amazing about parking in Britain is how vehicles can get in and out of the smallest spaces. Cars are tucked away in front yards (called gardens), back yards, alleys, and odd, irregular spaces in such a way that it seems that they must have crept in with fractions of inches to spare or have been lowered into place from great cranes. Americans who must park frequently in Britain need to become students of geometry once again.

Some Hazards of Driving on the Opposite Side of the Road

The first thing to remember is never to refer to driving on the opposite side of the road as driving on the "wrong" side. Even if nearly all of the countries in the world keep to the right, the British, the Japanese, the Irish and people in a few ex-colonies continue to drive on the left, and for them, at least, it is definitely not the "wrong" side.

Before embarking on the first experience of driving on the opposite side, be sure to become familiar with the locations of all of the gadgets and buttons, more intently than one would with a rental car in the United States. The reason for this is that the gadgets, just like the steering wheel, will be on the opposite side also. To have the windshield wipers activate instead of an expected turn signal can be very disconcerting in heavy traffic. It takes a while to get used to operating the gear shift with the left hand. On many non-automatic cars available for rentals in Britain the gearboxes will involve peculiar motions, and in heavy traffic one does not have the time to find and study the little numbers on the gear shift. Although the cheaper cars do not have them, a tachometer is helpful because it will give a good indication of whether or not the driver is moving through the gears properly.

The first few moments of driving on the opposite side may be harrowing, but remember that it is not as difficult as it seems during the first few miles. Most experienced drivers adjust to it fairly easily.

It is important to remember that the steering wheel should always be on the side where the white line, or as the British say, the divider is or ought to be. In America this means that it is on the left of both the car and the steering wheel and in Britain it is on the right of both the car and the steering wheel. To keep from straying into the wrong side of an unmarked road, always imagine a white line right outside of the driver's window.

Turns may be the most difficult feat of all because they must be negotiated just the opposite way from turns in the United States. The left turns are short and sharp, just as our right turns are. To make a right turn in Britain, remember to swing wide, out across one lane and into another. Always keep that divider line, real or imaginary, close to the steering wheel side.

It takes a while to get used to judging distances on the left, or the passenger's side of the car. Experienced American drivers more or less automatically calculate distances on the passenger's side when this is on the right side, but when it is on the left their perceptions might be far enough off to scrape curbs or worse.

Square Dancing with Cars: The Roundabouts

Roundabouts are vehicular merry-go-rounds that pop up with maddening frequency, every time there is a junction of roads. Lack of resources and space has dictated their construction instead of the safer, but more expensive and space-gobbling American cloverleafs which handle major intersections in the United States. They are like the traffic circles fast disappearing in the northeastern United States.

Roundabouts funnel traffic into a circle, and roads shoot off the outer rim in different directions, like spokes of a wheel. Drivers are forewarned of their approach by signs showing circles or oblongs with spokes to imitate the physical reality coming up. Yet the more complicated signs really do require more time for study than a fleeting glance. Once in the roundabout, traffic roars behind the driver who is straining to locate the proper exit marker to leave the vortex. Cars cut in and out, some making dramatic entrances and exits. The driver hopes that his or her exit will be undramatic, but sometimes the desired slot is missed entirely. The only thing to do then is to keep on going all the way around the circle again. In fast-moving, busy intersections, steering wheels are clenched.

The author confesses that the first time or two that he drove in Britain he did not know the rules for roundabouts and generally slopped into them and slopped out again, sometimes observing exasperation towards him on the part of other drivers in the same merry-go-round. There were also a number of near misses. Since roundabouts involve perhaps the most difficult set of maneuvers to be encountered in driving in Britain, some of the rules, studied subsequently in an official drivers' handbook, are worth presenting.

1. Slow down and be ready to come to a complete stop at the broken line across the road at the entrance to the roundabout.

2. Look to the right and if a car is coming, stop. Cars to the right in a roundabout have the right of way. If a car coming from the right is distant enough around the circle, and you can get ahead of it without impeding it, you can go ahead. This is a judgment call, and it takes some experience to get it right. This is one of the most dangerous moments in the procedure because Americans do not always look to the right in a roundabout. Their instincts from years of experience tell them to look to the left, and sometimes when they look to the right too late they see nothing but a big grille.

3. Position yourself in the proper lane before entering a roundabout. If the road leading into a roundabout only has one lane the question will be whether to turn on the left turn signal, the right turn signal or no turn signal. The left turn signal means that you want to go out on the first spoke to the left. The right turn signal means that you will want to go out on a spoke all the way around to the right. No turn signal means you more or less want to keep on going straight ahead, once you clear the spokes on the left.

4. If two or more lanes lead into an intersection, those taking spokes off to the left should be in the left hand lane and have that turn signal on. Those in the right hand lane should have their right hand turn signal on and be ready

to go all the way around and exit on a spoke going off to the right. When there are two lanes, those wishing to go straight ahead, that is, on a spoke leading off on the other side of the circle in the same direction, can be in either lane, without a signal on.

5. If the spoke is missed, do not panic. Just keep going around the circle, avoiding those going off, and being alert to those who might be coming on, some of whom, visiting Americans perhaps, may cut out in front of you too suddenly. Your exit will come up again, and if you miss it again, you can go all the way around once more.

Once a visitor gets the hang of roundabouts, their beauty can be appreciated when good British drivers do a delicate ballet (or is it a square dance?) with precise timing and exact positioning. In fact, roundabouts can be rather exciting, with the knowledge that the crunch of an accident is being avoided by only seconds and a few feet. This does give zest to the spectacle. Yet when the driver is tired from a long haul, roundabouts lose all of their thrill and simply become annoying obstacles.

Ordinary British Roads and Some of the Signs and Other Things Drivers Encounter on Them

British roads range from the sublime to the ridiculous. All too many of them tend to be tortuous, consisting of a never ending series of curves, turns, dips, angles and bends, interspersed with roundabouts. Towns, trucks, people and unexpected road hazards slow up every road. Ordinarily a twenty-mile drive is an easy ride of twenty minutes in a Western state; in Britain, a twenty-mile drive along a secondary road can be an ordeal lasting over an hour.

The worst British roads are the very minor ones. Some are almost incredible, such as the one-lane tracks that have dense bushes and trees growing up on both sides. On some roads, the foliage meets overhead so that driving is like going down a long, twisting green tube. Suddenly, out of nowhere, an oncoming car can appear, and both cars will have to scratch into the vegetation so that they can pass each other. Sometimes the lanes are so narrow that one of the cars will actually have to back up for a considerable distance to find a place where a passage can be attempted. It is said that drivers always know they are on a minor road when they hear the grass brushing on the left side. It is also said, and the author has experienced it, that drivers know that they are on a minor road in Cornwall when they hear the grass brushing on both sides!

Road repair areas are handled in a most casual way in Britain. For example, at places where there is room for only one lane of traffic, Americans would have someone holding a sign to stop or go slow, preceded by warning after warning of an upcoming hazard. British operations, by contrast, might have only a portable stoplight at each end of the hazard, leaving it up to drivers to stop or proceed without supervision.

Stoplights themselves function somewhat differently from the way they do in the United States. The yellow light will come on in-between the transformation from red to green. Also, at some intersections a red light will be on for some directions while a green arrow will be on for traffic to go straight ahead. Usually when a green arrow is on simultaneously with a red light in America, it indicates that a turn is permissible.

British road signs can be frustrating. They are small and crowded on ordinary roads and often it is difficult to read them. Directions and distances are given on signs that have green backgrounds. Some of the very best signs are right down on the roadways themselves. Immense letters, numbers and arrows will be permanently embedded in the roadways to indicate which lane to use in order to take the desired road.

Here are some other signs worth noting: Two small circular signs on a post with a black slash (/) on them indicate that the national speed limit can be pursued, which is 60 m.p.h., 70 m.p.h. on motorways. Very often it seems that this is an excessive allowance, given the twisting and dangerous nature of many of the roads. It can be argued that the American limit of 55 m.p.h. for ordinary roads would be much more suitable for these places.

Similar circular signs with a blue background, a red rim and a red x in the middle of them mean no stopping. Such signs mark clearways. Two little cars on a circular sign, a black one to the left and a red one to the right mean no passing, or, as the British would say, no overtaking. A red sign with a broad white stripe running through the middle of it from left to right means no entry for vehicles.

Along major roads there will be green signs with slashes on them in a series — three, two and then just one. These are countdown markers for an exit.

A triangular sign with a notched black circle in it indicates an upcoming roundabout, and it will be followed by a sign bearing a detailed diagram of the roundabout. An upside down triangle with "Give Way" in it is equivalent to an American "Yield" sign.

These signs and many more are included in good road atlases, and they should be studied so that the most important of them can be memorized before the key is turned in the ignition of a rental car.

How Most British Drivers Drive

It is much easier to study how British drivers drive and emulate them than it is to continue to putter about as if you were in downtown Des Moines or Dayton. Smoothly integrating with the traffic flow will be a decided advantage, and in the long run it will be safer also.

Overall, the British are good drivers. They have to be, given the road and traffic conditions. Americans driving in Britain can count on most of the other drivers on the road being quick, alert and precise.

On major roads in Britain, cars travel almost bumper to bumper in a steady maddening roar of traffic. Even the most polite British drivers tailgate in a manner that would be exceptional in any state, including New York and California. The American driver in Britain who continues to follow the rules from drivers' training and leaves one car length of space per each ten miles per hour of speed will soon find that someone will zip into that space. Sometimes two cars will zip in almost simultaneously.

It is customary for British drivers to give a quick flash of the headlights to signal other cars. This is not an official, legal signal, but custom has made it standard practice on British roads. Lights on European vehicles are engineered to allow this signal to be made easily. A quick flash of the headlights in daytime or of the high beam at night means: "I see you" or "I know what you are up to" or "Go ahead. I am watching out for you." This very polite and civilized practice is often very helpful in Britain's very difficult driving conditions. Perhaps it can be applied advantageously to American traffic in the future.

Much of this flashing goes on when cars opt to pass. Passing in Britain can be a breathtaking experience. All two-lane roads with traffic flowing in opposite directions magically become three-lane roads in the minds of British drivers when they make a move to pass. The British driver does not always wait until there are no oncoming cars, as any sensible driver would do in the United States. British drivers just go ahead and pass, feeling secure in the assumption that the oncoming driver will see him or her, flash, and then pull far over towards the side of the road so that the passing car, the passed car and the oncoming car can all be accommodated, if need be, three across, at one split second of time. Driving in Britain affords many such thrilling moments. By the way, it is illegal not to move over as far as possible when an oncoming passing car is roaring down a hitherto non-existent middle lane.

Another characteristic of British drivers is that they are very reluctant to put their headlights on. They are likely to drive about in the gloom of dusk or bad weather with only their parking lights on. In London and other lighted urban areas, British drivers think that parking lights are sufficient even in the dead of night. A cynic said that the decision to go from parking lights to headlights does not occur until the driver cannot see five feet beyond his fenders, what they call their "wings." As British drivers sail through darkening gloom with just parking lights on they sometimes create the appearance of a swarm of fireflies zooming down a busy road in formation.

Keen observers have noted that the British class system imposes itself on motoring also. Rolls Royces, Jaguars and big Rovers do seem to push the smallest of the Vauxhalls and Fords out of the way with sublime arrogance. Like big fish and small fish swimming in an aquarium, big, expensive, powerful cars and small, cheap, underpowered cars do not appear to have the same right of way in Britain.

The Shock of Petrol (Gas) Prices

A recent maverick candidate for the American presidency came up with a budget that called for a 50 cent increase in gas taxes for each gallon of gas. Many Americans thought this proposal outrageous. Yet it would take over five increases of 50 cents to match the cost of unleaded gasoline in Britain in the early 1990s, a time when the dollar is weak. The author paid closer to $4 per gallon on a recent trip to Britain.

Despite the fact that there is more petroleum off the Shetlands Islands than in Kuwait, and Britain is a net exporter of it, there has been a long tradition of applying very heavy excise taxes to fuel.

Bear in mind that the British imperial gallon is a bit larger, equal to five American quarts instead of four. Gasoline, or petrol, as it is always called in Britain, is usually sold in liters, which is spelled *litre* in Britain. A litre has just a bit more volume than an American quart, so a rough and ready way of calculating petrol prices is to multiply the litre price by four and then multiply this by 1.6 at the present exchange rate for a pound. A rough calculation of 47 pence for a litre of petrol would be one pound and 88 pence, or $3.00 for an American gallon.

More and more petrol stations feature unleaded gas now, which is dispensed from green hoses in the U.K. Also, note the brand "Q 8." It is presumably from Kuwait.

TRAVEL BY RAIL

The Advantages of Taking the Train in Britain

Although British people complain about the cost and declining service and cleanliness on their rail system, it offers much for those who come from America where rail travel is reduced to a few routes maintained by Amtrak.

It takes just a glance at a Britrail map to realize that the rail grid in Britain is still elaborate, despite some recent paring of less traveled routes for the sake of economy. Trains still go almost everywhere; service to important destinations is frequent and trains are usually quite punctual.

Rail travel is therefore a very good alternative to driving in Britain, especially for those who wish to avoid the special hazards and difficulties of driving on strange roads on the opposite side of the road. For those who wish to compromise and combine both forms of transportation, Britrail and car rental companies offer rail passes that can be used on random days, say eight out of two weeks, so that train travel can be interrupted at cities and towns where cars can be picked up for local travel. Travel agents have the most up-to-date information on what is being offered.

British trains vary enormously in appearance and performance. Less-traveled routes have small, rumbling trains that are more like trolleys. The main routes are connected by the powerful "Intercity" diesel trains, which Americans would call express trains. In between the streamlined 100 mile per hour plus Intercity trains and the quaint trolley-like trains are others, fast and slow, some with sparse modern interiors in which everyone faces forward, and others with upholstered compartments, curtains and shades that appear to be from old film sets.

Incidentally, the smallness of Britain and the speed and quality of the rail system guarantees that divorced and mobile parents can travel almost everywhere to see their children in less than a day.

Rail travel has become quite expensive in the second half of this century. It used to be said that the wealthy drove automobiles and the poorer people traveled by train. Now poorer people are likely to be out on the roads in an old clunker and more of the affluent are escaping the hassles of driving by taking the fast trains.

Trains are good places to observe people deftly. All kinds of British people can be found on trains, ranging from brightly dressed football (soccer) fans to staid businessmen complete with *The Times*, briefcase, dark striped suit and umbrella. Often British travelers will politely, subtly and silently observe the American observer. Since the convention is that strangers do not talk to each other, Americans must initiate conversations in most instances. Although most Britons will quite willingly talk to visitors at length, they will not be likely to hail strangers in the breezy American manner.

Britain was the pioneering nation for rail travel, just as the United States has been the pioneering nation for air travel. While air travel has lost much of its glamour in the United States in recent decades, most older Americans can remember when flying was so romantic and exciting that many popular songs were written about it. The same sense of adventure surrounded train travel in 19th- century Britain, when the speed, power and magnitude of the railways dazzled the Victorians. Therefore, British people tend to have a soft spot for railroads, which is manifested in the number of nostalgic excursions by trains and locomotives taken out of museums and the very rail museums themselves, which are elaborate and numerous.

Some Special Hints for Using Britrail

If possible, try to book seats in advance. This can be done at the railroad station at the Britrail Tourist Office. On many trains, half of the seats are backwards and only a third are likely to be by a window. Booking ahead helps to get desired seats.

Without a booking, the traveler might encounter long lines at the ticket windows, so be sure to be in the right line (queue) for the right destination and the right class of ticket. In all seasons but the middle of the summer train interiors may be chilly, so carry extra clothing.

Several British cities, London, certainly, and places like Canterbury, have a number of stations. This is an inheritance from the time that competing private railroads maintained their own stopping points. It is wise to know at what station in a given city the train you are taking will arrive. In taking a taxi, requesting "the railroad station" will be insufficient information in many locations. It is necessary to specify what station. Sometimes connections have to be made in cities from one station to another. This can happen in Glasgow, Manchester, Birmingham and London. Be sure that you have enough time to get from one station to the other.

Prices for tickets can vary greatly. It seems that there are always special offers for excursion fares or reductions on certain days. The best place to check on these discounts is right in the station itself, where they are advertised on posters.

When at the ticket window, remember that a one-way ticket is a "single" and a round-trip ticket is a "return ticket." Keep your tickets handy. They will have to be shown or given to railway authorities either on the train or at the exit gate.

TAKING THE BUS

The best that can be said about British buses is that they are cheap, often costing less than half of rail fares to the same destination. The worst that can be said is that they may turn out to be roaring rattletraps. Americans should not expect ordinary British buses to have the comforts of large interstate buses at home. In fact, most do not even have toilets. If the visitor is lucky and gets aboard a shiny, new vehicle, the journey ahead must nevertheless involve getting through all of the bottlenecks of British traffic compounded by the fact that the bus is a big object to be wedged through the narrow, crowded streets of British towns and villages.

Long distance journeys on British buses can be tiring on a crowded vehicle, particularly for non-smokers who are too close to the fumes of the smoking section. The infrequent rest stops can bring the traveler to the grimmest and dingiest of British cafes. Even so, buses go almost everywhere at low cost, and so provide another opportunity to observe ordinary, workaday Britain.

SHOPPING

With America being "malled to death," why spend precious time shopping in Britain? The author has asked this question of many Americans in Britain who were on their way to some emporium instead of a museum or gallery. Shopping just preoccupies many Americans. To be sure, souvenirs for relatives and friends and unique items that cannot be purchased readily in the United States are worthy of shopping forays. But for most goods, shopping is far better, far easier and, certainly these days, far cheaper in the United States.

What are the good buys in Britain? Books, certainly, because excellent bookstores, new and used, abound. London has Foyles, which is purported to be the world's largest bookstore—an operation that spans a street. Antiques and old furniture are also good buys, often when found at open air markets that have great quantities of bric-a-brac. But small shops in out of the way places can yield what may be perceived as treasures also. In addition, some people like to buy English clothes, particularly sweaters and tweeds, which are ordinarily of high quality, but do not come at particularly good prices.

What can spoil bargain hunting for books and antiques and old furniture is a crippling exchange rate between the dollar and the pound. When the dollar is weak, bargains will be few. When the dollar is particularly strong, as it was decades ago, bargains will be abundant. Remember, too, that a stiff Value Added Tax, or V.A.T., is slapped on almost everything. In 1991 it was up to 15%.

Americans can avoid the V.A.T. on expensive items that they want to take home by asking for a "personal export" form from the store clerk. Not all stores have them and many stores will not provide them unless a certain purchase value is reached. These exemptions apply only to goods purchased within three months of the time that the purchaser departs from Britain. Ask a store for more details.

Most ordinary shopping in Britain is not much fun. Shop assistants, often called clerks, are not, as a rule, as helpful or as friendly or as well informed as they are in the United States, where retailing is more of a polished art. When items are out of stock, a common occurrence, great vagueness often prevails about when the next shipment will arrive. Special orders for goods may take an unconscionable amount of time to arrive.

In most towns, shops are concentrated in one area, along a main shopping street called the "high street." Most of them are small and specialized, the way shops were in the United States half a century ago. But supermarkets are showing up in more and more places, another aspect of Americanization. They are more crowded and have longer check-out lines, but they are similar to the American chain stores. Late night shopping is appearing in more places, but closing times tend to be around 5:30 p.m., meaning that crowds on Saturdays are enormous. What is open and what is closed on Sundays is bewildering.

Harrods in Knightsbridge is perhaps the most famous store in the world. It is supposed to have everything. Note the large number of affluent customers in turbans if you go there. Marks and Spencer, oddly called "Marks and

Sparks" by many Britons, is a reliable chain store, sort of a British Montgomery Wards.

GETTING ALONG WITH THE BRITISH

British Characteristics to Look For

Educated persons everywhere know how damaging stereotypes can be and how a great variety of humans and human behaviors exist in any population category. Even so, some behaviors and social patterns show up with sufficient frequency in Britain to be labeled national characteristics. Of course, some Britons will have none of them, but most are likely to carry on with at least some of them to some degree. It will be helpful for Americans to know how British people differ from themselves so that social or business situations will be easier to handle effectively.

Politeness

Americans in Britain will tend to be polite, but in their own informal, folksy and breezy manner. British politeness is different. It has a ritualized predictability, an expected formality.

While Americans will often hold doors open for people following them, they will not do it in the prescribed, ritualized British manner. This includes automatically casting a glance over the shoulder to see who is coming next, holding the door like a machine and primly acknowledging the "thank you" from the next person with a nod or a smile.

In Britain, "please" and "thank you" are involved in just about every human transaction. These words are spoken automatically, sharply and without hesitation. They are normal, necessary and expected parts of the sentences involved. Sometimes there are elaborations, such as "thank you very much indeed." Americans appear at their worst when they say such things as "Give me..." or "Would you let me have..." or "I'd like..." or "I want...." Omitting "please" immediately labels the American as a boor, a label confirmed when "thank you" or "thank you very much" is omitted at the time goods or services are supplied. Note that the British say "Could you please bring me..." instead of "Would you please bring me..." because the assumption is that the person certainly would do it if he or she could.

The Northern English tend to be less formal than their southern counterparts. They are apt to say "ta" for thank you, which is similar to the American "thanks." Curiously, British people do not say "You are welcome." Instead, another "thank you" might take its place.

Americans can practice to match the politeness they will encounter in Britain. They can rehearse aloud by saying a clear "please" for everything and a clear, articulated "thank you" for everything. Have someone pay close attention to your efforts who is prepared to signal with a nudge when you forget. When in Britain, observe how the British do it and follow suit.

Sacred Queues:

American visitors in Britain are likely to spend much more time standing in long lines, which are called "queues" in Britain, which is identical to the French word for "tail" and is pronounced "cue." Long lines indicate Britain's crowded condition. It is possible, for example, to have up to twenty-five people queued up in the fast lane of a store belonging to the most modern supermarket chain in Britain. Moreover, the ordinary neighborhood butcher shop in the high (main) street can have long lines stretching out to the sidewalk on a Saturday morning.

The queues are sacred. They stand for fairness, justice, discipline and order — the very best that British civilization has ever offered — so woe to the American who is too casual about his or her place on one of them. British queues form quickly and naturally. They are noted for being peaceful, straight and disciplined. Everyone seems to know where his or her place is and where everyone else's is as well. The mob scenes of pushing, shouting, shoving to the front and milling about in many Continental countries, particularly Mediterranean ones, and in many Third World countries hardly ever happen in Britain. Compared to the Italians and the French, Americans do form orderly lines fairly well, but not nearly as well as the British do. The occasional American visitor who aggressively tries to slip towards the front may hear the mutter "bloody Yank" coming from the long, patient line.

Restraint of Emotions and Enthusiasm — British Reserve

British people in a queue are almost invariably calm, cool and collected. "Unflappable" would be another word for this attitude which is a pronounced British characteristic. Emotions are restrained and enthusiasm is minimized.

This contrasts sharply with much American behavior, which often features loud and noisy demonstrations of emotions. Consider how American audiences tangle with groups such as representatives of the Environmental Protection Agency or a school board or either side on the abortion issue. For a long time pop psychology in America has encouraged people to express their emotions fully. Another characteristic of American behavior is a very pronounced enthusiasm for whatever is at hand. At best, it gives a drive towards accomplishing something; at worst, it puts people in other people's faces too forcefully.

Understatement is the way the British put the damper on enthusiasm. To call something "very good indeed" is the equivalent of a rave of appreciation in America. When someone excels in a sporting event, polite observers may allow a "well done!" or a "good show!" American fans would jump up and down, shouting, hugging, crying and screaming at a similar feat. These comparisons do not hold when rowdy British football (soccer) fans are considered, of course. Restraint is also absent from the very House of Commons itself in its loud, raucous and often highly emotional debates.

A perceptive Czech once observed that people from the Continent give themselves an air of importance by talking, while an Englishman does so by holding his tongue. This reserve carries over into social situations, and it has inspired many ethnic jokes about the English. English people newly introduced to one another sometimes sit on the edge of their chairs in painful awkwardness while they earnestly cast about for a safe, impersonal subject to discuss. They usually hit upon the weather.

Breezily open Americans act differently. Give an American a chair and a drink, and in ten minutes he or she will be in the midst of important aspects of one's life history. British people usually have to know one another for a time before allowing exchanges about their backgrounds, or about the strengths and weaknesses operating in their lives.

The openness of Americans is often appreciated by Britons in contrast to their own caution. What they often do not perceive is that many Americans have a deeper and hidden wall of reserve of their own, well behind their smiling openness.

The class consciousness of British people may play an important role in reinforcing social reserve. All too often, British people are rapt players at the game of defining people in categories of class and status. Therefore, information about backgrounds and lifestyles may not be given out readily.

In one social circumstance the British are clearly more open and egalitarian than Americans. Older people are not so discriminated against or segregated or shunted aside or shipped away as they are in the United States. Respect for the elderly is clearly indicated by how they are spoken to without condescension by younger people. Moreover, social activities in Britain, such as dances, do not have the usual age segregation patterns that occur in the United States, where persons in one age group feel awkward if another age group is present in substantial numbers. In Britain, people of all ages seem to enjoy activities in mixed age groups.

One resolutely held conviction seems to have something to do with British reserve, namely the belief that they belong to the most civilized society on earth and that as individuals they are the best examples of what civilized human beings are supposed to be. This self-assured egotism of the British was once conveyed starkly by a woman who declared: "If it were not for the weather, England would be the best place on earth to live because the people are the nicest one can find."

Respect for Privacy

British reserve can be considered part of an almost sacred respect for privacy that prevails. Individual space, freedom and rights are all respected. Perhaps that is why Britain has been the homeland of so many colorful eccentrics.

Respect for privacy is undoubtedly in large measure a response to the extremely crowded conditions found over most of the island. The number of inhabitants per square mile in England is not that far behind the figure for Japan, so heightened respect for privacy can be seen as a necessary adaptation to a situation where houses, apartments, and even non-related people sharing living arrangements tend to be crowded in upon one another. Space is a luxury in Britain.

Concern for privacy has many manifestations. Windows are covered with lace curtains. Gardens have protective hedges. When strangers gather at breakfast in bed and breakfast establishments, they need not talk after saying good morning. On trains and in other public places, people do not talk to each other. These are outward manifestations. Important events in private lives and private feelings tend to be screened off similarly, even from friends.

Some aspects of life in Britain seem to contradict this respect for privacy. First, when conversing, British people tend to stand much closer and invade what Americans consider private space. An American who asks directions of a stranger will be surprised at how close the stranger stands when providing information. Second, in eating establishments people are often seated at tables that are already occupied, which sometimes takes Americans aback. Space is not wasted as it often is in American restaurants. Third, British people until recently have been much less careful about allowing tobacco smoke to invade the privacy of others. Anti-smoking prohibitions have not gone as far as in America, and it seems that a higher percentage of Britons still smoke. Often very old people and very young people can be seen taking the last puff right down to their yellowed fingertips. That smoking should be so popular in Britain seems odd because tobacco is very heavily taxed and many brands of cigarettes are of questionable quality.

Materialism

One of the frequent criticisms that some Americans make about their own society is that it is so materialistic. World travelers know that materialism is rampant throughout the world. Americans are outstanding not simply for being materialistic but in that they are so good at acquiring large quantities of the coveted materials. Do not be surprised if ordinary Britons are not as interested in the local castle or cathedral as much as they are in how many pounds they can find in their pay envelopes and in what very specific things they can buy. Britons' intellectual energies are often consumed by carefully calculating what they can afford and how they can add to their possessions over time. The difference between these Britons and their American counterparts is that Americans have had an easier time doing it, at least up to the present.

There is a long tradition of frugality in the backgrounds of the majority of people living in Britain. Clothes are bought that will last. Spending on luxury items is frowned upon. Lavish displays of consumption, including food consumption, is thought to be vulgar. Getting good buys and making pounds stretch wisely are the keynotes of British materialism.

Precision in Language Use

A very high value is placed on how English is used in Britain, and many Americans soon come to the realization that, up against good British conversationalists, their pronunciation is comparatively sloppy, their vocabulary underdeveloped and their verbal agility inadequate. All of this can be intimidating for Americans, but it is much more so for less articulate Britons themselves because it is in the realm of language that their class, educational background and status are starkly revealed.

Americans who are in Britain for a long time discover that their enunciation becomes clearer and more distinct. American tendencies to slur the ends of words or to drop final "g" participles are overcome. In time, Americans are likely to put out more effort in constructing lucid and artful sentences. Of course, this can be carried to extremes of imitation, as when the American "a" becomes the British "a" that sounds like an "ah" as in the pronunciation "toma-htoes." In a way, those Americans who try to abandon all of their native sounds seem somewhat phony. Improvements in American speech in Britain occur in large measure because speaking well is so obviously highly regarded in Britain, to the extent of being treasured as an art by educated persons. Visitors who can express themselves well in standard English are always esteemed, no matter what foreign national accent they may have, "broad American" or any other.

When it comes to many place and family names, English pronunciations can deviate widely from spellings and Americans can be expected to make mistakes. For example, Leicester is pronounced Les-ter, and Worcester is pronounced Woo-ster. Derby is Dah-by. When in doubt, just ask how a place or personal name is pronounced and expect surprises.

One curious deviation from precision in language use is the upper class tendency to use words of great exaggeration during rather loud but unemotional conversations. For example, something can be described as "terribly boring" or "awfully boring" or "frightfully boring." A favored item can be described as "smashing" or "jolly good." These are, of course, the stereotypical upper class pronouncements that Americans have always found very amusing.

Shouting is Shunned

If an American in Britain shouts in an argument with a

British person, he or she loses the argument virtually automatically. Shouters are perceived as those persons who have failed to handle the intellectual content of a disagreement and must raise their voices in order to compensate for their dim intelligence. This attitude is difficult for many Americans to deal with because they have been raised with examples of heroic shouters, such as John Wayne, who raise their voices when something callous, unfair, cruel or dishonest has been perpetrated. Yet shouting in Britain produces counter-productive reactions; the more the American shouts the more smug the Briton becomes. The Briton knows that he or she has won at that point, although victory might be signaled only by the lowering of the head to repress a flickering smile or by dumb resignation at having to deal with a barbarian.

In a classic Anglo-American exchange, a Briton might warn: "You are shouting!" which might bring on the all-American riposte: "There is something to shout about."

There is an English characteristic called "bloody-mindedness" which is hard to define. Someone is "bloody-minded" when they are impossibly stubborn and utterly uncooperative, frequently in a clumsy or awkward manner. Americans might encounter a bloody-minded clerk or garage supervisor. Such people have to be taken on if they cannot be bypassed.

The way for an American to engage in a dispute in Britain on an equal footing is, first of all, to lower one's voice and keep it low throughout the argument. Second, stick to the facts exclusively. Never go to an *ad hominem* argument, that is, an argument that attacks or puts down the opponent personally. In general, well-educated British people argue in lowered voices, taking up the facts precisely. Yet there are less than polite Britons, such as irate bus drivers who will, when exasperated, shout at Americans. The thing to do in such circumstances is not to respond in kind. Instead, keep your voice low and stick to the facts! This method, by the way, can even be effective in the United States!

The Image of Heroic Retreat

Despite their many victories over several centuries of international conflict, the British love to dwell upon those episodes when they were outnumbered and surrounded. They always seem to favor the underdog in combative situations, and they love to cast their heroes in such roles. Heroic retreats and last stands, in which courage and fortitude were displayed against staggering odds, are given special celebration. For example, the most treasured memories of World War II seem to be Dunkirk and the Blitz of London rather than the crossing of the Rhine, the reoccupation of Singapore and Hong Kong or the conquest of western Germany. Similarly, isolated colonial battalions that went down fighting hordes of spear-throwing savages in remote corners of the world are celebrated in paintings, songs and stories. So are heroic failures. Explorers who froze in arctic or antarctic wastes or the misguided Light Brigade that was sent into the cannons' mouths in the Crimean War have a special place in the collective memory of the British.

Maintaining cool, determined courage in a hopeless position seems to be the very essence of heroism for the British. Perhaps it comes from their emphasis on the study of the ancient Greeks, who stressed the same kind of heroism. Perhaps it comes from their canons of sportsmanship, which lay stress on how the game is played rather than on winning. What really counts for them in sport is expending effort and playing fairly. The fellow who gives a situation a good try is tops, regardless of failure in the attempt.

Public Safety

Regardless of occasional outbursts of violence in Britain from Irish terrorists, teenaged toughs, and outrageously barbaric football fans, Britain's urban environments are still among the safest in the world. Some unpopular sections of London, Glasgow and Liverpool may not be safe at night, but such locales are exceptions. In nearly all other British towns and cities, American visitors of either sex can feel safe at all hours. Compared with American cities, Britain's crime rates are extremely low, the inhabitants predictably peaceful, and the police present and efficient. It is somewhere near twenty-five times more likely for a serious crime, such as rape or murder, to occur per 100,000 persons in the United States than it is to occur per 100,000 persons in Britain. So it is safe to go out at any time in nearly all of Britain.

CONFRONTING AMERICAN CHARACTERISTICS IN BRITAIN

One of the best ways to comprehend the dimensions of one's own nationality is to leave that nation for a time. When Americans become immersed in the British environment, they are often startled by revelations of their own national characteristics. Normal, natural behavior at home can suddenly become aberrant behavior abroad. As a result, certain characteristics stand forth in stark relief as typically American, despite the infinite variety and diversity of Americans and American behaviors.

One complication arises from the fact that many Americans have chosen to live in Britain permanently, some of whom are noted for blending into the environment rather easily. They may speak in a very British way, with lowered tones, and their manners might be noteworthy for impersonal understatement. Many of these expatriate Americans have an East Coast background featuring a high level of education, and they are likely to be professionals. American visitors might not even be able to identify them as fellow countrymen.

The British are, of course, quite used to them, and they are also very used to the Americans who stand out glaringly as such because floods of American tourists have poured into Britain regularly for decades. The British know what to look for and what to expect as standard American characteristics. Most of the Americans who have never been abroad, on the other hand, may be seeing them in stark relief for the first time.

Loudness

The first and foremost American characteristic is loudness. Americans seem so much louder in Britain than they do at home. They can be heard coming a mile away. They shout to each other across open, public spaces, which is something Britons ordinarily do not do. Americans seem to be bellowing, howling and gesticulating everywhere. They can even be heard roaring over the rattles and crashes in cheap British cafes.

Of course, there are millions of quiet Americans who would not be noticed for their volume in Britain or anywhere. But a trip to Britain will prove that there is no silent majority among tourists. To be sure, tourists are likely to have high spirits from the fact that they are on vacation. Even so, British people who are polite will make a point of always approaching a person closely before speaking. What could be more American (with the possible exception of apple pie) than a loud shout echoing down twenty-five yards of an historic British street: "Hey! Did you see this over here?"

British shouters exist also, but they are immediately dismissed as the ill-bred, ill-mannered and ill-educated.

American Clothes and Americans Wearing British Clothes

Loud clothes are another indication of the American presence. Americans can be spotted at a considerable distance along a crowded British thoroughfare by the bright colors they wear, often in strange combinations. Americans don ski-style clothes for travel in winter and California-style, casual clothes for travel in summer.

As a rule, British people tend to dress in a more staid and sober manner, wearing more high quality, well-tailored items than Americans do. Across the board, they tend to have fewer but better items of apparel. Consequently, the ups and downs of fashion have less of an impact for most Britons. Britain is certainly much less a throw-away society when it comes to clothes. In fact, in most long queues one can usually spot at least a few "old dears," or older ladies, who tend to sport hats and coats that look as if they are well preserved from the days of World War II.

Many Americans rush to buy and wear British clothes since tweeds, sweaters and other well-made items comprise some of the best bargains that the country has to offer. Yet even wearing British clothes, Americans still present some contrasts. An American man will often sport his Harris tweed jacket on occasions when more formal dress is required. His British counterpart will tend to have on a very good, conservative suit instead, and wear Harris tweed for country weekends or sporting events. After all, such are the occasions for which these wonderful coats were designed. By the way, they seem to last forever.

Young Americans rush to buy and wear the latest avantgarde British fashions whether they go to Britain or purchase them at home. In this field since World War II, Britain has come up with some startling innovations. Colorful, daring and innovative pop fashions continue to blossom in Britain. Actually waves of British fashion have been taken up one after another by Americans. For a time it was the Carnaby Street mini-skirt look, and for a time the "mod" look, later the "punk" look appeared. All sorts of accoutrements have become for a time fashionable, including dyed and radically shaved hair, and metal studded leather wrist bands and collars. By the time the latest fad penetrates to the American interior, say Iowa or Nebraska, British youth will be on to something else.

There is a very considerable difference between who buys and wears youthful British fashions in the two countries. In America the affluent young suburbanites with disposable income are likely to take up the latest popular fashion. Most of these enthusiasts plan to go to college and pursue high-paying careers. By contrast, the very innovators of these styles in Britain are the young people who have little to look forward to. These are the people whose educations come to an early end and whose work lives begin at some boring or unpleasant jobs that have no future. The shocking, new, daring, colorful and often outrageous styles are their way of making a statement in life, which is something they cannot do in any other sphere. It may be all that they have going for them. Such young Britons are not likely to feel that they have much in common with those affluent and upwardly mobile young Americans who seek to imitate their exterior images.

Pragmatism, Speed and Efficiency

Up until now, Americans have had the reputation of being the world's foremost pragmatists, which means, roughly, that they are the most keenly interested in having things work. Americans want to solve problems, get answers and get whatever needs to be done accomplished. Spiritual, philosophical and aesthetic considerations are not their central focus.

Americans are also noted for demanding speed and efficiency from themselves and from people of other nationalities. They want things done without delay and with predictability. Almost everywhere in Britain, pragmatic Americans who live by the clock find themselves frustrated by slowness and inefficiency. Many things are accomplished only after maddening delays, and much is done in the most roundabout manner. There are several ironies here. In the Victorian era, the British themselves were the foremost pragmatists of the world, similarly noted for their speed and efficiency. At the same time, American life was still basically agrarian, and the United States imported efficiently earned British capital. Another irony is that the British exhibit the same impatience and bewilderment when they deal with the Irish, which is an old theme in Anglo-Irish relations. In recent years yet another irony has emerged. The Japanese are now advising their nationals making trips to America to expect to find a lesser degree of speed and efficiency than at home and to be prepared for times when inept Americans will allow plans to go amiss.

One prosaic example involving road repairs can serve to show how the American who takes speed and efficiency for granted can be in for culture shock in Britain: When Americans decide to fix a road intersection by widening it, they are likely to send in a fleet of trucks and equipment and a small army of workers. After a short period of time engulfed in tar and noise, they will transform the intersection and move on elsewhere. A typical British operation at an intersection will involve fewer people, and smaller and fewer pieces of equipment. What is truly remarkable, though, is that the process seems to drag on forever. The road workers are called "navvies," a carryover from the time when they built railroads, and they seem to slog on at their own sweet pace. For example, when a board is needed from a distant pile, one man may go to fetch it, slowly and deliberately, and carry it back even more slowly and deliberately. He is not likely to do it alone because someone will saunter along with him, perhaps to make sure that he picks up the right board, or to make sure that it is balanced securely on his shoulder, or, most likely, just to take a break.

At one such seemingly never-ending road repair site, the author, who regularly passed by it on foot, asked in March whether they planned to finish off the project in July. After a long pause and a searching glance heavenward, a navvy answered in the most innocent and gentle of all Irish brogues, "Which July?"

Cleanliness

Another American characteristic is the demand for a high degree of cleanliness, something that is not sufficiently available in most of Britain and even less so in many parts of the Continent. In Britain the American preoccupation with cleanliness is perceived as an obsession as they daily shower, shampoo, and splash on chemicals. Britons are often amused at what they see as a fetish of cleanliness. For example, the reassuring messages about sanitation inscribed on the paper bands put around toilet seats in American motels are likely to provoke strong laughter from

Britons unaccustomed to them. Americans, on the other hand, are not amused at the lower standards of cleanliness they find throughout Britain. Americans in the cheaper British hotels have one of the worst manifestations of culture shock when they discover that they either have to take tub baths or wash themselves at a sink. Some of them exhibit a peeved reaction that can be called "shower withdrawal syndrome."

Boastful Affluence

The Americans who are so clean and so loud in Britain are from the ranks of the affluent, with relatively few exceptions. After all, the poor and the struggling have to stay at home trying to make ends meet, unless they are adventurous students who go to Britain on a shoestring.

Thanks to the old images from Hollywood and the new images from TV serials, Britons expect Americans to be affluent. Raw statistics on per capita income do show Americans considerably ahead of their British counterparts, although both nationalities are certainly far ahead of most of the world when it comes to commanding goods and services.

Even so, the disparity between British and American affluence is exaggerated by the fact that financially comfortable Americans in Britain display a penchant for boasting about size. Americans tend to go on about how much larger all sorts of things are at home when compared to similar items in Britain. Americans make frequent invidious comparisons about cars, refrigerators, TV sets, apartments, bathrooms, kitchens, gardens and yards. Americans also boast about the size of farms, parks, the number of doctors available and the number of students at various universities. The message is painfully clear: bigger is supposed to mean better.

British people do share the blame for this boasting because some do ask visitors to make comparisons about the size of their refrigerator or car or kitchen with similar items back in America. Perhaps they do this because it provides a topic guaranteed to generate American enthusiasm and animation.

Naturally, the most enthusiastic and animated of Americans are the Texans. The British have a particular fascination with them. The stereotype of the Texan as a particularly loud and exceedingly boastful individual who behaves in an outrageously familiar and friendly manner is often highly esteemed in Britain. Perhaps this is because the Texan carries some American characteristics to their most extreme manifestation. The British love to listen as Texans almost lose control of themselves as they describe how huge and wonderful and spectacular things are in the second largest state in the Union. Dull by comparison are the Canadians or the New Englanders who look and sound much more like the British themselves.

CHAPTER TWO

Travel: What to See in Britain
WORKING OUT A STRATEGY

Why A Strategy to See Britain is Necessary

A STRATEGY is needed simply because Britain has just too much to see and experience. Britain's area of less than one hundred thousand square miles is so rich with attractions that trying to fit just the highlights into the duration of a trip soon becomes an overwhelming task. What is available has to be assessed. Priorities have to be cited. Highlights have to be segregated from all that is available. To do this is to shape a strategy, and strategies, if they are not too rigid or demanding, can make the costly recreational and educational experience of travel efficient and, in most cases, more pleasurable.

Even the most experienced visitors to Britain, those who have been there dozens of times, can always find another historic town, or another ancient site, or another stately home, or another interesting valley that they have never seen before. Similarly, a yearly visitor to London can find another neighborhood, another museum, another impressive sight or another charming corner tucked away somewhere that he or she never saw before. What is more, the most experienced of American visitors almost inevitably arrives on his or her latest trip with a list of places that "must be seen." New lists always keep coming to mind. The point is that Britain is so rich and varied in its civilization that it would take several lifetimes to experience it all.

Here are some examples to illustrate the problem of Britain's richness: I have been going back fairly regularly since the 1960s and on two occasions I have had the opportunity to live there for the better part of a year in two separate locations. Nevertheless, for my next trip there will still be a list of "must see" places that I have never had a chance to get to. Even in a very limited location the offerings can be remarkably rich. For example, a student who went to study at Swansea in south Wales wrote that he was able to go for walks to ruined Norman hill forts, Bronze Age cairns, "lost" medieval towns, castles, early Tudor fortified manors, medieval churches, pre-historic caves, shipwrecks, medieval quarries, and a variety of burial sites. No part of the United States has such intense concentrations of historic sites. Moreover, I know people who initially visited the southeastern tip of Britain and on subsequent visits they have gone back to the same general area, despite all of their vows and plans to move on to other regions of the island. They just get bogged down seeing favorite places once again plus stopping off at the sites in the immediate vicinity that they passed up the last time.

Of course, there is nothing wrong with sticking to a favorite part of Britain. It is a restful alternative to racing all about the island at a frantic speed to take in all of the featured places that travel books tout during a vacation of limited duration.

With only a small segment of one lifetime available to see Britain, perhaps as short as one to three or four weeks, how is it possible to get the most out of it? The worst thing to do is to try to encompass everything. It simply cannot be done. The only result will be frustration, exhaustion, and the feeling of having been dragged past all sorts of things that blur in the memory. What is more, it will seem like work, like a run through a high pressured salesperson's circuit. Reality and plain common sense demand that limitations be imposed. Shortcuts need to be considered.

Practical Shortcut: Seeking Your Own Special Quest

Since Americans are such romantics about Britain, few arrive without some special quest in mind, something that they personally have always wanted to see. It may be a classic tourist attraction. It may be from an image appreciated as a child, or from an adolescent longing, or from an adult fantasy.

Whatever it is, this special quest should not be tucked away into a long list of obligatory things to see and do. It should be indulged in, featured, given a whole chunk of precious time and given top priority. Everyone should try to have imagination and reality touch, as they often do beautifully in Britain.

The nature of such special quests in Britain varies from person to person, and what might seem extraordinarily special to one individual might seem insignificant or even silly to another. Such is the variety of human responses. Dare to do what might seem silly to others! Besides, as any British person will agree, that is one of the most important reasons why people have vacations!

One example of a special quest involved a young American who had always wanted to ride a horse in a London park. It made no difference that her trip to Britain occurred in mid-winter. In foul weather, London stables ordinarily do not rent out their horses. Nevertheless, she persisted, and on one fair day she got her horse from a stable that was so far from a park that she had to ride her steed through dense and frightening London traffic before she reached the park's paths. Yet no one had to ask her whether the time, expense and trouble were worth it, because her face gave the answer.

Another example was the visitor who just had to see James Herriot's Yorkshire, and, if possible, observe the famous veterinarian himself. Whole troops of Americans go off to otherwise grim Liverpool to worship at the shrines now dedicated to the Beatles. Others have made pilgrimages on the London underground railroad to the grave of Karl Marx in Highgate Cemetery in the northern part of the metropolis. More romantic visitors have chased the memory of King Arthur in the west of England, at places such as Glastonbury. There are those who firmly believe that Shakespeare's villain, Richard III, was one of the most unfairly maligned figures in all of history. These people are drawn to York because Richard spent so much of his time in that city. Some people go down to Portsmouth to walk the deck of the flagship of their hero, Horatio Nelson. His ship, the *Victory*, is beautifully preserved at a magnificent maritime museum.

A special quest for a large number of Americans is Stonehenge. They can be seen flocking around the great prehistoric stone circle at any time of the year, some of them much imbued with the occult significance of the place. Another popular special quest, particularly for those keen on literature, is Shakespeare's home town, Stratford-upon-Avon. Literally droves of Americans go through his birthplace, and to Anne Hathaway's cottage, and walk about the town.

In Britain closet royalists come out of their closets. Seeing royal palaces and the changing of the guard and whatever royal panoply is going on, to say nothing of gaining a glimpse of a royal personage, turns out to be the special quest of countless citizens of our egalitarian democracy.

The author remembers going on a rather silly special quest of his own many years ago. Impressed by John Fowles' novel, *The French Lieutenant's Woman*, long before it became a film, I went to Lyme Regis on the south coast of England to seek out the setting. Viewed objectively, this was not a wise allocation of time because I was an historian working on a research project in the libraries of London with a very limited amount of time available on that particular trip to Britain. Why should I look for the scenes of an English novel when I do not teach English literature? Yet it was great fun to wander about in Lyme Regis and today I remember each scene from the book vividly but I am not at all sure about which research project I was working on at the time. What I had done was to achieve my own special quest.

These are just a few examples of special quests. The reader may have one or more of these in mind already, or something entirely different, or perhaps a special quest has not been fully formulated yet. The thing to do is make time available on your trip to Britain for it, even if this means cutting other items from an itinerary. It will be worth the time and the effort to seize that special quest because you will never forget your achievement. Other experiences of a trip to Britain may fade to dim recollections, but the special quest will always be vivid. Make it priority number one!

Another Shortcut: Do Not Make Scenery a Top Priority

When it comes to looking at scenes of natural beauty, many Americans, particularly those from the West, are rather jaded. They have mile upon mile of celebrated and uncelebrated spectacular scenery literally in their backyards. For example, there are many little-known places in Colorado familiar to the author which would be swarmed over if they were in Europe, sites that would probably be furnished with all sorts of colorful legends and romantic names.

While America is one of the best endowed countries in the world when it comes to scenic areas, Britain is more modestly endowed. The places that are usually cited as the best scenic attractions in Britain are: the rough country and the coast in Devon and Cornwall; the rough country and the rolling hills of Yorkshire; the mountains of Wales and Scotland; the charming Cotswold village region; and the Lake District in the northwest of England where famous poets sat about chilly shores in the drizzle. Some also cite the White Cliffs of Dover, but the problem there is that the cliffs look best from out in the English Channel. It is extremely difficult to see them from a good angle from the landward side.

All of these beauty spots of Britain put together comprise but a tiny fraction of the acres upon acres of natural beauty in the United States. Moreover, places of natural beauty in Britain almost invariably have swarms of people appreciating them to death. There is nothing in Britain to match the Grand Canyon, the deserts of Arizona, the multicolored plateau of New Mexico, the majesty of the Rockies, the thick forest of the Great Smokies, the swampland of Florida or the brilliance of New England in early October.

National parks and monuments are very popular vacation destinations for Americans in their own country. Britain has several national parks also, but they are less extensive and generally less impressive and they often include a large area of ordinary farms and rural settings within their borders. British national parks should not figure as top priorities.

Outside of these noted scenic areas, and also outside of the large, ugly, industrial areas and the miles upon miles of sprawling suburban housing, Britain's countryside presents pleasant, undulating green plains, some ridges of dark green hills and some nicely wooded vistas. Everywhere the vegetation is lush, with richly scented, gorgeous flowers blooming during the warmest part of the year. While all of this is pleasing to the eye, it is gentle and unspectacular. Such countryside makes a fitting background for the old towns, cities, castles, cathedrals, museums and other historical and cultural sites that visitors should concentrate upon seeing.

It is wise not to make scenery a top priority. If outstanding British scenery is encountered along the way, well and good. For example, the author saw the brown, hulking Yorkshire moors while on the way to the beautiful and historic seaport town of Whitby and the wild coastline of Cornwall appeared while I traveled from seaport to seaport. Remember that on such a densely populated island, towns, cities, houses, shops, roads, railroads, power lines and all sorts of other manifestations are likely to be thick almost everywhere. So when in Britain, seek out civilization before scenery.

Another Practical Shortcut: Staying in Green England and Avoiding Black England

Black England refers to the industrial areas, where the coal, smoke and soot and the wastes from modern manufacturing and mining darken and scar the landscape. It is the region of slag heaps, cooling towers, railroad shunting yards, and great pylons that march to the horizons. It resembles scenes along the worst portions of the New Jersey Turnpike, so it is no wonder that tourists do not go to towns in the black area as a rule.

Even so, visitors ought to see at least one of these industrial centers, just to appreciate the fact that a workaday, hardbitten England exists side by side with the quaint and beautiful land of castles, cathedrals and Tudor half timber. What is more, it is likely that visitors will find many people in these places who appreciate the rare sight of a tourist. Also, no matter how industrialized or newly built up, most towns in black England will have something of historic interest, such as a very old and special church tucked away up a side street.

Black England is primarily in the northern and western part of England. The English portion of Britain can be divided into two zones. In the south and east there is an undulating, well-watered, broad plain, broken now and then by a line of gentle green hills; In the west and north of England, rough, broken country predominates, with parts of it forming well-worn mountain ranges.

Up until the nineteenth century, civilization was centered upon the great plain because in agrarian societies the fertility of the soil, the ease of farming and the length of the growing season together determine where the population will be the most dense. Therefore, England's broad plain has had the richest history and most of the oldest towns. Ever since the industrial revolution, however, large populations have concentrated where the subsoil resources have been the most ample. Towns and cities sprang up in colder, more barren regions of England which were sparsely populated before the demand for coal and iron intensified. These towns were ugly in the beginning and they are ugly or nondescript today.

The south and east did not remain unindustrialized. But the kinds of industries that tended to establish themselves in that region were craft industries and industries that are lighter, cleaner and more modern, what we would call "high tech" today.

Among the cities of "black England" are Leeds, Liverpool, Rochdale, Birmingham, Crewe, Macclesfield, Wolverhampton, Northampton, Bolton, Huddersfield, Oldham, and the towns around Newcastle-upon-Tyne. While Leicester, Derby, Nottingham and Sheffield have many charming Victorian attributes, they are also essentially part of workaday Britain. In Wales there are heavy industrial concentrations around Newport and Cardiff. In Scotland, Glasgow and the towns around it were developed on account of old heavy industry.

Other Practical Shortcuts: Thinking in Categories

Another way of dealing with the problem of having a limited amount of time to spend on Britain's fabulous abundance is to think in categories. There are just too many British castles, cathedrals, museums, galleries, great houses, palaces, medieval towns, historic cities, seaports and absolute "must-see" places in London. A lifetime is hardly long enough to see all of Britain's attractions, so forget about reaching even a substantial percentage of them during a two- or three-week sojourn. Even so, a short stay can allow a visit to some good examples in several different categories. For example, if a visitor is able to spend some time exploring one magnificent Welsh castle, he or she can return to the United States rich in memories of that experience even if a dozen more castles in the vicinity were bypassed. Return trips can be planned to see some of the others.

Here is a sensible way to group Britain's attractions: London is in a category by itself, and does have some places that everyone should see. Scotland and Wales are each unique areas, and deserve special consideration. Castles, cathedrals, stately homes, and historic towns and villages each form a practical category. A few special places, such as battlefields and highly specialized exhibits outside of London, can be put together in a category of their own. Individual preferences will determine how much precious time will be allocated to each category. Those with a greater interest in military history might want to spend more time in castles. Those interested in furniture, china, decorations, art and architecture may wish to see a number of stately homes instead. Romantics may wish to pursue their search for the perfect English village. Those with spiritual concerns may wish to pass more time in cathedrals and churches.

People who can afford to travel to Britain many times often become "collectors," meaning that they keep tallies of items that they see, putting each place down on a list. Some people collect cathedrals, or castles, or stately homes, or towns. Others make a point of noting every blue plaque that they come across in London. These discreet but attractive designations mark notable residences in London where famous people lived.

Each of the categories mentioned above will now be taken up separately, with appropriate travel hints. Short, workable, but very incomplete lists of suggested sights conclude the consideration of each category.

LONDON

The Uniqueness of London

London is a world unto itself, unique and different from the rest of Britain and unique and different from the other cities of the world. It is said that all of Britain can be divided into two parts: London and the rest of it. Nothing in the United States can compare to London. One out of every eight persons in Britain lives within the borders of greater London, a percentage that would be even higher if the whole metropolitan region were taken into consideration. Almost seven million people live within just over 600 square miles, giving a population density of over 11,000 per square mile. No urban concentration of comparable importance exists in any American city. Roughly only one out of every thirty-three Americans lives in New York City. Moreover, London has the importance of New York, Washington, Philadelphia, Boston and everything in between all rolled into one great circular-shaped metropolis. One odd-sounding description that seems apt is that London is a giant head belonging to a rather small body.

London is the center of government, trade, finance, the arts, publishing, theater and urban culture in general. It is clearly one of the most exciting places on the whole planet. As the noted eighteenth-century sage, Dr. Johnson, wisely remarked: "He who tires of London tires of life."

London is also a world city, sharing that designation with very few other metropolitan centers. It has been argued that only New York and San Francisco fit that description in the United States. All the rest of the cities in America and Britain are more or less provincial. Just what makes a world city? They are cosmopolitan in outlook and composition; having black, brown, yellow and white people sharing it; dozens of languages are spoken in them; they have the magnetism, size and importance to pull in able, ambitious and energetic people from all over the world. Visitors to world cities can feel this status. World cities seem to bask in the notion that they are true centers of human life on the planet.

Coming to Grips with London's Geography: Dividing London Up

Greater London

London stretches in all directions from its center along the Thames. A great ring road makes a wide circle all around it, crossing under the Thames in the east and over it in the west. Traffic thunders along this ring road at a fast and heavy pace, going off on roads heading into London or roads heading away from the metropolis. Beyond the ring road is another wide circle consisting of a patchy green belt.

A vast series of bedroom neighborhoods made up of hundreds of thousands of row houses or semi-detached houses fills greater London, making it one of the most densely packed urban regions in the world. Beyond the green belt are countless commuter suburbs, many of them formerly rural towns and villages, which are now connected to London by rapid train service. With some costly exceptions, these suburbs do not feature the detached, ranch-style wooden or brick houses surrounded by ample lawns and yards that comprise so many American suburbs. British suburbs tend to have smaller houses on more cramped streets.

Greater London itself is connected to the inner centers of the metropolis by the underground, called the tube, which sends the spokes of its rail lines considerable distances in all directions from the Thames. At key underground stops, rail lines disgorge commuters into the greater London system. Considering all of the people and space involved, the system works with surprising efficiency, at least when there are no strikes, accidents or acts of sabotage.

South of the Thames

London can be divided up into four broad areas very conveniently. The Thames River (pronounced Tems, with an "e" as in elephant) snakes through the metropolis, dividing off south London. South London is not particularly interesting. Some important buildings do line the southern bank of the river, such as the National Theatre and Lambeth Palace, where the Archbishop of Canterbury officially resides. There are also a number of large hospitals. But sprawling southwards from the bank is a vast, grim grimy urban area, consisting primarily of uninteresting residential blocks. After wartime destruction, large parts have been rebuilt in rather massive and stark concrete.

The East End and the City of London

North of the Thames another division can be made between East London and West London. In the eastern part of the metropolis the City of London proper can be found, a rectangular-shaped area that hugs the Thames and at one time comprised the old, walled Roman and medieval London. Today the City has a thriving business community reminiscent of lower Manhattan. The Bank of England, the Royal Exchange, Lloyds of London and a host of other worldwide companies have their headquarters in the City of London. The Tower of London and the new Museum of London are other attractions in the vicinity. An army of soberly dressed British businessmen descend upon the City daily, and on weekends the area can be as deserted as Wall Street on weekends.

North and east of the City is the East End proper. It is famous for its working class cockney neighborhoods. During World War II, the area was severely bombed, particularly along the port section stretching eastwards along the Thames. The scars of the Blitz are still deep, despite the massive new concrete complexes and modern buildings that have gone up. The old neighborhoods have irregular skylines because so many buildings were destroyed and have not been replaced by anything more than parking lots. Some people who did not like the prewar shabbiness of the area sometimes refer to the Blitz as urban renewal on a grand scale that was carried out by the *Luftwaffe*.

The East End does have many similarities with London south of the Thames. It, too, is a vast residential area for poorer people that is largely grim, gray and relatively uninteresting. Nevertheless, there is a vast open air market along Portobello Road on Sundays that evokes echoes of the London of Charles Dickens in its sights, sounds and, above all, its characters.

The West End

The West End is a misnomer because it really comprises the heart of central London. Development has continued westwards over the centuries, and it now extends far to the west of the so-called West End. Nevertheless, the name "West End" has stuck from the time centuries ago when it comprised the new and fashionable part of London.

The West End has the greatest tourist attractions. It is here that the visitor is likely to spend the most of his or her time in London because so many important and interesting places are clustered together: museums, theaters, famous squares, shopping streets, Parliament and some palaces. For that reason it deserves the detailed geographical consideration following.

Coming to Grips with the Geography of Central London

Newcomers to London are well advised never to go out without one of the handy folding maps of the metropolis which are readily available from tourist authorities, bookshops and newsstands. The very best of these maps have the tube (underground railway) stops superimposed so it is possible to know at a glance which stop to aim for. Maps from the British Tourist Authority, 64 St. James's Street, London SW 1A1NF, are very good.

The richness of the few square miles of central London is simply amazing. Getting around in this milieu is not so easy at first because the streets curve into and away from one another at odd angles and the squares and streets leading to them seem all pushed in on one another. Visitors are often confused trying to find their way from one major hub to another. "Can you tell me how to get to Leicester Square?" is a question so often heard in a broad American accent on London's streets, with variations of the question

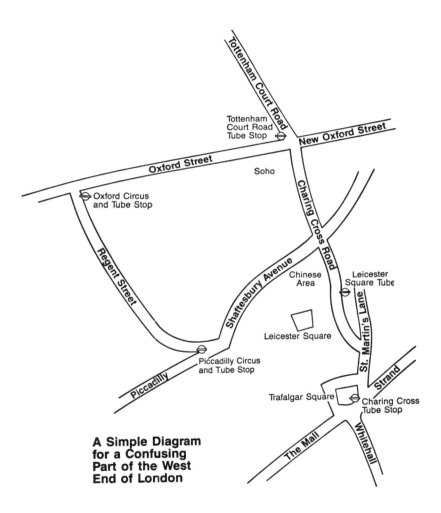

substituting Trafalgar Square or Piccadilly Circus for Leicester Square.

These three hubs seem to be the best places to begin to sort out central London's geography. The three form a roughly irregular triangle (see the diagram). Piccadilly Circus is London's Times Square, having a reputation for brassiness, loudness and crudeness. But it is much less dangerous and degenerated. "Circus" means a place where roads come together. Remember that Piccadilly Circus is roughly to the west of Leicester (pronounced "Les-ter") Square. Regent Street feeds traffic into Piccadilly Circus from the northwest, and Shaftesbury Avenue brings traffic from the east. Leicester Square is at the very heart of the theater district. Note that the square itself is just to the west of the London underground stop of that name.

Of all the sights in the London area, Trafalgar Square is probably one of the three most memorable, along with the Tower of London and Parliament. Who can forget Nelson's column, the floodlighted fountains and the great bronze lions? Trafalgar Square is just southeast of Leicester Square via Charing Cross road. Flanking Trafalgar Square itself are the National Gallery and the National Portrait Gallery. The Royal Academy is some distance, actually closer to Piccadilly Circus.

Trafalgar Square is an excellent departure point for the avid urban hiker. Whitehall is a great road leading directly south, past government buildings and the colorful Horse Guards to the Houses of Parliament and Westminster Abbey. The Mall is another great road that leads southwest to Buckingham Palace. The Strand is the first segment of a major street leading northeast. After a while it becomes Fleet Street, then Ludgate Hill, where it passes St. Paul's in East London and then Canon Street, where it leads up to the monument erected after the Great Fire of 1666. The Tower of London is not far from the monument. Only strong hikers should start out on Fleet Street with the Tower as the destination.

Many of London's other major attractions are not far away from this triangle of hubs. Running east and west, but north of these hubs is one of the busiest shopping streets in all of London, brassy Oxford Street, particularly the stretch of it between Oxford Circus and Tottenham Court Road (pronounced totten-em). Between Oxford Street and the lines drawn between Leicester Square to the east and Piccadilly Circus to the west is the Soho district, where Karl Marx once lived. Today it is a place for foreign restaurants intermingled with enterprises of all sorts dealing with sex. Just up behind Trafalgar Square, towards Shaftesbury Avenue, are the densely packed streets of London's remarkable Chinese district, featuring a large number of splendid and varied Chinese restaurants.

The best way to get to and away from central London is via the tube or the underground because it is fast, direct and efficient. (See the section that follows this one for practical details about using the tube.) The Tower of London will require a stop at Tower Hill station; the Houses of Parliament can best be reached from Westminster station; a whole group of museums can be reached from the South Kensington station. These include the Victoria and Albert Museum, the Natural History Museum and the Science Museum.

Getting Around in London: The Underground

Driving a car in central London is a chore, just as it is in Manhattan in New York. Individuals are better off using public transportation. Most Londoners do most of their travel on the underground, otherwise known as the "tube." It is London's remarkable subway system which provides abundant and rapid public transportation all over the London area. Buses roar everywhere over the surface of the metropolis, of course, but their routes, numbers, criss-crossing and diverging can become very confusing for the visitor. It is much better to depend on the tube because it is usually faster and more direct than any surface transportation.

In addition to being convenient, the underground is very

interesting historically and sociologically. Most trains and stations are old, evoking memories of World War II, when people took shelter from Nazi bombs in the system's caverns. All sorts of interesting people from all over the world and from all walks of life can be observed on the tube, but the conventions respecting privacy in crowded places require that such observations be made discreetly. Conversations rarely occur, and when they do, they are usually between people who know each other and voices are ordinarily kept at low levels. Every so often a loud and obnoxious drunk will destroy the atmosphere, but travelers are in general free from the physical dangers and intimidation found too often on the New York subway system.

Since the underground radiates far out from the center of London in all directions, commuters in many outlying areas of greater London can be within a half hour or 45 minutes of Oxford Street or Piccadilly Circus or Charing Cross Station or the financial center, the City proper. Beyond the underground network, and connecting to it, is a commuter rail system. Taken together, these railways enable literally millions of people to work in the metropolis without having to spend excessive time commuting.

Practical Hints for Using the Underground

At first the system seems difficult, but with some practice the visitor becomes delighted with his or her ability to zoom all over London. It can become great fun, especially when the person has a pre-purchased pass for unlimited rides.

The first step is to get a free little folding map of the underground, called the "Journey Planner," available at all the stations. At first glance, the routes look much more complicated than they actually are. Notice the different colors for the different lines. Notice also the stations that appear as little solid notches. Observe that some stations are designated by round circles and others are designated by three-quarter circles that merge with other three-quarter circles. If a station has a circle or a merged circle, lines can be changed at them. This cannot be done at stations indicated by notches. At stations where changes can be made, prominent signs direct passengers to the other lines.

When you are riding on the tube, look at the diagram of stations on the wall of the car above the windows. You can mentally tick off the stations one by one on this chart because it gives only the line upon which you are riding. You can easily coordinate this chart with the "Journey Planner" folding map.

Here are some other things to notice on the map: The Circle Line makes a complete but oblong circle. Observe, also, that some lines branch. For example, at the upper center of the map, the Northern Line has one branch going to Edgeware and another to Mill Hill East and another to High Barnet. For those heading inward to the center of London these outward-bound destinations do not make much difference, so any train will do. But for those heading north, away from the center, it is vital to get on the train going to the right branch. Large, electronically changed train arrival signs hang over platforms at stations where trains arrive on their way to one of several branches. These signs indicate which trains will arrive and when, and in what order.

Fares can be paid in three different ways: First, tickets can be bought at the booth in the station. Second, with exact change in hand, possible lines to the ticket booth can be avoided by using one of the machines issuing tickets. Look for your destination on the lists that are printed over the machines and use the appropriate one. Note also how tickets are validated and turnstiles opened at busy stations by inserting them in slots. Just watch what other people do at such places. The third way to pay a fare is to purchase a pass that enables the owner to travel anywhere on London's underground or on London's buses or, in the case of some passes, on both. Such passes can be purchased at travel agents in the United States at no extra charge. These passes can be real money savers and are highly recommended. Without them the cost of getting around in London can mount quickly and alarmingly for those on a tight budget.

One more hint needs to be given: Americans and other visitors to London have a penchant for standing idly all over the escalators. Signs clearly insist that they stand over to one side so that people may hurry up or down them. Even in remarkably polite London, hapless tourists who stand on the wrong side can be barked aside, shoved aside or run over by individuals who are in a big hurry.

London's Taxis

For the relatively affluent, London's taxis provide an excellent means of transportation from point to point in the metropolis. The drivers are reputed to be the best in the world on account of the detailed knowledge of their vast urban environment, their skill in driving through heavy and fast traffic, and, in most but not all cases, their courtesy. All of London's cab drivers must pass rigorous tests on the geography of the streets before they are licensed to ply their trade.

Their black cars are huge, inside and out. Five people can get in with ample leg room and space for bags. Those cabs with a yellow light gleaming at the top are for hire. Unlike in America, nobody can sit up with the driver.

London's Theaters: A World Class Highlight

What bullfighting is to Spain, opera is to Italy, rich cuisine and painting is to France and films are to California, theater is to London. The metropolis has been famous for dramas, musicals, operettas and ballets throughout the world for many centuries. To put it succinctly, theater is the greatest cultural phenomenon in Britain.

London has been the Mecca for countless actors, some of whom succeed brilliantly while others work long hours for low pay when they can find work. In actuality, the overwhelming majority of people in this huge pool of talent work at other things most of the time. For them, and for their audiences, the lines are the most important part of their craft. For American theater, the visual impact of sets and costumes counts for more than in Britain.

The bedrock of theater in Britain is Shakespeare, which has trained generations of actors and gives them opportunities to make a living in their difficult profession. Shakespeare is constantly being revised, reshaped, redone and sometimes bizarrely presented by ambitious producers, directors and actors. Yet the classic productions never cease to go on, not just in London but at the Royal Shakespeare Theatre in the bard's home town of Stratford-upon-Avon.

There are dozens of theaters in London. Among the more famous are the National Theatre, the Garrick, the Drury Lane Theatre, Covent Garden, Haymarket and Sadler's Wells. They cluster in the vicinity around Leicester Square, bright and busy every evening. Many of the interiors are still elaborately Victorian or Edwardian, and gently seedy, adding to the overall effect.

Everything else is available also, from mysteries and romantic farces to wrenching drama and spectacular musicals. While it may be difficult to get tickets to a big hit, unless they are purchased far in advance, there is always something good to see. Perhaps it will be the big hit of a few months or years ago. The best place to buy tickets is at the window of the theater itself in the afternoon. Tickets bought at booking offices will cost something extra for their fee, and may involve an awkward exchange of their vouchers for actual tickets at the theater. Sometimes special outlets sell remaining tickets at half price for that evening's shows. Ask about for such bargains. Another way to economize is to purchase tickets for bad seats at enormous discounts. The disadvantage is that part of the stage may be out of sight or it may be a physical torture to strain across a railing to see it or perhaps binoculars may be necessary.

Designations for seat locations within a theater are different in Britain: Orchestra seats are called the stalls; the mezzanine is called the dress circle; the first balcony is called the upper circle and the balcony may be called the gallery.

British audiences have their own peculiarities. They tend to dress up more than Americans do, and they are wonderfully quiet. When anyone transgresses this custom of silence, a distinct shushing sound will erupt, and the guilty will be quiet, if they are British, that is. Also, at comedies Americans will miss many jokes because they pertain to current affairs or topics that are obscure to those who live in the United States. Yet a good comedy will have many good jokes that will register internationally.

A Short List of London Sights that Should Be Seen

Around London Bus Tour — One of the best ways to start out in London is go get an overall basic orientation and a quick view of the great sights by taking the Around London Bus Tour provided by the London Transport Service. Fairly inexpensive tour buses leave Piccadilly Circus regularly. Places along the way can be noted for a return visit later on.

The British Museum — This is one of the most spectacular museums in the world that sprawls for acres and contains one of the most extensive and diverse collections of exhibits ever amassed. Included are exhibits as varied as a mass of mummies, marbles from the Acropolis, Japanese ceramics, gorgeously illustrated hand-made books, vast stamp collections and priceless documents from English history. Greek, Roman, medieval, Egyptian, Assyrian and British antiquities are on display in dazzling abundance. The specialist in any one of these fields will be delighted. The British Library, one of the best in the world, is housed in the center of the museum, but admittance is restricted to ticket holders.

The Houses of Parliament — These famous buildings should be seen, but perhaps from the outside only. Lines for admission tend to be long, and tying up a whole afternoon to get in may not be a worthwhile investment of time.

Either the House of Commons or the House of Lords can be visited. The buildings are strikingly Victorian in decor, inside and out. They are pseudo-Gothic, which is what the romantic Victorians who built them in the mid-19th century wanted. Many of the murals inside seem to be right out of the pages of Victorian children's history books. If pressed for time, a walk around the outside and a few appreciative glances up at Big Ben will suffice.

The Tower of London — The Tower of London is an historic treasure because of the great events and people from English history associated with it. Beefeater Guards, drawn from specially selected veterans, serve as informative guides. The best way to see the Tower is on one of their lively tours, which is included in the price of admission. At the Tower one can see the old Norman keep, a dazzling display of armor and weapons and the Crown jewels. Newer sections jostle the old for space, but the locations where grisly historic events took place still evoke the past wonderfully. These include the gate where traitors were brought in, the place where bodies of murdered princes were found, and the exact spot where Anne Boleyn and other victims of Henry VIII's wrath were beheaded. The Tower of London is in the East End, near Tower Bridge, which is often wrongly called London Bridge, and wrongly thought of as medieval. It is actually late Victorian. Expect the Tower of London to be extraordinarily crowded, so select an odd hour on a weekday to go.

Westminster Abbey — Westminster Abbey is right across from the Houses of Parliament. It is here that most of Britain's illustrious dead are laid to rest, including famous kings, queens, poets and statesmen. The ancient church, much of which was built by Edward the Confessor, has been the place where the kings and queens of Britain have been crowned. A series of chapels, some of them very ornate, take up a substantial portion of the edifice. For those interested in Tudor history, the chapel of Henry VII is of paramount importance, as is the tomb of Queen Elizabeth I. There is also a Poets' Corner of interest to all those concerned with English literature. The cloisters allow a

Approach to Canterbury Cathedral

Ruins of Fountains Abbey, Yorkshire

St. Giles High Kirk, Edinburgh

Balmoral Castle, Scotland

York Minster

Clifford's Tower, York

Street in Lavenham, East Anglia

Bolton Castle, North Yorkshire

Ruins of Laugharne Castle, Wales

Scene from London's busy West End

Street scene from Lewes, southern England

Restored interior of the Provost's House, Aberdeen, Scotland

Brighton Pavilion

Penshurst Place, southern England

Coast of Cornwall

Interior of Haddon Hall

good stroll that can evoke the far past, despite roaring traffic nearby.

Other London Museums and Galleries in Brief — London is one of the very few world centers for our Western Civilization, and as a result it has a concentration of museums and galleries that may be unsurpassed by any other city in the world. Individual interests vary greatly, so here is a list of other museums and galleries that are quite popular, some public and some private, some to enlighten and some to entertain. With these, as with so much else in Britain, it is foolish to rush through as many as possible in as short a time as possible. It is far better to select a few of particular interest and to take these in at a good pace. Save the others for future trips.

Two world-famous art galleries are right on Trafalgar Square: *The National Gallery*, which houses a vast collection of British and European paintings, and the *National Portrait Gallery*, where all of the most famous figures from British history are on view. Either the Charing Cross or Leicester Square tube stop will take the visitor there. Paintings from the last two centuries, mostly British, can be found at the famous and crammed *Tate Gallery* which is to the southwest close to the Thames. Take the tube to Pimlico to get there.

A cluster of museums of lie close to Cromwell Road in the southwest. The *Victoria and Albert Museum* has a huge collection of various fine and applied arts. The *Science Museum* is nearby and should not be missed by people interested in engineering, transport, including railroads, mining, and communications. The rather old-fashioned *Natural History Museum* with fossils and specimens of minerals, plants and animals from all over the world is nearby. The South Kensington tube stop is the one to get off at for all of the museums in this cluster.

For those with a keen interest in anthropology, the *Museum of Mankind* has new and fascinating displays. It is part of the British Museum, but housed separately. Take the Piccadilly Circus or Green Park tubes to get there.

For those interested in military history, the *Imperial War Museum* has many striking exhibits, particularly of the era of world wars. Unlike nearly all museums, it is south of the Thames. Take the tube to Lambeth North or Elephant and Castle.

For London itself, the new and excellent *Museum of London* has exhibits from prehistoric times until the present day. Take the tube to either St. Paul's, Barbican or Moorgate.

Two commercial museums in London deserve mention. One, *Madame Tussaud's*, is old and famous, and the other, the *London Dungeon*, is new and gaining popularity. Madame Tussaud's is the best known waxworks in the world, containing all sorts of contemporary and historical figures, many of them amazingly lifelike. There are classic exhibits of the worst scenes of the French Revolution and a heroic evocation of the Battle of Trafalgar. It can be reached by taking the tube to Baker Street. The London Dungeon thrills children of all ages attracted by horror. It features the gruesome and grotesque, including the plague, hangings and violent, nasty aspects of history. Take the tube to London Bridge.

STRATEGIES FOR SCOTLAND

What Is Special about Scotland

The Scots enjoy working at maintaining their own distinctiveness, and in this they are helped by the legacy of a long period of development as a nation separate from England. The two nations were officially joined only in the early 18th century, and the last Scottish uprising took place in the middle of that century. Before that, Scotland was an independent kingdom for centuries, with its own institutions, including its own Parliament and laws, its own national music and dress, its own customs and special foods, and its own language. Once English was introduced in the Lowlands, the Scots developed their own very distinctive way of rendering it, called the Scottish burr. Scotland also had its own ancient university, St. Andrews.

Scotland fought England in many wars, often forming alliances with England's enemy, France. On several occasions during Anglo-French wars, Scottish forces attacked through England's back door, the northern border. Many brutal battles took place between the English and the Scots over the centuries, the last of which was the Forty-five, an uprising of Highlanders in favor of the exiled Stuart pretender to the English throne. It occurred in 1745, just thirty years before the American Revolution began. For a time the English were so adamant against Scottish nationalism that they banned the use of the bagpipes and the wearing of the clan tartans.

Technically, Scotland was never conquered. England and Scotland were first joined together in 1603 when a Scottish king, James VI, also became king of England as James I. James VI and I, as he is often known, was the closest heir to Queen Elizabeth I, who died unmarried. It took another century to make the union official rather than just through the person of the monarch.

Today Scotland has its own great metropolis, stately and beautiful Edinburgh, and its own vast, depressed industrial belt along the Clyde River, which includes Glasgow.

A special feature of Scottish geography is that it has so many wild and beautiful places in the Highlands, where clear, rushing mountain streams are reminiscent of those found in the American Rockies. There are also gaunt, almost bare mountains that are covered with those singular Scottish plants, rough dark heather and tough, beautiful yellow gorse. Scotland even boasts of a ski area in its mountains. There are also deep, dark lochs, or giant lakes. In the west and north of Scotland are scattered picturesque islands that are regularly swept by wind and rain.

Scottish Characteristics and Speculation about their Origins

Ordinarily stereotypes should be shunned because they

can do so much to harm human relationships. Yet behind many stereotypes lie some partial truths. This certainly seems to be the case for the proverbial Scottish thriftiness. The Scots do not seem to waste anything, and they do make very careful and open efforts to find out about prices and values. A stark geographical reality has made thriftiness a necessity over the centuries. Scotland has been a very poor country for that long period of human history when agriculture dominated the economy. The soil is hard with rocks and flint in most places, and the growing season is short. Most of the rugged and beautiful stretches of Highland Scotland simply cannot produce much food. It is a fact that the ancestors of most Scots huddled in their chilly, rain-pounded cottages or slate gray buildings eating oatmeal. Big spenders do not come from such environments.

Another aspect of the Scottish stereotype is dourness, an adjective that means thinking before they speak, and then speaking a few well chosen words and making sure that the hearer understands. Dour behavior is serious and sober, without a sense of humor. The Scots have also been regarded as straight and honest in their dealings, although great sticklers for detail and proprieties. These characteristics have made so many Scots able administrators throughout Britain and, in the past, throughout the British Empire. It has also made them effective businessmen, lawyers, scientists, bankers, and doctors. Scots have functioned for centuries as the capable deputies, or second in command, for British business operations. Oddly, the Scots have not produced many outstanding political leaders in modern times.

Scottish nationalism is understandable because of their separate, independent development for so many centuries and their wars with England. While it is a potent force, a majority of Scots probably realize the advantages that come from being in a United Kingdom. The British government has certainly tried to respect Scottish and Welsh sensitivities by accepting some forms of regional autonomy and by recognizing cultural differences. For example, it is not unusual for BBC announcers to speak with a distinctive Scots dialect. Another example of acceptance of Scottish distinctiveness is the use of Scottish pound notes issued by the Bank of Scotland. Scottish pounds have exactly the same worth as British pounds, and in most places they can be used without difficulty. One difference is that the single Scottish pound is paper, while a British pound is only in coin. Less obvious, Scottish law still has its distinctiveness; the established church in Scotland is Presbyterian, not Anglican, and local government is distinctive also. For example, Scotland has provosts instead of mayors, burghs instead of towns. There is also a Secretary of State for Scotland who takes over many functions that separate ministries carry out in England and Wales. Last, but certainly not least in the hearts of the Scots, they have their own national football (soccer) team.

The Scots and their descendants are all over the world. The English have joked that the British Empire was created so that the Scots could have a large area in which to make money. The Scots have retorted that if it were not for the famous regiments of Scots soldiers, such as the Black Watch, the British Empire could not have been created in the first place. The Scots have always seen their regiments as the best in the British army. Such banter reveals the ongoing rivalry between the English and the Scots, which is usually friendly and appreciative, but sometimes it can take on an edge.

Scottish stereotypes prevailing in America tend to be very favorable, depicting the Scots as democratic, friendly and utterly thrifty. By the way, Americans do sometimes err in calling them "Scotch," which is the proper name for a beverage, but not for the Scots people.

The Scottish stereotype in England retains the thrifty aspect, sometimes stretching it into a mean stinginess. The English are apt to stress aspects of Celtic wildness in the Scots also. At their worst, the Scots are depicted as drinking to excess and being tactless, crude, coarse and loud. Some unfriendly critics have suggested that these negative traits explain why the Scots have a reputation for getting along with Americans, since Americans at their worst are supposed to manifest these characteristics also. In Scotland, the worst stereotype of the Englishman can be just as unflattering. He is seen as effeminate, silly, insincere, devious, stiff, haughty, unfriendly and so cold-blooded that most human feelings have been drained out of him.

These stereotypes, friendly and unfriendly, along with those for the Irish and the Welsh, figure in that endless series of jokes that begin: "Once there was an Englishman, a Scotsman, a Welshman and an Irishman...." American visitors are advised not to join this play upon national differences that have been created by geography and history over the centuries.

Getting the Most out of Scotland

Many Americans travel to Scotland to see where their ancestors came from, and this in itself is rewarding, no matter how poor or barren or industrialized these places may be. Others travel to Scotland to enjoy the beauty, as countless English people have done over the centuries. Queen Victoria herself was so enamored of the cool, wild Highlands that she spent considerable time in her Scottish castle, Balmoral. While many visiting Americans will enjoy the scenery immensely, others, particularly those from the more scenic parts of America, may not find Scotland's beauty overwhelming. They may also take note of the fact that historic sites thin out in Scotland, and that nearly all of the castles and cathedrals are smaller than in England and that many of the newer towns look too new.

Getting the most out of Scotland requires making a personal assessment of how high a priority should be placed on observing natural beauty. It takes time and effort to get up into the Highlands where the wildest, most open terrain and the best mountainous panoramas can be seen. The opportunity to see many historic sites may have to be sacrificed if the visitor has only a limited amount of time to spend in Britain.

For those oriented more towards British history and culture, time may be better spent in Scotland south of the

Highlands. Edinburgh, St. Andrews, Stirling and Aberdeen, plus the little towns and villages down the coast from Aberdeen are excellent alternatives to a prolonged journey through the Highlands.

Scottish cathedrals, castles, cities and other sites have been integrated into the short lists for special categories.

STRATEGIES FOR WALES

What Is Special about Wales

The Welsh are extremely proud of their history, which is often generously mixed with legend. They see themselves as the original and true Britons, the people who fought with the Romans long before Anglo-Saxons arrived. When the Germanic Anglo-Saxons invaded, the outnumbered Britons fought them also, until the Anglo-Saxons pushed them into the hills of the west, which became Wales. There they remained, a fierce, pastoral, tribal hill people until English kings sent expeditions to subdue them. The great castles of Wales testify to the force that England brought to bear to conquer and control them. Militant contemporary Welsh nationalists claim that the conquest was never complete, right down until the present day. Some of them deface English names on road signs and agitate for more Welsh language programming on radio and television. A substantial percentage of the Welsh population regularly speak at least some Welsh today, often as a conscious national statement. There are efforts to maintain Welsh in the schools, where English is often a second language, and through a great variety of cultural activities, especially those centered on the Welsh speaking chapels. Newspapers as well as radio and television broadcasts in the region are in Welsh.

A vivid stereotype of the Welsh exists. It has them as magnificent singers, especially in choruses. They are also supposed to be talkers of quick wit who are likely to be somewhat sly, shifty, and devious. The Welsh are also seen as more romantic than the English, which means that they are more emotional and temperamental, and, consequently, unpredictable. This is supposed to link them to the other Celts, the Scots, the Irish and the Bretons of Brittany in France. Yet they differ from the Bretons and Irish, but not the Scots, in that they are staunch Protestants. The physical dimension of the stereotype has them as short, dark-haired and dark-eyed. The best stereotypical image has them singing hymns in plain Protestant chapels in a beautiful and remote countryside.

Among the famous Welshmen of history have been Henry VII, the founder of the Tudor dynasty; David Lloyd George, the Prime Minister during World War I; Dylan Thomas, the poet; and Richard Burton, the actor.

Getting the Most out of Wales

Everyone who goes to Britain should spend at least some time in Wales for several good reasons. Wales has its own atmosphere and pace, which is more provincial and slower. In many ways, a visit to Wales is like a visit to another country. Despite its small size, it has an amazing number of picturesque historic sites, often set against the background of hills or mountains or seashore, or a combination of them. Wales also tends to be less expensive than England.

It seems that no other place in the world has so many magnificent castle ruins in a relatively small area, thanks to the efforts of vigorous English kings to build them as strongholds in order to incorporate Wales in their realm. They succeeded, and left an incomparable boon for tourism in Wales.

The northwest corner of Wales is probably the best place to go if time is limited. Conway, Harlech, Caernarvon, and Anglesey are all close together, and Snowdonia, a National Park noted for its high peaks, is right in the vicinity. Small towns, some of them ancient and walled, are delightful in Wales.

The castles, cathedrals, towns and other sites in Wales

have been incorporated into the short lists for special categories that follow.

CASTLES

Strategies for Seeing Castles

Castles and cathedrals are the two most significant kinds of medieval buildings; castles reveal the warlike, struggling nature of the era while the cathedrals demonstrate its soaring faith.

Britain has several hundred castles of various sizes and in various stages of disrepair. It would be difficult to find any place in Europe with such a great variety of them crammed into such a small land surface. Therefore wherever one stays, a castle will be near.

The problem of which castles to see and which to bypass will always confront the visitor to Britain. Since castles come in several varieties, it is likely that each individual is more likely to enjoy one kind more than another. Some visitors prefer uninhabited, ruined castles and some prefer those which have been repaired, added to, and inhabited down to the present. Even castle ruins come in varieties: Some are mere odd heaps of stone and bits of wall that children and dogs clamber over merrily, for which there is no admission charge. Some ruins are enormous, covering acres, consisting of great walls and turrets of rough gray stone. They have lost some of the appearance they had in the Middle Ages, when they had bright, stuccoed exteriors and light painted conical roofs that flew colorful flags. These ruined castles are often owned and operated by the National Trust, and are accessible for a modest fee. (This variety, incidentally, is the author's favorite kind of castle.)

Some castles or parts of them have been lived in until the present day, and may appear as private residences or they may be converted to hotels. They will vary considerably in majesty and, for those offering accommodations, price.

There is another variety of castle which seeks to evoke the atmosphere of an amusement park along the lines of Disneyland. Such castles may have giant wax historical figures, or, worse, animated giant historical figures that lurch about in a manner reminiscent of Dr. Frankenstein's creations. There will also be piped in "historical" music, a troupe of extras in costumes, perhaps music from some of the extras, and perhaps a small menagerie strutting about, especially peacocks and ducks. These Disneyland-type castles look as if considerable money has been invested in their resurrection. The few genuine pieces or parts remaining from the Middle Ages are lavishly supplemented by neatly manufactured modern items. Interiors will be bright with color, rich in paneling and fresh with new paint. The price for tickets is astounding.

See the short list of castles at the end of this section for suggestions about which ones to see.

The Significance of Castles

Castles were strong, defensive structures placed in strategic locations that were intended to be royal strongpoints. In actuality, the noblemen who were supposed to man them in the name of the king often used them against the crown. Such castles came to represent the strength of local, feudal authority instead of the power of a distant monarch. Great, predatory noble families made castles their homes and bases of operations as they played the grand medieval sport of war. Before cannons were developed, a well stocked and well-garrisoned castle could hold out against extremely long sieges.

Wales has a group of spectacular castles. These were originally intended to be English outposts in a conquered but still rebellious Welsh tribal countryside. They were usually built comparatively rapidly, which gives them the architectural harmony of construction from one time period only. They were allowed to fall into ruin after the Middle

Ages in part because the Welsh always saw them as the physical symbols of English domination over them.

Some Helpful Terms for Understanding Castles

A *barbican* is the outer fortification, or the outwork.

A *breastwork* is often a temporary defensive work, breast high.

The *donjon (dungeon)* is the main tower or the keep of the castle. Often the cellar or the deep interior is referred to as the donjon and is the grim place where the prisoners were kept.

The *keep* is usually the strongest part of the castle, designed to be the last place to hold out in a siege.

The *parapet* can be an outer wall.

The *portcullis* is a grating of strong bars of wood or iron that can be suddenly dropped across the gateway of a castle.

The *rampart* is the embankment surrounding a castle upon which the parapet is raised. Sometimes the term includes the parapet.

The *turret* is a small tower rising above the walls. The great castles would have many of them.

A Short List of Castles

Balmoral Castle — This was Queen Victoria's favorite retreat, probably because it was in such a scenic part of Highland Scotland. Today the Victorian atmosphere still pervades it. Balmoral is still the official summer residence of the royal family, but visitors can stroll about the gardens and see the ballroom and some exhibits near it.

Bolton Castle — Bolton Castle is a stark building in a bleak setting in North Yorkshire. Mary, Queen of Scots, was imprisoned there, and there is a display of her chambers. This castle is not spectacular, but it does have atmosphere.

Caernarvon (sometimes Caernarfon) — This castle has gained everlasting fame as the place where a succession of

Princes of Wales have been installed. It is a large, grim mass of a castle ruin on a river, one of the huge fortresses constructed in Wales by Edward I in the 13th century in order to hold Wales for England. Today it contains a regimental museum.

Conway — This is undoubtedly one of the very best castles in the world to visit, enhanced as it is by the small walled town that it once protected. It is partly in ruins and can be explored thoroughly. Even its tallest turrets can be climbed. Mountains, the sea, an estuary for small boats all help to enhance the vista.

Conway was built in the relatively short time of just a few years by Edward I in order to help hold Wales for England.

Dunnottar Castle — This castle is perched on high rocks at the very the edge of the sea, in one of the most dramatic settings imaginable for such a structure. Its history is filled with violence and tragedy. It is near Stonehaven, just south of Aberdeen on the northeastern Scottish coast.

Deal — Deal Castle is on the southeastern tip of England. It is low, squat and mostly empty today. It is more modern than most English castles, since the Tudors built it to guard the southern beaches. It is designed to utilize artillery pieces.

Edinburgh Castle — This huge, sprawling castle astride a huge rock dominates the skyline of Scotland's capital. On a clear day the view of the city from the battlements is marvelous. Most of it dates from the 16th century, but it has been added onto over the centuries. Many famous personalities and events of Scottish history are connected to the castle. Today there are military museums among the complex of buildings on the rock.

Harlech — Harlech Castle is a splendid ruin in a splendid mountainous setting. It is another castle built by Edward I to hold Wales in the 13th century. It once guarded an inlet of the ocean which has since become dry land. It was here, during the Wars of the Roses, that heroic Welshmen defending it inspired the stirring anthem, *Men of Harlech*, a song dear to all the Welsh, especially in times of crisis.

Hever Castle — Hever Castle is one of the castles-cum-amusement parks run for profit. Money has been poured into this old home of Anne Boleyn and the Astor family to make it a special attraction in southeast England. There is a maze, a children's playground, Italian gardens, and rooms that have been restored to what was imagined to be their Tudor magnificence. The long gallery at the castle contains 25 Tudor figures in full costume for those who like "the Disney treatment" for the past. The castle also hosts jousts, concerts and various exhibitions.

Kenilworth — Kenilworth is about as romantic as castle ruins can get. Only parts of the great walls and chambers made of red stone exist today. It is the place where Queen Elizabeth I and her favorite, the Earl of Leicester, cavorted. It contains an interesting display of its own fascinating history, particularly about the Tudor era. It is near Warwick Castle and the city of Coventry.

Pembroke Castle — This castle is in an interesting Welsh town and has important historical connections. It is reputed to be the oldest in Wales and the seat for the Earls of Pembroke for 300 years. It is the birthplace of Henry VII, the first of the Tudors. During the Civil War the castle changed hands between King and Parliament. It has a 75 foot tower and walls that give good views, although much of what was inside the walls is gone.

Stirling Castle — On the basis of sheer magnificence, Stirling Castle is said to be the only rival of Edinburgh Castle in Scotland. Situated on a high hill, it was designed to guard the main route from Lowland Scotland to Highland Scotland. It became the favorite residence of early Stuart monarchs and is therefore steeped in Scottish history. Many buildings are on the castle's rugged hill, and there is an interesting Regimental Museum of the Argyll and Sutherland Highlanders.

Tower of London — See the list of London sights that should be seen.

Warwick — Warwick Castle is impressive in its gigantic walls and towers, and remains very well preserved today. It is now owned by a private firm which has installed various features to amuse the large crowds that arrive from everywhere. There are animated mechanical displays of wax-like figures to illustrate events from Warwick's past, costumed attendants and other touches of show biz. Admission, naturally, is expensive.

Windsor — After nine centuries, huge Windsor castle is still in full operation as a royal residence, just over 20 miles outside of London and in the flight path from Heathrow airport. It is the largest continuously inhabited castle in the whole world. It contains private portions, the royal apartments and library, as well as many areas open to the public, which troops through in large numbers. Windsor also contains the burial place of many important members of royal families. The fire of 1992 severly damaged much of it, but substantial portions remain open to visitors.

CATHEDRALS

Strategies for Seeing Cathedrals and Abbey Ruins

With only the possible exception of France, Britain is the best place in the world to see the grandest medieval cathedrals. Cathedrals are as important to the British landscape as national parks are to Americans. Just as each national park is different and the source of ardent pride for local people, each cathedral is unique and the glory of its particular locality. Each cathedral has a different atmosphere and special features and characteristics. No two cathedrals are even remotely alike.

It is amazing how medieval cathedrals can still dominate the skylines of British cities in this century of high rises. Even though our age takes massiveness in architecture for granted, the size and grandeur of ancient cathedrals remain breathtaking.

There are over forty Anglican cathedrals, most of them old, which were taken over from the Roman Catholic

Church during the English and Scottish Reformation era. The Roman Catholic cathedrals in Britain are, therefore, newer structures. Along with the confiscation and alteration of cathedrals in the Reformation came the destruction of many monastic settlements and their impressive abbeys, or monastic churches. Today several of these places have enchanting ruins.

Every visitor to Britain must make a point to see at least some of the most famous cathedrals and abbey ruins. Some people make a point of "collecting" them by giving themselves credit for each one that they see. The lucky ones, who either live in Britain or visit regularly, can hope for a complete collection. Visitors who have a limited amount of time may be able to see just a few of the more famous ones. Some of them are less impressive than others. In fact, some of the abbey churches which survived the Reformation might be more magnificent than some of the smaller cathedrals. Consult the list at the end of this section to help make choices.

As with many other good things in life, overindulgence in cathedral viewing can result in exhaustion. Despite their distinctiveness, the characteristics of cathedrals may begin to blur for the American newcomer to Britain who tries to see too many of them too rapidly. This is certainly the case for those who avidly take photographs inside and outside of various cathedrals and then cannot figure out which shot pertains to which cathedral. It is much better to savor just a few of them well and put some really good ones off for another visit.

The Significance of Medieval Cathedrals

Medieval cathedrals become even more amazing when the society that created them is contemplated. Since most medieval people were peasants living near the subsistence level on manors, how did this society muster enough social energy to construct edifices on such a magnificent scale? As with Stonehenge, cathedrals reveal the overwhelming, compelling force of religion in human life.

The medieval view of life on earth for most people was grim: life was expected to be short, nasty, filled with toil and pain, disease, disappointment and death. The specter of starvation or plague or mysterious fevers was never far from anyone's thoughts. But life in the world to come, after death, in heaven, would be glorious. Magnificent cathedrals brought a little bit of heaven's majesty down to earth, where medieval people were transfixed by awe and wonder at the color, artistry and music contained in this soaring architecture.

Cathedrals enabled heaven and earth to touch. Each cathedral was rooted in the earth, in the middle of masses of graves. People were buried one on top of the other in nearby grounds, under the cathedral, in the cathedral walls, and each of the most important people had their own richly carved sarcophagus in some prominent place along the cathedral aisles. All around the dead flowed the living, all those who frequented the cathedral, celebrated by carvings and statues of all sorts of people and creatures, some saintly, some wicked and some ordinary. Above, towers and spires reached skyward dramatically, touching heaven itself. So the whole cathedral represented the dead, the living and the life after death. What could be more important to medieval people than to put their concept of the universe into physical form and allow these sublime edifices to signify both their worship of God as well as what they perceived as their relationship with Him?

Some Hints for Cathedral Viewing

Despite the uniqueness of each and every cathedral, all have some basic similarities. All are built in the shape of a cross, with the east end pointing towards Jerusalem. Each was the base for the jurisdiction, or diocese, of a bishop. All of the cathedrals were built slowly and painstakingly, often over several centuries. Salisbury cathedral is something of an exception, since it erected in a relatively short period of time, all in just one century! All of these cathedrals were, of course, Roman Catholic edifices originally. It was in the sixteenth century that they became cathedrals of the Church of England, or Anglican cathedrals. Many of them sustained some damage, destruction and remodeling from the more zealous Protestants thereafter.

In some ways the twentieth century is proving to be much more destructive of medieval cathedrals than the flare-up of Protestant excesses in the sixteenth and seventeenth centuries. Experts estimate that auto and industrial exhaust has eaten into the stonework to the extent that the damage of all the previous centuries put together cannot match the destruction of our own polluted century. This explains the many campaigns to fund their preservation. Cleaning and repairing these gigantic structures is such an ongoing struggle that it seems impossible to see any cathedral in Britain without encountering scaffolding over at least one of the major surfaces.

Visitors should take their time in cathedrals. If each took centuries to build, there is no sense in rushing through in fifteen minutes. Purchase a guidebook, take a tour, or listen in on one of the phone commentaries that may be available at strategic locations for a minor fee. The information from these sources may seem overwhelming and daunting. Bear in mind, however, that you should not try to understand everything in church history, art history or architectural history that will be thrown at you. Digest what you can understand of it and be open to impressions and feelings and savor these buildings and what they contain.

Some Helpful Terms for Understanding Cathedrals

A small, specialized vocabulary will help a visitor get around in a cathedral. The signs, the phone information systems, and the church assistants who help tourists around all use a number of specific terms not often heard in America, probably because this nation lacks European-style cathedrals except for a few examples on the East Coast. Below is a list of helpful terms and a diagram to enhance your visit. Basic terms commonly known and used in America, such as aisle, altar, arch, dome, spire and steeple, are omitted.

Terms for the Floor Plan

The *apse* is a projecting extension of the cathedral, usually semi-circular, with vaults, and is in the east end of the building.

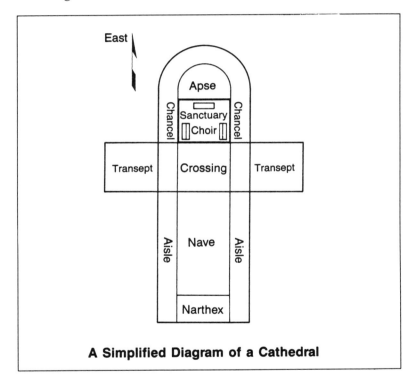

A Simplified Diagram of a Cathedral

The *chancel* is usually to the east of the nave (see below) and includes the choir and the sanctuary.

The *choir* is the part of the chancel between the sanctuary and the nave which is occupied by singers or the clergy.

The *crossing* is the place where the transept and the nave intersect. It is usually square.

The *narthex* is the area leading to the nave. It was originally a porch or a vestibule. Now it may be a place for informal conversation, posting notices or for the selling of souvenirs.

The *nave* is the main west-to-east body of the cathedral. It usually extends from the main entrance to the choir.

The *sanctuary* is where the altar is placed.

The *transept* comprises the two lateral arms of the cathedral, north to south. These are the arms of the cross shape of the building.

Terms for Decorations, Objects and Some Other Locations

The *altarpiece* is a work of art, often consisting of one or more painted panels, that is placed in a space above and behind the altar.

An *arcade* is a series of arches with their columns, and is often roofed.

A *boss* is a raised or projecting ornament on a wall or ceiling.

A *chapel* within a cathedral is usually a chamber or a recessed area for subordinate services of prayer and meditation. Chapels usually have separately dedicated altars.

A *choir stall* is a seat in the choir, often elaborately decorated and enclosed.

A *cloister* is a covered passageway at the side of an open court, usually walled on the side farthest from the court and colonnaded (having a row of columns) on the other side.

A *crypt* is an area under the main body of a cathedral, underground, and usually utilized for burials.

A *flying buttress* consists of a mass of arches jutting out from an upper wall or vaulted ceiling. Its purpose is to take on the weight of these upper structures. Flying buttresses usually extend themselves out and down on the outside of the cathedral.

The *font* is a receptacle for holy water or baptismal water.

A *fresco* is a wall painting executed on freshly spread plaster.

A *gargoyle* is really a waterspout, made in the form of a grotesque human or animal form. Gargoyles project from buildings and once served to frighten worshipers as images of demons.

A *minster* is a monastery church, and can be an important cathedral as well. York Minster is an example.

A *ribbed vault* is a vault, or arched masonry ceiling, that is supported by a skeleton of compartmentalized arches.

A *sacristy* is a chamber where the vestments, or religious garments, and sacred utensils are stored.

A *see* is the official seat of a bishop and the center of his jurisdiction. His chief church will be the cathedral.

Tracery refers to ornamental designs, often interlaced with branching lines.

Terms Referring to Styles of Decoration

The following terms can become confusing because nearly all cathedrals have additions in different styles from the style of the primary construction. The following terms are arranged in chronological order.

The *Norman* style was executed massively in heavy masonry; arches are huge, thick, round and adorned very simply. The Norman style was a variety of the Romanesque style.

Romanesque is the term for the general style of architecture of the early Middle Ages, up to the coming of Gothic style. From the 1000's on, it was characterized by the use of round arches and many arcades.

Gothic was the style of architecture characteristic of the Middle Ages from the twelfth to the sixteenth centuries. It featured tall, slim architectural masses supported by flying buttresses. Ribbed vaulting and pointed arches were other characteristics. In England, three varieties of Gothic style developed: *Early English Gothic* was the first version of the Gothic style in England, and was characterized by *lancet* arches, which are narrow arches that come to sharp points.

The *Decorated Style* came next. It was characterized by geometric tracery, or interlaced geometric designs.

The *Perpendicular Style* is the name of the later stage of English Gothic, appearing in the late fourteenth century and afterwards. Arches became extremely slender and gracefully pointed.

A Short List of Cathedrals and Abbeys

Canterbury Cathedral — This is the most famous cathedral in England for several reasons. It is the seat of the Archbishop of Canterbury, the leader of the whole Church of England. It is built on the site of St. Augustine's first church. St. Augustine was sent from Rome in the late 6th century to convert the heathen Anglo-Saxons. It was also in this cathedral that St. Thomas à Becket was martyred in the 12th century. The place where this occurred is marked in the cathedral, and for a long time it was a shrine, the very place to which the pilgrims of Chaucer's *Canterbury Tales* were headed. The cathedral is huge and magnificent, one of the best to see in Europe, with fascinating tombs and memorials and an ancient crypt.

Coventry Cathedral — Coventry Cathedral is so striking and so unique that many people make a special stop at this busy industrial city just to see it. Coventry itself was brutally bombed in World War II, and very few parts of it are old. Most of the city has been rebuilt, and the same is true of its cathedral. It is a striking modern building, whose shape, glass, modern statuary and splendid, huge tapestry, *Christ in Glory*, are truly remarkable. The old shell of the bombed cathedral is attached to the new one, and contains poignant pleas for peace and reconciliation.

Durham Cathedral — Durham Cathedral may be in one of the most impressive medieval defensive positions in Britain. It soars above steeply wooded sides. The inside is equally impressive, with a powerful Norman nave. This cathedral is regarded as the finest example of a Norman cathedral and the greatest Romanesque church in Europe. During the English Civil Wars radical Protestant soldiers were quartered in and about the cathedral, and they stripped many embellishments which they regarded as Catholic.

Fountains Abbey — Fountains Abbey is a wonderful monastery ruin near the city of Ripon in the north. It was founded in 1132 by the Cistercians, and was one of the most important centers of monastic life in England. The ruins were landscaped in the 18th century and today the immediate vicinity affords some of the most attractive walking paths in the north of England. Other historic attractions are on the estate connected to the abbey today.

Lincoln Cathedral — Lincoln Cathedral is set on a high hill, and dominates the town below it. It has a striking appearance with its great towers looming high against the horizon, reminiscent of Canterbury. The interior, like the interiors of so many cathedrals, is a composite from many eras, but some portions of old English decoration are treasured.

Rievaulx Abbey — This old abbey ruin is pronounced *ree-vo*. It is said to be the very best in all of England, although Fountains Abbey can mount a challenge to this assertion. The setting for this Cistercian abbey, in the Yorkshire moors with a high terrace above it is magnificent.

Salisbury Cathedral — Salisbury is justly famous, and not only because of the striking beauty that was inspiration for countless famous and lesser known artists. Unlike other cathedrals, it was built on a single concept and, for cathedral building anyway, rather rapidly, taking only 60 years to erect everything except its magnificent 404 foot spire. Some crusaders were laid to rest in this cathedral, and it protects one of the few remaining copies of Magna Carta.

St. David's — This is a gem of a small cathedral in a charming small town in western Wales. The town has to be called a city because the cathedral is there. It is a shrine to the patron saint of Wales, who is buried behind the altar. While it is an ancient building, built in the 12th century, it was substantially redecorated by the Victorians. The nave is still solidly Norman, however. What is unique about St. David's, besides its smallish compactness, is the fact that it is built in a hollow, or vale. Instead of going up a hill to a cathedral, which is a regular occurrence, at St. David's visitors must walk down steps to it. There are also interesting ruins of old church buildings.

St. Giles Cathedral — This huge and historically famous church is along the historic Royal Mile in Edinburgh. It is the place where the Scottish Reformation actually began in the 16th century when an Anglican prayerbook was rejected by the Presbyterian congregation. It is a squat cathedral without the soaring beauty of many English cathedrals and it has been much restored and refurbished over the centuries but the square central tower remains similar to its appearance when it was completed in the late fifteenth century.

St. Paul's Cathedral — This cathedral in the east end of London ranks with Westminster Abbey in importance. It is huge, actually the second largest church in the whole world. This magnificent structure in the East End of London somehow survived the mass bombings of World War II. It is the greatest church built by the greatest English architect, Sir Christopher Wren. It was completed in 1710 and served to replace the cathedral destroyed when London had its huge fire in the late 17th century. Since then it has been the scene of a myriad of historical events, including weddings and funerals. The interior is a museum for the famous dead. Monumental art of various kinds abounds in a formal, austere manner. This is truly a national cathedral for a national church.

Tintern Abbey — Tintern abbey ranks with Fountains and Rievaulx as the most beautiful church ruins in Britain. It is in a peaceful valley in Wales, and the green grass has captured much of it. Poets have been inspired by it for centuries.

Wells Cathedral — This ancient cathedral is one of the most beautiful in all of Europe. Its inception dates from the 12th century, but its towers were completed only by the late 14th century. Its high, massive west front is said to have the most extensive array of medieval sculpture in Britain, consisting of hundreds of figures. Wells also has a medieval clock that has survived.

Westminster Abbey — See the section on London sights that should be seen.

Winchester Cathedral — It is impossible for many people

to think of this charming cathedral without recalling that wry popular song about it from decades ago. It has the longest nave in Europe. It is well situated in an historic town which was once the capital of England. Therefore the cathedral is associated with many famous events and persons.

York Minster — This is a cathedral church which is one of the largest in Britain. It is the seat of the Archbishop of York, the second ranking Anglican leader. The size of York Minster is hard to appreciate because it is surrounded by little houses. Yet it can be viewed quite well from the outside by walking around on the remaining medieval walls. York has some of the most spectacular medieval stained glass windows in Europe, particularly in the east end, where the Biblical story from the creation to the Apocalypse is told. Some say that only Chartres Cathedral in France has a better display of glass.

STATELY HOMES

Some Strategies for Seeing Them

Britain has over 500 stately homes, which are actually grand country homes, a reflection of the power and opulence of the landed classes over the centuries. In the agriculturally rich south, particularly around London, there are scores of them in each county. Britain is different from other countries in that so many present and former homes of the upper classes have been thrown open to the public. The Labour Party is to be thanked for striking down the privacy of these bastions of the upper classes by imposing steep inheritance taxes and land taxes.

Deciding on how many stately homes to visit involves a very subjective decision. It depends upon the degree of one's interest in interiors, furnishings and china. Then again, it may depend on the historical connections of places. Blenheim Palace, for instance, may be on a list of things to see because Winston Churchill was born there and because it was originally a grand gift to celebrate the victories of the first Duke of Marlborough. Still another reason for choosing a particular stately home might depend on what comes with it. Some have zoos attached, including some with lions that amble about on the lawns. Others have collections of old motor cars or early airplanes. Many strive for an amusement park atmosphere, with many attractions to delight children. Beautiful gardens, which clash less with the historical appearance of these places, serve as a major attraction for many stately homes, reaching the heights of their beauty from April until June.

It is easy to overdose on stately homes. There is just too much stuff in them, too many portraits of lesser known or hardly known ancestors, too many dim, creaky interiors, too many references to ill-remembered minor figures connected to the past or present owner's family. After a while, impressions of various stately homes can blur. Just what house has a certain room, hall, decoration or fountain can be mixed up easily.

Visits to stately homes can be expensive. The top attractions cost from $15 to $18 per ticket. Doing three or four top priced houses in a single day can be compared to the cost of going to Disneyland, particularly when the extra costs of parking, gift shop items and refreshments are factored in.

Just who owns them can be confusing. Some have been sold to the National Trust; some are operated by an organization known as the English Heritage; some are sold to independent commercial operators; and still others continue to be owned by aristocratic families that are out to make pounds from the curiosity and envy of the masses.

Even when these great buildings have been sold off to the National Trust to pay the steep taxes on inheritance or on land, special arrangements are often made to allow the resident family to occupy a portion of the structure in privacy. In some cases the owners retain the property with the proviso that it is open to the public for a portion of the year. A number of the titled former owners or present owners actually enjoy walking about to mingle with the visitors incognito.

The Georgian Heritage

Some of the stately homes began as medieval manor houses and were added onto over the centuries, often with incongruities from one wing to another. Nevertheless, some of the most striking stately homes are from the Georgian era, or the 18th century, when the landed classes were dominant. Most of the great families had their "big house," or mansion, or seat, in the countryside. These were often great and gorgeous structures, and they tell something about reality of the power of the landed classes compared to royal power in Georgian England. The dozens of palatial Georgian mansions were built for aristocrats and landed gentlemen as well, and not for the dull members of the royal family of the eighteenth century. By contrast, on the Continent monumental buildings were very likely to be royal buildings.

The baroque and rococo styles were in full bloom on the Continent in the eighteenth century, the former powerful and the latter highly decorative. English baroque buildings tend to be rare. Compared to the Continent, English neo-classical styles and buildings were generally more restrained, proportioned and less highly ornamental. Their interior decorations repeated classical motifs, drawing inspiration from ancient Greece and Rome. Usually light, delicate colors were used in the eighteenth century: gold, silver, light blue, pink, white and lavender. Jasmine Wedgwood china, popular in the United States, gives some indication of Georgian decoration.

A Short List of Stately Homes

Blenheim Palace — Blenheim is so massive and grand in detail that it has been called England's Versailles. The difference is that it was built for a prominent English family rather than for the royal family. It is one of the grand baroque structures in England, having been designed and constructed in the early 18th century by Vanbrugh. It covers many acres. Winston Churchill was born in the palace, and lies buried in the nearby Bladon churchyard. The setting and gardens match the grandeur of the buildings.

Chartwell — Chartwell was the home that Winston Churchill bought and adored. His most peaceful hours were spent here, and his busy attention to it is marked everywhere, from ponds he constructed to walls he built to paintings he executed. The spirit of Churchill haunts the place. Anyone truly interested in him needs to visit Chartwell. It is a pretty place, and fairly large, but it is not a grand historic house. The Churchill connection makes it special.

Chatsworth — This is a gigantic house in Derbyshire, originally built in the sixteenth century and extended considerably in the late 17th and early 18th centuries. It is the home of the Duke and Duchess of Devonshire. The furnishings, tapestries painted walls, the elaborate ceilings, staircases and the chapel are all outstanding in their richness. The grounds and gardens are in proportion to the house, meaning that they are enormous and elaborately landscaped and justly famous. Chatsworth powerfully conveys an impression of the grandeur of the British aristocracy in the 18th century.

Hampton Court Palace — Anyone visiting this truly magnificent palace just outside of London can feel close to Henry VIII quite easily. Henry VIII's right hand man, the ebullient Cardinal Wolsey, built this sprawling, rambling red brick Tudor palace for himself, but when he fell from grace Henry VIII claimed it for his own. It sprouts hundreds of chimneys and the entrance has ornate Tudor carvings. Later on Wren added sections to it. Today elaborate gardens surround it.

Hatfield House — Hatfield House has been associated through the centuries with the Cecil family, which first rose to prominence as servants to Elizabeth I. Members of this family have served Britain in high political roles ever since. Hatfield House is one of the major Jacobean, or early 17th century houses in Britain. It has an exceptional staircase, tapestries, and furniture.

Hughenden Manor — This was the home of one of the most dazzling figures of Victorian Britain, Benjamin Disraeli. Unlike many other famous houses that have been added on to over the centuries, Hughenden Manor was and remains a Victorian home. It has been carefully preserved by the National Trust so that many rooms look exactly as they must have to its famous owner. It is in Buckinghamshire, near High Wycombe, and therefore not far from London.

Knole House — This is a magnificent Jacobean, or early 17th century house in the south of England, although its foundations date from an earlier time. It has many literary associations, since it was in the possession of the Sackville family for nearly 400 years. Its tapestries and furnishings are of special merit.

Longleat House — In this century Longleat House has been turned into something of a Disneyland, with an animal park, a lion park, and various other amusements. It would be a remarkable place to visit without all of these distractions, because it is a striking Elizabethan building, a true triumph of Renaissance architecture in England. It is just south of Bath, and belongs to the Marquis of Bath, who is the entrepreneur in charge.

Newby Hall and Gardens — Located near Ripon, in North Yorkshire, Newby Hall has the special advantage of not being overwhelming. It is small enough to be thoroughly explored and savored in an afternoon visit. Its yellow-walled Regency dining room and its rococo tapestry room are gems of decoration. It is one of England's impressive Adam houses, named after a noted architect of the 18th century. Surrounding it is a gorgeous 25-acre garden.

Palace of the Holyrood House — This spacious old building is at one end of the royal mile in Scotland. It is the official residence of the British monarch when in Scotland. It was largely rebuilt in the late 17th century. At that time a hack artist was commissioned to paint portraits of over 100 Scottish kings, which he did with humorous effect. Most of them resemble each other and the English monarch, Charles II, who commissioned the artist. Holyrood Palace has associations with Mary, Queen of Scots, and a plaque on the floor marks where her favorite, Rizzio, was stabbed to death by furious Scottish lords.

Penshurst Place — Penshurst Place, just south of London, does have atmosphere. It retains the impression of its original use as a medieval manor house, although it was added on to extensively in the Elizabethan era. There is still an excellent 14th century hall. It is the birthplace of Sir Philip Sidney, the famous soldier, poet and statesman of the Elizabethan era. The furniture, tapestries, armor, paintings and acres of gardens and parks make it a place well worth visiting.

Royal Pavilion — This is one of the strangest and most exotic buildings in Britain. It is in the seaside resort town of Brighton. It is in an exotic, oriental design, built for the Prince Regent in the early 19th century. It has onion domes, minarets, and a grand mixture of Chinese, Indian, Gothic and Egyptian inspiration in its interior.

COLORFUL HISTORIC CITIES, TOWNS AND VILLAGES

What follows is perhaps the least adequate short list in the whole book. Without doubt, many attractive and historic towns and villages have been omitted because the author does not know about them or has not yet spent time in them. So an apology is due to those readers who know Britain well and who are dismayed at the omission of their favorite historic place which they feel should be included on this short list.

Those that do appear on the following short list have been selected on the basis of their overall atmosphere rather than size. In other words, a key criteria has been whether or not these places still retain some of the look and feel of what they must have had centuries ago. Places that have not been engulfed by modern urban sprawl and that have a cathedral or many half timbered buildings have been candidates for inclusion.

Some people like to go to little out of the way places that have strange sounding names. Britain offers the following: Blubberhouses, Foul Mill, Great Snoring, Mop End, Mousehole (pronounced *mousel*), Piddle, and Ugley.

A Short List of Historic Cities, Towns and Villages

Places are in England unless designated as being in Scotland or Wales.

Aberdeen, Scotland — Aberdeen has been transformed considerably by the boom from North Sea oil. It is a big, bustling city with many reminders of its quieter and solid past. Aberdeen has a hard appearance due to the fact that so many buildings are made out of granite and other kinds of gray stone. One very nice thing about Aberdeen is that its public historic attractions are free. Provost Skene's House is an early building carefully furnished to evoke the authentic past very successfully. Marischal College dates from the late sixteenth century and has a museum featuring ancient treasures. For those interested in the sea, Aberdeen's Maritime Museum has much to offer. There is also a nice provincial collection of art at the Aberdeen Art Gallery.

Canterbury — Although Nazi planes ruthlessly sought to destroy this city in retaliation for bombings of historic towns in Germany, two-thirds of Canterbury fortunately survived. With a magnificent ancient cathedral, several historic gates, old inns, the ruins of a Norman castle, and excavations of Roman buildings, Canterbury is a gem. It is a fairly small city, but it has a thriving modern section in addition to its ancient center. It is a very popular place for tourists from France to visit. Tourists from everywhere will enjoy walking all around the historic streets of this beautiful municipality. Canterbury should be very high on everyone's list of places to visit.

Bath — Bath was long known as a famous spa. Its wealthy devotees of the eighteenth century were responsible for the splendid Georgian architecture that predominates, including the two great crescents of apartment buildings which remain truly impressive to this very day. Bath's abbey and Roman remains are other attractions of this lovely town.

Braemar, Scotland — This is but one of many Highland Scottish towns, and a particularly beautiful one. The author saw deer strolling down a side street here, and a rushing mountain stream that could have been one of the best in his native Colorado.

Brighton — Brighton is and was many things. It is a seaside resort with great amusement piers and a strip of amusement parks along the seacoast. It also has the Royal Pavilion, a striking early 19th century pleasure palace for royalty which is well restored. There is also an interesting art gallery and a notable aquarium. One part of Brighton also has a rough side, with some beggars and groups of people who are not conspicuous in other British towns of comparable size. Today many people living in Brighton take the commuter train in to London.

Bristol — Bristol is a large city in the southwest of England, from which countless emigrants departed for America. Bristol has many beautiful buildings and cultural events are frequent. Nearby is an historic suspension bridge which is lighted for the holiday season.

Cambridge — Cambridge is one of the two great ancient university towns in England. The other is Oxford, which has a thriving industrial sector as well as an ancient university. By contrast, Cambridge is more quiet and sedate. Part of the vast and scattered university complex is open to the public at certain times, so that strolls along the river and through some of the medieval quadrangles and choirs become highlights of a visit to Cambridge. Be sure to check with the porters about what is open to visitors.

Chester — Chester is located in the northwest of England

and has much to offer from its rich past. Chester has unique arcades called "the Rows" that are a two tiered shopping complex in striking half-timbered style. There are old city walls, a unique cathedral, places that evoke the Civil Wars of the 17th century and some places that have Roman remains.

Chipping Campden — This is one of the most pleasant of a number of towns that are not far from London in a region called the Cotswolds. Picturesque villages sprinkle rolling hills. Sheep farming and the wool industry gave prosperity to this region. Other noted towns in the region are Morton-in-Marsh, Chipping Norton, and Bourton-on-the-Water. This charming part of England can only be seen properly on foot or by car.

Durham — Durham is a northern city whose impressive castle and cathedral are set in a powerful defensive position on a peninsula with steeply wooded sides. The castle has been amalgamated into the University of Durham and now houses students and, in off season, visitors. The Durham Cathedral is one of the best in Britain, as mentioned elsewhere. The town itself is quiet and pleasant, although it is set in a mining region.

Edinburgh, Scotland — Edinburgh, capital of Scotland, is one of the most historic cities in Europe, and has its own stark, slate gray beauty. What is amazing about Edinburgh architecturally is that the cramped confines of the old walled city inspired builders to build upward, so that there are tall buildings, alleys, closes and courts. Beyond the walls a newer city stretches, one that is laid out spaciously because the fear of invasion no longer prevailed. Edinburgh is second only to London in having a concentration of museums, art galleries and historic sites. The National Gallery of Scotland is superb, featuring not only Scottish artists but European artists from the Renaissance to the 20th century. There is also a Scottish National Portrait Gallery, as well as a Scottish National Gallery of Modern Art. The Scott Memorial on busy Princess Street is unique with its heavy Victorian Gothic appearance, which is appropriate for the author of so many Victorian Gothic novels. The "Royal

Mile" is a magnificent axis for history, running from Edinburgh Castle at one end and Holyrood Palace at the other. John Knox's house and St. Giles Church are among the sites that lie in between.

Harrogate — In recent years Harrogate has become an important town for conferences. It is a solid, essentially Victorian, resort town that is noted for its extensive floral displays. Harrogate can serve as a jumping off place to visit historic sites in and around the ruggedly beautiful Yorkshire dales.

King's Lynn — This is a charming old market town and port in East Anglia that has many old buildings dating from its days of great commercial importance before the railways made its inland river trade dry up. It has churches, a guildhall and a fine 18th century customs house. Sea trade and market activity still continue.

Lavenham — Lavenham is a delightful small town with a large number of half-timbered buildings dating from the time that it was a center of the wool trade. Its old church, inn and guildhall are three special gems from the past.

Lewes — The town of Lewes along the coast of southern England has a considerable amount of historic atmosphere due in large part to its irregular streets which are built on hills. The conquering Normans made it a stronghold and built a substantial castle, some of which remains. There are many attractive older buildings in the town, including the Anne of Cleves House, where one of Henry VIII's divorced wives lived with her head firmly and safely on her shoulders.

Lyme Regis — This delightful small town on the southern coast of England drew attention as the scene of both the book and the film *The French Lieutenant's Woman*. It is protected by "the Cobb," an ancient breakwater that creates an artificial harbor.

Norwich — Norwich is the largest and most important city in East Anglia. It has a large and significant cathedral, a huge castle with interesting exhibits and many old buildings and crooked streets. A special feature of Norwich, both past and present, is a large, open-air market.

Oxford — Oxford is one of the two ancient university towns in England, the other being the quieter and more sedate Cambridge. Oxford has a large industrial sector in a nearby suburb and busy traffic with London, which is not all that far away. Oxford's great attraction, of course, is its university, part of which is open to the public at certain times. Some of the towers can be climbed, affording marvelous views, and there are good walks along the river and through some of the older quadrangles. The extensive Ashmolean Museum is another top attraction.

Rye — Rye is one of those delightful old ports rich in history and utterly charming because it never has had the opportunity to grow and sprawl and become modern the way successful rival towns have. The main reason for this is that the coastline shifted, leaving Rye isolated inland. Many buildings are half timbered, with tile roofs, and these buildings, along with many dating from the 18th century, charmingly ascend the hillsides. Old World charm is still retained, especially along the cobbled streets that remain. The old days of smugglers are easily recalled in this setting. It is readily accessible from London.

St. Andrews, Scotland — St. Andrews has much to offer, including an ancient university and ruins of a sprawling castle. The town has many connections with Scottish history, since it was the coronation site for many Scottish kings, a stronghold for John Knox, and the site of considerable religious strife during the Reformation. For many American sportspersons, it is to golf what Cooperstown, New York, is to baseball: the St. Andrews golf course is where it all began. American devotees of the sport have been known to smack balls about in blinding, cold rain just to say that they have done it there.

Stirling, Scotland — Stirling is in one of the most strategic locations in Scotland, along the main route from the Lowlands to the Highlands. To control the area, a magnificent castle was built on the hill that dominates the town. (See Stirling Castle on the short list of castles.) Leading up to it are crooked streets with historic buildings lining them. Stirling is a pleasant, modestly sized city and most of its highlights can be seen within one day. Outside of Edinburgh, it is one of the most historic towns in Scotland and well worth a visit on a trip further north.

Stratford-upon-Avon — This town is a must for all of the passionate admirers of Shakespeare. They can see the streets where he walked, the house where he was born, the church where he is buried and the river he crossed so many times. There is also the lovely Anne Hathaway house in nearby Shottery. Older inhabitants say that so many tourist buses roar into the area that it is reminiscent of the preparations for the D-Day invasion. Such popularity has had some negative effects, particularly in making Stratford a tourist town, filled with souvenirs and people jaded towards new faces. Nevertheless, the National Trust tries to make the exhibits in and around the town accurate and accessible, and the National Shakespeare Theatre in Stratford is world famous. If your love for Shakespeare is ardent, do go to Stratford-upon-Avon; if not, you might think about skipping it.

Warwick — Besides having a marvelous castle, mentioned earlier, Warwick is a charming small town, good for walking around. Delightful old buildings abound. Incidentally, a church in Warwick contains the remains of Elizabeth I's favorite, the Earl of Leicester.

Winchester — Winchester was the historic capital of Wessex, the kingdom of King Alfred. It has a famous cathedral and a castle where many famous kings held court. There is a very questionable round table in the castle that is supposed to be that of King Arthur. About a mile from the castle is the St. Cross Hospital, a charitable institution that has handed out bread and beer to travelers for centuries. Winchester also has a famous public school where youngsters wear traditional uniforms.

York — York is an historic gem of a city in northern England. It is one of only two archiepiscopal sees in England, and was the most important city in the north of England all through the medieval period. It is the northern counterpart to the southern archiepiscopal see, Canterbury. It is still a city that has a medieval look and feel about it, despite its role as a busy, bustling modern center of its region. Just walking around York is a treat. There are long stretches of the old city walls extant, and it is possible to hike along them to see superb views of York Minster, one of the largest cathedrals in Britain. The narrow street named the Shambles has long been a popular subject for illustrations. Sixteen medieval churches and several city gates, as well as the riverfront on the Ouse, all help to give York its special charm. Among the outstanding attractions are Clifford's Tower, the stark 13th century keep of York Castle, the York Castle Museum where the everyday life of the past century is recreated and presented, and the York Story, an accurate audio-visual presentation of York's history. York is also the home of the huge National Railway Museum and the Jorvik Viking Center, both popular places to visit.

Some Special Historic Places, Including Battlefields

Until recently, Britain did not develop and display its battlefields to the extent that they are exhibited in the United States. A few of them are simply marked by a plaque, saying that here a certain contest was fought. Marston Moor outside of York is a case in point. The scene where this great Parliamentary victory over the royalists took place in the English Civil Wars is simply marked by a small concrete marker. What is more, the moorland has been transformed by cultivation. In order to get information about details of the battle, not unmixed with folklore, it is necessary to chat with local people who are interested in it.

Some battlefields have been given more extensive treatment as the value of presenting history for tourism has been more fully realized. Below are a few examples of British battlefields worth seeing and several other places that defy ordinary classification.

Battlefield of Bosworth — All of English history was changed by a battle fought in the Midlands in 1485. Many remember the famous scene in *Richard III*, where the stricken villain shouts: "A horse a horse, my Kingdom for a horse!" Whether or not he really said it is questionable, but the fact that he was slain in the heat of battle by the forces of his rival, Henry VII, is one of the more significant facts of English history. Henry went on to found a dynasty that ruled until the opening years of the 17th century.

The battlefield is well worth a visit, especially for those with keen historical interests. It is not easy to locate on a map, and a car is required to visit the site. The way to find it on a map is to draw a line to the west of Leicester, and just a little south, and another line north from Coventry and just a little east. The battlefield is roughly where the lines intersect, near the hamlet of Sutton Cheney. This place is between two roads that run north to south, the A447 and the A444.

The battle scene is pleasant farmland today. Visitors are kept on paths that lead through gates. While walking the battlefield itself, they must use their imaginations to envision the course of events, because the only indications of the conflict on the ground today are two pennants, one for the main position of Henry VIII and the other for Richard III. Nevertheless, the whole scene becomes clear and vivid to those who first spend time at the visitors' center, where exhibits, models of the battlefield and a short film explain the events of those critical days in 1485. Those matters which still remain mysteries to this day, such as the motivations of those who switched sides, are presented undogmatically and open to interpretation. The center is very modern and very carefully conceived. In sum, a trip out to Bosworth Battlefield is well worth the effort.

The Battlefield of Hastings — Most people know that in 1066 all of English history was changed when the Normans defeated the Anglo-Saxons at the Battle of Hastings. The actual field of battle is several miles from the town of Hastings at a place called Battle. An abbey, now a ruin, was built at the site by the victorious Normans. Today visitors are treated to a detailed audio-visual presentation that brings the contest back to life. The battlefield itself has markers at key locations, and it is possible to walk along the top of the slope the Anglo-Saxons held for most of the day, although the buildings of the abbey crowd that position. It is more impressive to start on the Norman side and walk up the green, undulating hill, reflecting on the difficulties of unleashing attacks of armored cavalry in such a relatively confined space. The only battlefield hazard to be encountered by visitors today are scattered animal droppings.

Other British Battlefields — In modern times, the British have fought their battles all around the world instead of on their island. The last notable military contest in Britain was at the battle of Culloden, fought outside Inverness in Scotland, which marked the last of the Scottish risings in favor of the House of Stuart and against the Hanoverian kings of England. The battlefield, five miles east of Inverness, is preserved and can be visited. There is an audio-visual presentation and the graves of the clansmen can be visited. Bannockburn, where King Robert the Bruce won dramatically over the English in 1314, has a Heritage Centre nearby with exhibits and an audio-visual presentation.

Ironbridge and Coalbrookdale — The Ironbridge gorge in Shropshire, which is several miles long, has a complex of museums and displays that celebrate and explain the early Industrial Revolution. The world's first iron bridge still spans a river and can be walked across. Many original pieces of machinery are on display. Anyone interested in engineering or the era of the Industrial Revolution should see this complex.

Runnymede and the Kennedy Memorial — These two places are close together and just outside London on the Thames. Neither is spectacular. Runnymede, the birthplace of Magna Carta in 1215, is commemorated by a modern gazebo like structure, actually modeled on a domed classical temple. The Kennedy Memorial is a slab of stone with an excellent inscription from the words of the assassinated president. Both sites are within easy walking distance of each other. People who visit must be imbued with the importance of Magna Carta or President Kennedy or both, because there is little to see.

Stonehenge — This is one of the most popular historical monuments in the world. It towers dramatically on Salisbury plain, in the southwest of England. It is easy to see both Salisbury Cathedral and Stonehenge on the same day. Access to the monument has been curtailed somewhat in recent years, but the grandeur of this prehistoric testament to the overwhelming power of religion is undiminished.

The Victory at Portsmouth — Portsmouth, badly bombed during World War II, is the home of the famous *Victory*, Nelson's flagship at Trafalgar and the vessel upon which he died so heroically during his greatest triumph in 1805. Visitors can walk all through the large and majestic ship and visit an adjacent maritime museum also.

CHAPTER THREE

Understanding British Geography, Economics and Sociology
UNDERSTANDING BRITISH GEOGRAPHY

National Designations of the Parts that Make Up Britain: When to Say "British" Rather Than "English," "Welsh" or "Scottish"

AMERICANS often have problems with national designations in Britain. The official name of the country is the United Kingdom, abbreviated as U.K. Before World War II, "Great Britain" was the usual designation. Today "Britain" is still used, usually without "Great." All of these names refer to the whole of the largest island in that archipelago, or cluster of islands, known to geographers at the "British Isles." Of the remaining islands, only Ireland is of substantial size. Most of Ireland is, of course, a sovereign republic that is separate from the U.K. The rest of the islands are quite small, such as the Scilly Islands in the English Channel and the Shetlands and Orkneys, which are sprinkled in the cold waters north of Britain.

All of the people on the island of Britain can safely be called "British." This includes the English, the Welsh and the Scots, the three nationalities that are constitutionally united and comprise the "United Kingdom." Of the three nationalities, the English predominate overwhelmingly in numbers and take up most of the space on Britain. Recent tabulations of ethnicity in Britain put the English at 81.5%, Scottish, 9.6%, Irish, 2.4 %, and Welsh, 1.9%. The small percentage remaining beyond these four ethnic groups are from all over the rest of the world.

Most of the English were originally descendants of the taller and blonder Anglo-Saxons, the Germanic people who once drove the shorter and darker-haired Celtic people and other early types into the hills of the north and the west. Of course, the mixing, mingling and moving of people over the centuries have made the English population quite a hodgepodge.

The predominance of the English on Britain, along with their language, customs, laws and history, has been so strong that foreigners often make the serious mistake of calling non-English British persons "English." For a Welsh or Scottish person, this is as infuriating as calling a Coloradan a Texan or someone from Philadelphia a New Yorker. The Welsh are British, but not English; the Scots are British, but not English; the English are both English and British. Visitors should be very careful about this point. When in doubt, "British" is always a safe term.

The Parts of Britain: England's Regions

The largest component of Britain, England, can itself be divided into several regions (see map). East Anglia is a remarkably flat area bulging out on the eastern part of the island. It is similar in topography to the Netherlands, which is directly across the North Sea. The "Midlands" are in the middle of the rolling, undulating plains of England, and include the lands that are the farthest from the sea in all of Britain, which never exceeds a grand total of only 70 miles! There is a great conurbation in the west Midlands, centering around Birmingham. Very picturesque places are found in the Cotswold region just east of the Bristol Channel. The

Understanding British Geography, Economics and Sociology 139

The Parts of the Island of Britain

"West Country" is the region that juts out into the Atlantic along the southern tail of Britain. Since part of it is rough country, and there are moors, an irregular coastline and many charming seaport towns, it is deservedly popular with tourists. The westernmost counties of the West Country, Cornwall and Devon, are the busiest in the tourist season. The "south" is a term sometimes used to describe the counties south of the Thames, a region with a reputation for affluence, culture and, alas, snobbery.

The "north," an area actually north of the Midlands, contrasts sharply with the "south." It has many sections developed in recent centuries that are rougher and obviously more industrial than the south. Even so, the people living in the north seem less reserved and much more informal than in the south of England. Two important historic counties in the north are worth noting: Lancashire and Yorkshire. The former is associated with the very first developments of the industrial revolution. Old, historic Yorkshire, before it was divided up into North, West and South Yorkshire and Humberside, was so large that it was declared the Texas of England! The map shows the old, historic counties, not the new subdivisions. North Yorkshire has ruggedly beautiful stretches of green hillsides and valleys, called the Yorkshire Dales, and stark moorland. West Yorkshire is grimly industrial.

The Parts of Britain: Wales and the Welsh

Wales is not very large and not heavily populated when compared to England. England is over six times as large as Wales and has more than 47 million people. Wales has just over 2.8 million persons. Nevertheless, England and most of the English-speaking parts of the world have had a substantial Welsh addition to their populations. Note how often the typically Welsh name of "Jones" appears in America.

In recent decades Wales has seen an in-migration of English families who have taken advantage of rural settings and cheaper properties. Sometimes friction has developed between the native Welsh and newcomers who do not maintain traditional practices. For example, a new English owner might put a fence across his property and cut a pathway that ran through it for centuries and upon which all the neighbors had trod since they were youngsters.

The Welsh who have remained in their homeland are spread across a poor but lovely land. Blue hills, dark mountains, gem-like small towns and golden beaches are found throughout north and central Wales. In south Wales, a depressed conurbation runs along the southern coast of the region. Cardiff, the capital of Wales, and several other cities are located along this strip, which is dependent upon coal mining and industry. Even where most industrialized, Wales is rich with historical remains, particularly castles. Yet the best places to spend time in Wales are far from the factories and mines. See the section in chapter two entitled "Strategies for Wales."

The Parts of Britain: Scotland

Scotland is a Celtic region divided into a Lowland zone and a Highland zone. The Lowland zone stretches from the North Sea in the east to the Irish Sea in the west, just above the rough border country separating England from Scotland. Historically the Lowland zone was the most prosperous part of Scotland because it had the best farmland. The Lowland population is mixed with Anglo-Saxons, while Celts predominate clearly in the Highland region to the north. Edinburgh (pronounced Ed-in-boro), the captivating, romantic, ancient capital, lies in the eastern part of this zone, along an indentation of the ocean called the Firth of Forth. At the western end of the Lowland zone is the second most famous Scottish city, Glasgow (pronounced Glas-go, not Glas-gow), unfortunately noted today for extremely high rates of unemployment and considerable crime, as well as for industries that are old, tired and depressed. Nevertheless, the city leaders have made valiant efforts to make the old Victorian parts of it something of a cultural center.

Highland Scotland has Britain's most rugged mountains and best hunting, fishing and skiing regions. Such well-developed recreational opportunities make the Highlands a popular place for vacationers. While visiting Americans might enjoy the scenery and the small towns of this region, they should always recognize that the United States has vast recreational resources along these lines. Americans are better off spending their time in Britain at places that cannot be duplicated or surpassed at home.

A sprinkling of fairly new looking towns thinly covers the Highland zone. In the past, fierce tribal clans occupied Highland Scotland, warring upon each other and, when opportunities arose, raiding either the Lowland region or the north of England. Hardy Highlanders maintained their traditions of bagpiping, wearing tartans and kilts, and dancing in a peculiarly Scottish manner long after the Lowland Scots had become Anglicized.

Scotland's topography has some distinct features in addition to the existence of these two zones. Long indentations of the coastline carry ocean water far into the interior. These "firths" are similar to the "fjords" of Norway. The Firth of Forth, for instance, brings a long sweep of the ocean in just north of Edinburgh. In western and northern Scotland, a highly irregular coastline produces a vast number of islands and peninsulas.

Size and Density

From an American standpoint, Britain is incredibly small and incredibly crowded. All of Britain is only 94,226 square miles, which means that all of it fits into the single state of Colorado (104,247 square miles) with 10,000 square miles left over. Perhaps Oregon would be more appropriate for the purposes of comparison, considering its cool and rainy climate along with its similar size. By the way, Britain can fit into Texas almost three times.

Britain's comparatively small land area is home to a grand total of more than 57 million people, which includes approximately a million and a half counted in Northern

Ireland as a part of the United Kingdom. This total is between a quarter and a fifth of the American population of approximately 253 million. Britain now has just over 600 people per square mile, compared to the 68 per square mile in the United States. The American population density varies immensely from state to state: Alaska has only one person per square mile; Nevada only 10.9; Colorado, 31.8; Connecticut, 678; Rhode Island, 960.3 and New Jersey even exceeds the population density of England itself with 1,042 per square mile. When the population of Britain is considered on the basis of each of its component parts, it breaks down in this fashion: Scotland has 167 persons per square mile; Wales has 356 per square mile; and England has the formidable population density of over 940 persons per square mile, based on a population of approximately 47 and a half million. Clearly, with pun intended, England has the lion's share of the island of Britain!

These stark figures show what visitors soon come to realize: thick throngs of people are everywhere in Britain. In most places, the masses of shoppers are dense; thoroughfares are crowded; strollers are found in thick knots in the countryside; every historic site or museum or cathedral has an ample audience almost every hour that it is open. American visitors will come to appreciate the space and solitude available to them so easily at so many places at home.

While the density of population becomes readily apparent, the smallness of the country does not. There are so many regions, so many dialects, so many local styles and so much packed into so small a space that Britain really does seem like a much larger nation than it actually is. It feels as if Britain were once much more immense and had been shrunk in every direction some time ago. This contention may not be as silly as it might seem at first. Given the limited mobility of people during all of the centuries before the railways, a single mile had to seem a greater distance than today. To a medieval peasant, going even twenty miles was probably an awesome journey. So all of these aspects that we variously label as provincialism, localism and regionalism were deeply rooted in Britain over very long periods of time. Their survivals, plus the compacted intermingling of urban and rural areas, give a sense of size that is illusory.

The Topography of Britain: A Man- or Woman-Sized Country

One old generalization about Britain's land surface is that it is man-sized or, as we would properly express it, woman-sized as well. What this means is that nature does not overwhelm. There are no awesome and seemingly impassible deserts or mountain ranges nor are there any torrential rivers or formidable swamps. The rain-fed rivers of Britain gently flow towards the sea; the mountains are old and worn, and the highest peaks only reach a few thousand feet. There are no deserts, and most of the marshy areas were drained long ago. While the weather often is depressing and miserable, blizzards or heat waves that kill droves of people do not occur as they do in America. So, in general, Britain is a gentle, green country providing a most agreeable environment for masses of Homo sapiens.

Every now and then a freak storm will strike Britain with severity, as one did several years ago, when hurricane force winds uprooted trees in southern England. Outside of such extremely rare occurrences, whatever out-of-the-ordinary weather the British have is apt to be highly exaggerated, particularly in the more sensational press. For example, an ice storm that left a sheen of ice was once described as a "killer ice blizzard" because a motorist had skidded on it, hit a tree and died. When buses and trains occasionally have a problem with snow and ice, the situation produces headlines that scream: "Public transportation paralyzed!" All of these British journalists should be treated to a genuine storm whipping off the Rocky Mountains or a tornado in Kansas or Nebraska!

The Climate: The Influence of the Ocean

The effect of the Atlantic on Britain's climate is paramount. The ocean cools the island in summer and warms it in winter. Were it not for the warm flow of the Gulf Stream that brings water up from the south, Britain might have a climate similar to that of Labrador, which surprisingly occupies the same latitude as the British Isles.

Overall, due to the effect of the ocean, Britain's temperatures are moderate and predictable. High sixties can be expected in the summer and low forties in the winter, year after year. Stark extremes of weather, such as broiling days of over 100 degrees in the summers and bitter below-zero weeks in winter are continental phenomena found in places far inland such as the plains of Eurasia or the plains of the American Midwest.

The ocean plays an important role in shaping British attitudes and lifestyles. Insularity, which is defined as the condition of being an island surrounded by the ocean, gives a feeling of separateness and independence. The old joke about the headline that read "Fog in the Channel — Continent Isolated!" reveals something essential about the British viewpoint. Moreover, the ocean has always been a grand playground for British people, whether they sail on it or swim in it, or frolic at an array of seaside resorts. Also, seafood has been a much more important part of the traditional British diet than in most regions of America.

British Weather: Mostly Agony with Some Ecstasy

The ocean also brings rain very, very regularly in most years. Prevailing winds from the west lift clouds of moisture out of the Atlantic to drench Britain all year long. These clouds hang low and gray over the island day in and day out, with few exceptions. The most typical British weather forecast is for "sunny intervals," meaning that most of the day cloud and rain will prevail. Three hundred days with at least some precipitation per year can be expected in Britain, providing a stark contrast to the three hundred days or more of sunshine that is the boast of some of the states in the sunbelt. There are some parts of the

United States where people expecting normal weather expect sunshine; similarly, people in Britain expecting normal weather will expect overcast skies.

In the winter, visitors will find Britain cold and wet. In the spring, it will still be cold and wet. In the summer, it becomes cool and wet, and occasionally warm and wet. In the fall, it becomes cold and wet again. Since dreary gray skies and raw rain are inevitable in Britain most of the year, many British people become masochistic over the weather and dwell endlessly on how they suffer from it.

Nevertheless, the climate does afford a few compensations. Britain is always bright green. Even after the rare occasional snowfall, visitors can push the snow aside and see bright green grass growing beneath. The Atlantic moisture keeps Britain lush with grass and other plants all year long. As one resident put it, Britain has a marvelous climate for plants, but a climate that is less agreeable for people and animals. In the south roses can be seen blooming any month of the year, and at least some dormant but hardy green vegetables can be harvested during the coldest months of winter.

Britain's generally chilly mildness means that even in mid-winter, frosts, or times when the temperature dips below 32F, are specially reported on radio or TV. Snow is exceptional, particularly in the south. When it does accumulate, it is expected to turn to slush and go away by itself. If it does not, it is usually pounded into an icy gray crust on thoroughfares.

Overall mildness notwithstanding, the cold of Britain has a peculiarly penetrating effect that seems to cause chill that seems to go to the very marrow of the bones. Extremely high humidity is probably responsible for this. British people cope with these damp chills by wearing layers of clothes, particularly thick sweaters.

While many American visitors have a difficult time with the damp chill, they usually have an easier time than the British in experiencing the occasional hot and humid days that show up in July and August. Some noted quotations from the Paris edition of the New York *Herald Tribune* illustrate this point nicely. On one summer day it reported: "New York, high 84° clear and seasonably cool; Paris, high 78° warm; London, high, 72° continued hot." Some days later it reported "London, high 76°, no relief in sight." There are also authenticated stories of British workers who threw down their tools and refused to work when the temperature went into the low eighties, protesting against the "inhuman conditions" of labor in such heat. Dallas construction workers staying at working during a 100° heat wave provide an interesting contrast.

Even though it might not be appreciated, the chilly, wet rawness of Britain does stimulate people to keep moving and working. Activities such as study, research and reading seem easier to do on a cold, rainy day in Britain than on a gorgeous, warm, sunny day in the Southwest of the United States.

Finally, the climate does yield a very few exceptional days when it seems that there is no more wonderful place in the whole world to be than in Britain. Fortunately, these days do happen during the height of the tourist season. Some of these days are thick and moist and gray, when one can sense the heavy richness of life everywhere. Then there are those occasional warm days when the sun is radiant and all of nature simply bursts out in an overwheming tide of color and scent. Perhaps one such day is really worth two dozen miserable, rainy weekend afternoons. Perhaps the rarity of such lovely days makes them all the more appreciated, just as a glass of cool water becomes a treasure after a hike through a burning desert.

SIGNIFICANT ASPECTS OF THE BRITISH ECONOMY

Why Britain is Preoccupied with Economic Concerns

The worrisome state of the British economy is a topic

that seems to preoccupy Britons constantly. They maintain a perpetual gloominess about the economy, a pessimism not unlike their reaction to the weather.

There are some very good reasons underlying their grave concern over the fate of their economy. Size is a key factor. Britain's small, densely populated island simply does not have enough farmland to feed everyone. Therefore at least a third of the food consumed in Britain must come from abroad. A stroll through the shops of any high street (main street) reveals food products from various places, including New Zealand, Australia, Israel, Spain, France, the United States and Canada. British farms often specialize in producing high quality and expensive dairy, meat, fruit and vegetable crops, leaving the production of basic staples to those countries that have the vast acreage to grow them cheaply. Canadian or American wheat, for instance, has been cheaper than locally grown wheat in Britain since the 1870s. Much British land is given over to pasture, taking advantage of the lushness of plant growth to raise animals for wool and food. If plowed, much of this land could produce good crops, but the labor and investment for such crops would be too costly in most cases. By the way, anyone flying over Britain in the growing season will see many fields that are bright yellow. These fields grow an animal food crop with the odd name of "rape," which has become very popular in recent years.

America stands in sharp contrast as a food producer. It has a huge agricultural hinterland, a population spread more thinly across our landscape, substantial agricultural exports and surplus agricultural products bulging out of storage facilities.

America is also rich in raw materials, which also contrasts to the British situation. Unlike America, Britain is short of all kinds of raw materials necessary for industrial production. Britain's coal and iron mines once led the world in production, but the best has long been taken out of them. The list of raw materials that Britain must import in quantity is long, and includes timber, various fibers and many kinds of metal and ores.

Petroleum is an exception this picture. The United States must import an ever growing percentage of the petroleum it uses, even though it is one of the world's leading petroleum producers. Britain self-sufficient and an exporter of petroleum since 1980, thanks to a seemingly providential discovery of oil deposits under the North Sea in 1969. Without North Sea oil, dependence on imported oil would have been disastrous for the British economy. The fact that Britain has enough petroleum to export is sadly not reflected at what Americans call "the gas pumps," where the prices continue to be breathtakingly high, almost four times the price in the United States in 1992.

Besides exporting petroleum for a profit, how does the British economy pay for the necessary imports of so much food and so many raw materials? Britain manages to survive by living on brain power and skills that are applied to producing goods and services to meet overseas demand. In addition, many British firms are involved in banking, shipping and insurance services. The profits turned on such services can be used, eventually, to purchase food and raw materials. These are the so-called "invisible exports" of the economy. Many firms manufacture finished products from imported raw materials and semi-processed goods. Substantial quantities of these finished goods are then exported, thereby earning profit which can be applied to importing more raw materials and foodstuffs. This never ending cycle of services, exports and imports keeps the economy of this crowded island going.

Britain has an elaborately developed infrastructure suited for this economic activity. An elaborate financial network is superimposed on an old but workable system of docks, rails and trucking. A skilled work force with considerable technical and managerial expertise operates a series of factory complexes that range from the near obsolete to the ultramodern. Despite all of the complaints about the British economy, its level of development is quite high.

Given an economy that depends on its brains, skills and exports, the balance of payments question is crucial for Britain. The balance of payments measures exports against imports and registers either a surplus or a deficit. Britain's geography and demography, the sheer fact that so many people are crowded on the island, make the economy precariously dependent upon sustaining a favorable balance of payments.

Understanding British Socialism

Americans hear and read many peculiar, contradictory and often confusing things about the socialist component of Britain's economy. Socialism is a term usually employed in America in a pejorative manner, and conjures up images of arbitrary rule and rigid controls. Britain's socialism is democratic: It can be voted away at any time by a majority of elected representatives. It is also but one part of a dynamic economy that has larger capitalistic components.

Europeans are generally more sophisticated than Americans about the meaning and implications of modern socialism. It is not to be confused with the bankrupt communism that collapsed in eastern Europe just a few years ago. It is a concept firmly wedded to the democratic ballot box, meaning that if a majority of people in any country wish to dismantle some or all of what is socialistic, they may elect those representatives who are pledged to do so. This is precisely what has gone on in Britain recently, as Mrs. Thatcher's Conservative government, backed by an electoral mandate, has sought to remove substantial aspects of the socialist component from the British economy.

What really prevails in Britain and in many other European nations, such as France, Germany and Sweden, is not socialism but a mixed economy that has a strong component of socialism operating in conjunction with a strong component of capitalism. Under a mixed economy, markets have both considerable regulation and considerable freedom. Most of the political issues in these countries center on what the precise formula for the economy's mix should be. Politicians debate specific issues that boil down to whether there should be a little more or a little less of the capitalistic or the socialistic component. Nobody debates the need to have a mix; this is taken for granted, even by governments as staunchly conservative as those of Mrs. Thatcher.

Just what makes up the socialistic component? There is an extensive welfare system, including socialized medicine. In addition there are government controls over business and banking and the money supply. At one time many large scale operations were nationalized, or run by the state, but in recent years most of these large concerns have been privatized, or sold off to investors. It is worthwhile to consider some of these aspects in greater detail.

The Welfare State

The component of British socialism called the "welfare state" has been generally highly popular with the voters, so even the Conservatives will not try to dismantle it directly. So they nibble at the edges instead. Most British people take the welfare state for granted as a mark of a high civilization, and almost two generations have grown up since it was put into operation between 1945 and 1950. These generations have not known anything else but cradle to the grave welfare security. The system is simply regarded as normal in Britain.

The idea of a comprehensive welfare system is seldom appreciated by conservative Americans. For some of them it conjures the image of lazy people enjoying a secure, comfortable living without working for it. Some newspapers in the United States reinforce such negative images by spotlighting only the shortcomings and anomalies that crop up from time to time in the British system while ignoring the day to day achievement of effectively managing social problems in a humane manner.

Welfare means something quite different to British people than it does to conservative Americans. It means that there is a safety net under everyone, just as there is a safety net under trapeze performers in the circus. Everyone is assured of having the basics to sustain life, namely food, housing, clothing, health care and education. Drastic sickness, old age and unemployment are no longer haunting specters of financial catastrophe as they have been for centuries when ordinary people simply could not lay enough money aside as savings to cope with these situations. Becoming sick, old and unemployed are still unfortunate circumstances, but at least the sufferer knows that he or she will be taken care of by the society during those difficult times.

Of course, there is something of a welfare state existing in the United States also, although Americans are disinclined to call it that. Social Security, Medicare, Medicaid, food stamps and various other entitlements all help comprise our rather patchier and less complete and less carefully controlled system. We have the persistent problem that there are always people who suffer from its inadequacies, particularly those who fall between the cracks in coverage, or those who cannot be properly served by underfunded and overburdened operations. Another problem is that some persons and institutions find ways to take advantage of benefits improperly.

Aspects of the welfare state in Britain are always subject to criticism by British people, of course, but in general it is seen as a vast public insurance system, with everyone contributing and everyone eligible to draw benefits.

The National Health Service

The existence of British socialized medicine, called the National Health Service has long been a highly controversial topic in the United States. Until recently, most American physicians have been adamantly opposed to it, and American journalists have often held up some of its worst aspects to reinforce the prejudices against it on the part of their readership. Therefore a sympathetic consideration of the British system may be useful to counteract the negative image that has been built up over the years.

First of all, tourists who become ill or have an accident in Britain will be treated by the National Health Service without cost. Special insurance is unnecessary in Britain. In general, emergency services are quite good. Medics and ambulances can be counted upon for promptness and efficiency.

The more negative features of National Health will be encountered by long-term visitors who have medical problems that are not particularly urgent. Under these circumstances, British National Health will most likely seem frustrating on account of its delays, and it will allow invidious comparisons to be made with the fast, elaborate and expensive health care that the middle and upper classes in America have come to expect. Visitors have a way out, however, which is opting for private care. Many British physicians have decided to put more of their time or all of their time into private practice. There are also numerous private hospitals in addition to the public hospitals. It is estimated that perhaps 15% of British medicine is private now. So for a good fee, anyone in Britain, tourist or resident, can go to the head of the line (or queue) and receive either good or only fair treatment, depending on the skills of the doctor in private practice who treats them.

What really exists in British medicine are two competing and overlaid systems of medicine, one private and one public, one for the affluent and one for the poorer members of society. It is, in fact, a duplication of the competing and overlaid systems of public and private education. As in education, the private care sector has gained a reputation for being better among some but not all of those who have used it. The less fortunate and the less affluent have no choices and must use the National Health system and the state school system. Clearly, the emergence of this dual system was certainly not what the architects of the welfare state envisioned.

Everyone who has spent some time in Britain has either heard or experienced at least one or two genuine horror stories about the National Health Service. The standard themes involve incredibly long waits, crowded facilities, bungled operations and incompetent doctors or dentists. Many stories feature Commonwealth medical personnel, usually Indian or Pakistani, who have such difficulty with

English that it frightens the patients or causes a mistake in the treatment. Such stories, taken together, do point up a fundamental shortcoming of National Health: the system tried to do too much too fast with inadequate resources. To this day, Britain spends a much smaller percentage of its gross national product on health than does America. There are simply not enough doctors, dentists or medical facilities to go around to accomplish all of the ambitious tasks that the National Health Service has claimed as its responsibilities. To make matters worse, recent Conservative administrations have curtailed expenditures on health somewhat. At the outset, all persons in Britain were to receive free medical care, dental care, hospitalization, psychiatric services, prescriptions and even eyeglasses and dentures. These provisions were all too ambitious, so eventually various fees and partial payments had to be imposed for many of these services.

Yet even when all of the failures, shortcomings and horror tales about the National Health Service are taken into account, its striking achievements cannot be denied. For centuries, the majority of ordinary people in Britain were chronically deprived of basic health care. Vast numbers needed dentures or eyeglasses, or suffered regularly from some painful chronic malady, or had a health impediment that could have been corrected by treatment. This sad state of health was revealed when men were called up for the draft during the world wars of this century and a high percentage of them were found unfit for military service. Other statistics on life expectancy and the recurrence of epidemics also reflected the low standard of medical services available to ordinary British people before the National Health Service was instituted.

There have been dramatic improvements all along the line since National Health's ambitious programs have gotten underway. Much of the effort has been prophylactic, involving the regular screening of categories of people, such as children and underground miners. There have also been sterling examples of applied medical expertise that have surpassed the efforts of comparable practitioners in the United States. Take mammography, the screening for breast cancer, as an example. In the United States, errors of communication and interpretation can and do take place between general practitioners, specialists and radiologists, sometimes resulting in misdiagnosis and tragedy. In Britain there is a large, specialized institution that does the whole process of breast examination and nothing else, and is noted for its accuracy and its efficiency.

British doctors are paid much less than American doctors, but nevertheless most of them stay in Britain instead of emigrating for higher salaries. When told that he would make three or four times as much money in the United States as he did in general practice in Britain, one doctor told the author: "In America, medicine is a business. In Britain, I provide service in a healing profession. Doing that, instead of being a businessman in a white coat, is what is important in my life."

British doctors also seem to have a less exalted status than American doctors, and enjoy the same kind of social esteem accorded to other professionals such as engineers, lawyers (solicitors and barristers, that is) and clergymen. They also are much less troubled by malpractice suits. Doctors and dentists, not bureaucrats, are the people who run the National Health system, for the most part, sitting on boards, committees and commissions, drawing up the rules and handling the problems that arise. They are the people responsible for supervising, designing and disciplining the system within the limits of the resources available. Even so, they are much more free from the mountains of paperwork from insurance companies and government agencies that have burdened American doctors.

Despite the frequent delays, frustrations, overcrowding and understaffing associated with the National Health Service, the ordinary Briton does appreciate the fact that he or she has free medical service that is at least adequate most of the time. These Britons know that they are on a particular doctor's list of patients, and that they can see their doctor when needed. In turn, the doctor knows that he receives a fee for each of the patients on his roster, whether they need to see him or not. Compared to what ordinary and poorer Britons had before National Health, the system is a substantial improvemment. British people recognize this, and politicians dare not tamper with it. Even the physicians, who reluctantly accepted it after World War II, now are its champions, proud of the service they supply. So it seems that the only fair way to view Britain's socialized medicine is in the light of this historic perspective.

The Persistent Strength of British Capitalism

Despite the expansion of the public sector through the growth of the National Health Service, the welfare system, and government bureaucracies, well over eight out of every ten jobs in Britain are still in the private sector, meaning that these jobs are from a vigorous capitalism that continues to flourish, change and grow in Britain.

Britain shared in Western Europe's vast expansion of the regional economic base and a tripling in the standards of living in the post-war decades. New technologies were the engines driving this achievement. In Britain, notable advances were made in what is called high-tech sectors, including computers, robots, jet engines and scanners for diagnosing illnesses.

Much of the strength and vitality of British capitalism comes from the flexibility and incentives of entrepreneurs who are out to make a pound, whether the pound comes from American tourists, teenage music fans, fashion-conscious wives, visiting Arabs or simply anyone who is willing to spend. When considering the more spectacularly profitable breakthroughs in British popular culture since World War II, it is quite clear that no government direction or incentive could ever have developed and marketed the Beatles or the mini-skirt.

The capitalistic endeavors that made Britain such a power in the Victorian era live on in the mixed economy. Famous British firms still operate world-wide, and British resources of people, money and managing give strength to a diverse range of multi-national corporations. The City of London remains one of the world's great centers of high finance, ranking with Wall Street, Hong Kong, Singapore and Tokyo. The City is still noted for its speed, power and skilled professionalism.

Admirers of the British economic system claim that the best of capitalism has been kept and that its worst features of tooth and claw have been removed or ameliorated by the mix of socialism in the economy. It is a contention worth pondering.

CLASS AND GENDER IN BRITAIN

Class Consciousness

Feelings about class in Britain are pervasive, insidious and frequently charged with emotion. The United States does not have class feelings on anything approaching this scale, but subtle or blatant racial feelings, still pervasive even today, can be compared with the strains and tensions of lingering class feelings in Britain.

Class discrimination might comprise the very worst feature of life in Britain. American visitors will not encounter any class-conscious expressions directed at them because Americans stand outside of the British class system. In fact, class antagonisms are often flashed in such a subtle way that visitors might miss the inferences entirely.

Why do these class antagonisms exist? Various explanations have been offered. One argument sees class antagonisms going all the way back in history to the time that the upper landed classes imposed their dominance, first by force and then through heredity and wealth. Since Britain never experienced a French-style revolution, in which the lower orders rose to topple the upper class, the dominance of the upper class was never broken in Britain and members of it have continued to be influential to the present day.

An explanation for this state of affairs favored by the ultra-conservatives is that the most able people established their ascendancy by the laws of survival of the fittest long ago, and just as fast horses breed fast horses, able people have produced long lines of talented individuals. Therefore, it is argued, people in the lower classes are generally less able human beings of lower intelligence. Some go so far as to imply that those at the bottom have interests and activities that are much more animalistic than those of the people at the top. This argument goes on to declare that the people at the commanding heights of society have always been charged with the responsibility for maintaining civilization in the face of lower class barbarism. Therefore they deserve their privileges.

Another argument used to interpret class consciousness in Britain is that human groups have always had antagonistic disputes when it came to sharing the earth's riches. Since England has always had relatively few people of other ethnic stocks or skin colors, white Anglo-Saxon Protestants have divided themselves into classes in order to exercise rivalry and conflict. This view sees group antagonisms as natural to the species everywhere. Therefore, what could be more natural than that two similar American communities geographically close to each other on the nondescript plains of North Dakota become convinced that the members of the respective opposite basketball team are worthy objects of hatred? Long before the gymnasiums were built for these teams, rival tribes of Native Americans living very similar lifestyles undoubtedly fought each other in the same region.

Still another explanation, popular on the left, relates class differences to the economy. Since the means of production are owned by one group and the work is done by another group, classes must exist, and where there are classes there are class struggles. Such a point of view recognizes that groups of people exist who are of no economic value to the system. Such people are cast aside and barely maintained by a society whose key motivation is the acquisition of profit.

No matter which of these arguments or what combination of arguments is used to explain class antagonisms in Britain, nobody will deny their existence. A definition of class divisions is needed, but the dynamic changes of modern society make defining difficult.

An Attempt at Defining Classes in Britain

In the past, a fairly clear division into three classes could be perceived in Britain: upper, middle and lower, or, using alternative terms, the aristocratic (or landed) class, the bourgeoisie and the working class, which can also be called the proletariat. To simplify things, most people could be placed in one of these three categories by determining how they received their money. Those who lived off rents and payments on property that they owned, especially inherited land, were upper class. Those who shuffled pieces of paper around for a living, either in business or in one of the professions, were bourgeois or middle class. This class had a broad range, from high income bankers to low income shopkeepers and clerks. Those who actually touched work materials were working class or proletarian. For instance, the carpenter touched wood, the butcher touched meat and the plumber touched pipes.

In recent times, class definitions have been blurred. This has largely been attributable to the creation of so many semi-professional and technical jobs that may or may not be considered middle class. Some new definitions of working class have been tried out, but difficulties have arisen in applying them. Take, for example, the current definition of a working class job as one that the worker regards as repetitive, unchallenging and as likely to be carried out in generally unpleasant surroundings.

Growing affluence in Britain in recent decades has meant that considerably more social mobility has been injected into class structure. While a recent study found that 55% of Britons remained in the class to which they were born, 45% moved into another class. Most movement was upward, into the middle class and from the middle class to the upper middle class and beyond. Dynamic technological advances allowed a great expansion in the ranks of affluent professionals, managers, administrators, and technical experts. Many young people advanced beyond their parents' status to become pilots, computer programmers, broadcasters, television producers, journalists, sales managers, engineers, draftsmen, factory foremen, and accountants.

Many of those in the working class did not advance, and this has been attributed to unequal educational and environmental backgrounds. Perhaps the worst feature of the current class situation in Britain is the existence of what is called a "permanent underclass" at the very bottom of, or below, the working class. These people are "on the dole," what Americans would describe as being "on welfare," subsisting in ugly surroundings with little hope that they or their children will break out of the cycle of poverty. Their youngsters drop out of school without any training or any prospects for improving life. This segment of society is much more numerous and visible in America, but Britain has its own underclass also, and they can be found in the rundown neighborhoods of places like Glasgow, Liverpool and Leeds.

No matter how difficult it is to come up with definitions that fit a host of anomalies, there is a broad gulf in Britain between what is considered middle class and what is called working class. The gulf is confirmed by dozens of subtle and blatant indicators, revealing an individual as either "one of them" or "one of us."

Speech is the most ready indicator of class. In most cases, pronunciation gives class identity away before the first sentence is finished. There are only two ways to speak in England (but not in Scotland or Wales): properly or improperly. To maintain their children's proper speech, the middle and upper classes gladly spend their money on tuition at the "right" schools so that class and regional afflictions of speech will not contaminate them. Accent is one thing; choice of words is another. People on one side of the great gulf of class will say such things as "the missus," instead of "my wife," which is intoned by people on the other side. Hundreds of words used by lower class speakers are never used by those who speak proper English, and vice versa. Over time, a rich slang has developed in working class life, creating nicknames, abbreviations, and even rhymed words for all sorts of objects and situations. But should any of these slang terms be used accidentally in a setting where only proper English is acceptable, it can be construed as an embarrassing gaffe.

Other indicators of class abound, including the way people dress; the magazines and newspapers they read; how and where they spend their leisure time; what clubs they belong to; where they live; whether or not they own their own domicile; where they went to school; where they vacation; what cars they drive; whether or not they have a car; and what TV programs they enjoy.

All of these differences were much sharper before the age of television. Before World War II, George Orwell could single out certain striking behaviors of the working class, such as comfortably wearing hats indoors, taking cheese from the point of a knife and drinking tea from the saucer. Part of the "global village" effect of television has been to inform working class Britons about proper behavior, which they can clearly see acted out on countless sitcoms and other programs.

While class differences remain a constant source of humor in Britain, there are serious effects of class distinctions that are not at all beneficial. Because of class, sniggering contempt, hostility, rancor, jealousy and, at worst, outright hatred can flare, particularly when an event such as a strike brings class consciousness to the fore. At such a time, each side looking across the gulf of class seems to see a stereotype. To the employer and managerial classes, the working classes can appear particularly lazy, mean, gross, dirty, insensitive, unpatriotic, stupid and narrow minded. Conversely, workers see the employers as stupid and narrow minded, as well as spoiled, lucky, selfish, greedy, false, artificial and, at worst, truly vicious.

Another stereotype held by each of the classes is a favorable self-image. Workers regard themselves as the "real" people of the nation, the salt of the earth who do not put on airs. They are the people who do the essential hard work that actually keeps the nation going. Their demands, from this point of view, are only for a fair share of what they create through working. The middle and upper classes, on the other hand, see themselves as the brains behind the dynamism and decency of the nation, without whom the working classes would be hopeless slugs.

Bitterness over the gulf of class is unfortunately deep and enduring in Britain. It can surface in all sorts of places in addition to the workplace. It can come between doctor and patient, librarian and reader, householder and maintenance man, and ticket taker and passenger.

Americans and Class

Americans in Britain are often taken by surprise when such class feelings arise. Sometimes they are confused by tales of malicious behavior that one class casts upon another in a "them" versus "us" setting. This is because class consciousness of ordinary Americans tends to be blurred and undeveloped in comparison to that of British people.

There are several reasons for this. America has always been a more open, more expansive, less traditional society. In spreading itself across a continent rapidly, the United States has come to incorporate diverse regions and diverse populations. People who have strong regional accents are accepted at the very apex of American society. In newer parts of the United States, but to a degree in all parts, the dominant determinant of class in the minds of Americans is money instead of education, taste, behavior or various kinds or language. If one has large amounts of money, one is considered upper class, and if one has little, one is lower class. Those with a fair amount of money make up the mass in the middle. From a sociologist's standpoint, this is a glaring, sweeping oversimplification. To the ordinary American, it most often seems like the truth.

Ask Americans what class they belong to and nearly all of them will respond: "middle class." British surveys bring a response from over 60% of the population that they are "working class." Declaring allegiance to the middle class in America seems to involve maintaining a belief in the American dream of living well, either at present or in the future. It does not necessarily mean, as it does in Britain, achieving a certain level of education, maintaining certain forms of social behavior or holding particular jobs. Therefore many Europeans have great difficulty in understanding class in America. Sociologists must constantly refine and redraw the tests used in the difficult task of putting Americans in class categories.

This is not to deny that some broad divisions do exist in American society. For instance, there is a division between college educated and non-college educated. Even so, countless people take courses as adults and many get degrees late in life. There is also an old division between "blue collar" and "white collar" workers, but innumerable jobs, especially newer occupations, fall between these classifications.

While American doctors, lawyers, architects, engineers and investment bankers obviously belong to high paying and high prestige professions, a high percentage of the individuals holding such jobs undoubtedly at one time served in restaurants, held down repetitive factory jobs or worked at some other low paying, low prestige jobs side by side with workers who would go nowhere else. Americans know that the young person at the fast food outlet can become a senator or a scientist or a bank president some day. Americans are not "pegged" by what they do for a living during one period of their lives, and this is one of the great boons of living in the United States.

Of Men and Women

It is very difficult to generalize about the respective roles of men and women in Britain and the United States at this stage in history because there are all kinds of men and all kinds of women in any community, and they form all kinds of relationships. Undoubtedly, a highly significant and inexorable revolution in the relations of men and women and, consequently, of the structure of the family has been going on in the Western world. This vast social revolution is far from over, and since we are all caught up in it somehow, an understanding of its significance, implications and ultimate results is far from clear, whether we live in Britain or in the United States. What is clear is that it is a much debated and discussed matter, with emotions, interest and controversies operating at high levels of intensity.

Some facts about the advance of equal rights regardless of gender are clear. An Equal Pay Act of 1970 declared that men and women should have equal pay with men for doing the same job, but this law has been circumvented in many situations. By 1980 half of the married women of Britain were in the workforce, compared to only 10% in 1900. In Britain as in America, two incomes have been required to maintain a comfortable standard of living.

It appears that this formidable revolution has proceeded at a faster pace and has gone the furthest in the United States. Equal opportunities on a broad social and legal front have been achieved to a greater degree in the United States than in Britain. This is not to deny the successes gained by a long tradition ardent feminism in Britain, highlighted by the celebrated Suffragettes of the Edwardian era who championed women's right to vote. Recently, feminist groups on British campuses have taken notable avant-garde positions. Yet when the various activities of feminist and women's groups in Britain are taken into consideration, it appears that many of them are relatively isolated in positions far in advance of the mainstream of British women. Comparable American groups, it can be argued, are not as far out front in advance of ordinary American women.

Translated into daily circumstances, this means that most British women continue to act in traditional ways. They will be more apt to defer to masculine judgment, wit, knowledge, strength and understanding, as their mothers were purported to do. At the same time, they will seek to maintain a mysteriousness about their intuition, charm and spiritual powers. They may expect deferential treatment from men while they may seek to manipulate those men whom they openly acknowledge to be so wise and so strong. In other words, the male and female roles prevailing in the 1950s and in all of the previous centuries are far from finished in Britain for millions of people. American visitors accustomed to the new relationships in the United States might be taken aback by this. Americans of a more traditional caste might feel more comfortable in Britain over this matter.

There is an irony here. No matter how far behind the British drive towards equal rights may appear in comparison to developments in the United States, women in Britain have long been regarded as far in advance of the rest of the world. Even as far back as the sixteenth century the independence, assertiveness and freedom of English women was mentioned frequently by foreign visitors. Of course, these views were offered by males who securely dominated society. In that century, Elizabeth I enhanced appreciation of women's abilities, although she, too, played the game of feminine deference when it suited her purposes. In subsequent centuries, intellectual females in Britain gained worldwide renown in philosophy and literature. They included Mary Wollstonecraft, the Brönte sisters and George Eliot, who took that pseudonym in deference to male chauvinism. These women and the militant Suffragettes who followed them had to fight an uphill battle against the slowly crumbling bastions of male power and even more slowly crumbling resistance of male prejudice. The Equal Pay Act of 1970 is a case in point. It declared that women should have equal pay with men for doing the same job, but the law was not enforced and pay continued to be unequal in many places just because of gender.

Certainly Mrs. Thatcher has gone down as a politician of ability and authority, regardless of what one thinks of her political stance. Her example should have a significantly beneficial effect on the campaign for equal rights. For those of a different political persuasion, the example of Shirley Williams, an ex-Labour Party leader, should be encouraging. Many considered her as a potential Prime Minister until she lost her position by abandoning Labour for the new but now faltering Social Democratic Party.

When one contemplates how distant the prospect of a female President of the United States seems, it must be conceded that at the very top British women are ahead of American women. In both countries the direction does seem to be set towards greater and greater female participation in all of life's activities and tasks, with equal compensation for equal effort. Indeed, recently the advance in the standard of living in both countries has been maintained by both husbands and wives working. Gone are the days when there was a stigma attached to the married middle class woman who worked outside of the home. Today it is a necessity for most families.

One particular aspect of relationships between the sexes in Britain that should be mentioned before ending this section is the particularly British phenomenon of "chatting up." Naturally, males talk to females to impress them, and vice versa, everywhere, and no matter whether the games of the 1980s or the 1950s or 1050s are being played. What makes this a remarkably British pastime is the intensity of the phenomenon. Flirtation with words is something carried on everywhere by people of all ages in that country. Word games become very elaborate and are characterized by flashes of humor and cleverness. Here is yet another example of the great importance of language in this country. Rumor does have it, though, that when relations proceed far beyond chatting, Britons are apt to display an intensity that is both very serious and very quiet!

CHAPTER FOUR

Understanding Aspects of British Culture
LANGUAGE

The Queen's English and the American Dialect

ENGLISH certainly has come close to becoming the new international language, a status that only Latin once enjoyed in our civilization. Of all the hundreds of millions who speak English around the globe, it is impossible to tell just how many speak British English rather than the American dialect of English. Most Americans are not accustomed to having their language labeled a dialect, but by some definitions of language, that is exactly how it can be categorized. Of the parts of the world that emerged from the old British Empire, only Canada speaks American English. All of the other places throughout the world once under the British flag speak British English, sometimes with a particular local accent. Included are India, Malaya, Hong Kong, Nigeria, Kenya, Jamaica, Australia, and New Zealand, to name but a few.

American English shows up around the world among those who speak English as a second language, often because American businesses and military installations are so widespread. There are also countless thousands who speak American English because they studied in the United States. Nevertheless, in many quarters there is a consensus that British English is better English, a prejudice shared by quite a few Americans. In Britain it is a conviction.

The Importance of Language in Britain

Just how a person says something means much more in Britain than it does in the United States. Listeners are keenly attuned to pronunciation and vocabulary because in Britain speech is one of the best indicators to use in placing people within the categories of the pervasive class system. Unlike English in the United States, there is only one proper way to speak the language in Britain. Proper English can be heard on the BBC, in private school instruction, at the universities and in the mouths of properly educated persons all the way up to the Prime Minister and to the royal family itself. All other accents, all regional dialects and all use of slang are deemed below-standard English. Aspiring upwardly mobile persons pursuing various careers often become terribly frustrated when attempting to refrain from speaking the way they spoke at home and in their inferior schools. British ears are so keen that they can usually detect a person's educational background, no matter how hard he or she may work to contrive a "proper" accent.

Not everyone in Britain wishes to speak standard English. Scots, for instance, take great pride in their dialect, to the extent that they have insisted that the local BBC carry programs and employ announcers using the Scots dialect. Lower class Londoners enjoy their Cockney speech, rich in fast, amusing slang. People in the north of England feel that a person's ordinary, warm, decent qualities are revealed in the use of the local dialect. Visitors get a taste of this when bus conductors taking the fare say "ta" for "thanks" and call the passengers of the opposite sex "love." To these people and others who do not want to speak it, "proper" English usually connotes artificiality and snobbishness. For many it is the sound of people who have money, privilege and coldness.

How Americans Escape Language Snobbery in Britain

One of the worst aspects of British society is how speech can bring on painful self-consciousness for some people and deft snobbery on the part of others. The strained self-consciousness that British people experience in using their language enables the American visitor to appreciate the generally free and easy tolerance of language usage at home. Fortunately, Americans in Britain are free from this British game because they stand outside of British class relationships, a position guaranteed by their American dialect. Even so, language can put Americans in embarrassing situations. Using the wrong word or mispronouncing a word may draw mild criticism or mild amusement from such people as shop attendants. For example, "pants" in America means "underpants" in Britain, where pants are always "trousers." "Tomato" pronounced with an "ā" instead of "ah" is conspicuous in a British restaurant or grocery. But no American will suffer from having his or her education, social standing and family background quickly assessed by the spoken word.

The use of American English in Britain has a bright side. British people generally enjoy talking with Americans who are inclined to speak without inhibitions. Also, American English is the dialect used in much of imported light entertainment, and it is also the dialect used in carrying out many feats of high technology, such as space exploration, achievements that British people hold in such high esteem. Regional variations of American English are also appreciated in Britain. Southern or Texas pronunciations are relished in particular. Overall, the American visitor has a great advantage in that dialect and slang provide a ready topic for initiating conversations in Britain.

In a way, it is unfortunate that the New England accent was not selected as the standard speech for announcers when radio was developed in the United States. The bland Middle Western sound was selected instead, largely because it was the most neutral of all the American regional accents. Had the New England pronunciations become standard through use on the media, American English and British English would be much closer today.

Despite this, the sheer size of the United States guarantees that regional accents will flourish. Even American presidents have spoken with strong regional pronunciations, as the speeches of John Kennedy, Lyndon Johnson and Jimmy Carter testify. By contrast, it is difficult for a British politician to carry distinct, non-standard English into high office, unless he or she comes from the Labour Party's left or from Scotland.

Some Necessary Translations from British to American

Vocabulary in Britain and America has diverged ever since the Jamestown settlement in the early seventeenth century. An old witticism states that America and Britain are two nations divided by a common language. Today a rich variety of words, standard and slang, appear exclusively on one or the other side of the Atlantic. Also, shared identical words might have entirely different meanings in Britain from those in America, or, a further complication, the first meanings of words in Britain may be the second meanings in America, and vice versa.

While it is often amusing to discover differences in vocabulary on the spot, visitors are best forewarned and forearmed by studying the lists of translations that follow. These terms will also be useful for persons interested in British theater, literature and journalism. Undoubtedly most readers will already know how to translate many of these words from familiarity with these sources.

There are other lists of translated words in this book. See the section on driving for automotive terms; the section on food has its own list; so do the sections on accommodations and using the telephone; and the sections on education, cathedrals and castles.

The words in this listing have been grouped in three categories: cultural terms, very practical terms and potentially embarrassing words and phrases. The cultural terms will certainly help in doing everything from reading newspapers to going on tours. They include terms pertaining to religion, politics and geography. The practical terms are for day-to-day living in Britain, and the potentially embarrassing words and phrases are some of those verbal quagmires and pitfalls that exist whenever translations are attempted.

Cultural Terms

Athlete — This term is likely to refer to someone in track and field in Britain. The word athletics pertains to track and field sports.

Backbencher — The ordinary members of a political party, or the rank and file, sit on the back benches in Parliament.

Barrister — A barrister is a lawyer who pleads cases in court. Ordinary legal paperwork and minor business are handled by a solicitor in Britain.

Billion — A billion is a million million in Britain. The American billion is expressed in Britain as a thousand million. So a five billion dollar debt owed to an American bank would be spoken of as a five thousand million debt in Britain.

Boxing Day — This is a holiday on the day after Christmas, December 26, a time when many people give presents. The name comes from the old custom of giving boxes of presents to those owed gratuities, such as the postman.

Britain — As a geographic term or as a political term, Britain is the island which includes England, Scotland and Wales.

Brit — This is a slang abbreviation for a British person.

British — Any person or phenomenon from England, Scotland or Wales can properly be called British. The term can also be applied to many but not all persons in Northern Ireland.

Buckhouse — This is slang for Buckingham Palace, the usual residence of the British royal family, so the word may be used as a casual reference to them.

Celsius — This is the term used officially for the temperature. Fahrenheit is used in the United States in general. 0° Celsius is the same as 32° Fahrenheit; 10° Celsius is the same as 212° Fahrenheit, the boiling point of water.

Circus — This is a place where important streets intersect. Piccadilly Circus and Oxford Circus are examples.

City — "The City" means the old City of London, now a square mile comprising London's financial district. City in general is not used in Britain the way it is used in America. It means an urban area that has a cathedral. Thus, Coventry is a city, but nearby Warwick is just a town.

Cockney — this noun or adjective refers to working class East London culture and the accent that goes with it. Loosely used, it can mean a working class Londoner. Originally it meant someone who was born within the sound of Bow Bells, the bells of a church in East London.

Continent — British people use this term to describe the rest of Europe.

Corn — This is a word for all grains. The American word corn is translated as maize or Indian corn. It does not grow well in Britain, and is likely to be used as an animal food when available. Yet American sweet corn is regarded as a special American delicacy.

Corporation — This term means municipal government, what is called local government in many parts of the United States. The American word "corporation" means "limited company" in Britain, abbreviated "Ltd."

Council house or council flat — This refers to subsidized public housing. It is housing provided by the local council or local government.

Dates — Americans should note carefully that the British write dates thus: day/month/year, rather than the American style of month/day/year. There is logic in the British style because it starts with the smaller and goes towards the larger.

Demo — This is a popular abbreviation for "demonstration".

Dole — These are welfare payments, usually to unemployed persons. "On the dole" usually means chronically unemployed, perhaps similar to the American phrase, "on welfare."

East Anglia — This is the eastern hump on the map of England, a rather flat plain.

East End — This is the working class, Cockney, part of London.

Fleet Street — This is the street in London that has been noted for its journalism, but the major newspapers are now produced elsewhere.

Football — The American game of soccer is called football in Britain, where it is immensely popular. American football, rarely played until recently, is called just that.

Guy Fawkes Night — This is a carnival night of bonfires and fireworks on November 5. Children beg as they do in the United States on Halloween. It commemorates the capture of Guy Fawkes, who tried to blow up the king and the legislature early in the seventeenth century.

Gaol — This word is pronounced exactly like "jail" in American English and it means the same thing.

Holiday — This word is used in Britain for "vacation." We are "on holiday" means we are on vacation.

Home office — The Home Office is the government department responsible for law and order, domestic affairs and immigration.

Hustings — These are election meetings. The term formerly meant a platform candidates literally stood upon. It is always used in the plural.

Life Peer — A Life Peer is a new nobleman or woman who can sit in the House of Lords but cannot pass on the noble title. This new form of nobility was created in the 1950s. There are several hundred of them in the House of Lords now, and no new hereditary peers have been created for some time.

Limited Company — This is the British name for a corporation, abbreviated as Ltd., just as American corporations use Inc.

Ltd. — This is the abbreviation for Limited Company, what Americans call a corporation.

Midlands — This area is made up of the counties of England that are in the middle of the country, the place that features undulating plains farthest from the sea.

M.P. — This is an abbreviation for member of Parliament, the equivalent of member of Congress.

Navvy — A navvy is an unskilled day laborer. Originally navvies were canal and railroad builders. The term is often applied to road construction crews today.

Nip — This means sneak away, as in "nip out into the garden."

Number Ten — This refers to number 10 Downing Street, the residence of the Prime Minister where much governmental activity takes place.

P.M. — This is the abbreviation for the Prime Minister.

Provinces — This term refers to all of England outside of London.

Redundancy pay — This is what Americans would call severance pay.

Redundant — British use this term to mean unemployed. The number of redundancies refers to the number unemployed.

Rugby — This is a game somewhat like American football, but played without protective padding. It is also called "rugger."

Scotland Yard — This is the headquarters for London's Metropolitan Police.

Scottish — This adjective is preferred instead of "Scotch" because "Scotch" refers to a drink, although this drink is called "whiskey" in Britain. A person from Scotland is called a "Scot."

Send down — This means to expel or suspend a person from a university.

Soho — This district in central London was once known for foreigners and prostitution. Its reputation lingers but it is less dangerous and more quaint today.

Shadow cabinet — The political party out of office has a potential cabinet formed for the time when it will return. Opposition party leaders comprise this shadow cabinet.

Solicitor — Britain has two kinds of legal professionals. Solicitors do ordinary legal work, much of it paperwork. The barristers plead cases in court.

Stalls — This term refers to theater seats on the ground floor.

Stand for Office — In Britain, politicians stand for office; in America, politicians run for office.

Supporters — This is the word in sports for those whom Americans call "fans."

T.U.C. — This is an abbreviation for the Trades Union Congress, an organization of Britain's powerful unions.

West Country — This refers to the southwestern part of England, the long peninsula pointing out into the Atlantic containing Devon and Cornwall and adjacent counties.

West End — This fashionable and rich part of London is now in the geographic center, but the historic name is retained.

Westminster — Parliament and the government are situated in this area along the Thames west of the City of London.

Whitehall — This is a street housing most of the main ministries that runs from Trafalgar Square down to Parliament. The residence of the Prime Minister is just off it on Downing Street.

Work to Rule — Unions apply this to slow up and disrupt activity by rigidly adhering to rules and regulations.

Very Practical Terms

Here are quick translations of a wide range of regularly used and practical terms, ranging from some useful for shopping to some useful for seeking a toilet. See the list following for potentially embarrassing terms.

Advert — In Britain this is used as an abbreviation for advertisement. Ours is "ad."

Alsatian — This is the British name for what Americans call a German shepherd or a police dog.

Balaclava — This is a knitted hat which can be pulled over the face for additional protection from the elements.

Bank Holiday — This is a day when the banks are closed along with almost everything else. They occur at the end of May and the end of August, and are rather comparable to the American Memorial Day and Labor Day. Many other holidays are called Bank holidays, although only two of them are official ones.

Bathe — As a verb, this means to go for a swim, not to have a bath. By the way, Americans "take" a bath, while British people "have" them.

Billfold — This is used in place of wallet.

Biro — This is the British word for a ball point pen.

Book — To book means to reserve.

Boot Sale — Literally, a boot sale is conducted from the boots of cars, what Americans call car trunks.

Busker — Buskers are street performers, singers, musicians of various kinds, and dancers who solicit voluntary contributions from people passing by.

Camp Bed — A camp bed is what Americans call a cot.

Carriage — This word means a railway car. The only time that the word "car" is used for railroad coaches is for the railway cars of the London Underground.

Cheerio — This is a light way of saying goodbye which is quite outdated now.

Chemist — A chemist is a druggist in America.

Chemist's Shop — This is a drugstore in Britain, but it sells a narrower range of products than the American drugstore.

Chit — a pass or document or any piece of paper with significant writing on it can be called this.

Cinema — This means movie or movie theater in America. The term "pictures" is also used.

Cling Film — This is the British term for plastic wrap.

Cloakroom — This is a polite term for toilet in a place such as a restaurant.

Clothespeg — This is used instead of clothespin.

Cold — This usually does not mean ice cold as it does in America. Americans would use the word "cool" to describe what is called cold in Britain.

Constable — This is the proper term for policeman. The Chief of Police is the Chief Constable. Police Constable is abbreviated P.C.

Convenience — This is a polite term for toilet, meaning a public toilet, usually outdoors. Its full name is "public convenience."

Cot — This is a bed for a small child. What Americans call a cot is a "camp bed" in Britain.

Cotton — This word is used instead of thread. Instead of a "spool of thread," one asks for a "reel of cotton."

Cornet — This means "cone," as in ice cream cone.

Current account — This term in banking refers to what Americans call a checking account. Note, too, that checks are spelled "cheques," and that they are not ordinarily sent back to the person who wrote them, as they are for most checking accounts in the United States.

Cutlery — Americans will say "silverware" instead, even if silver is not involved.

Cutting the Grass — This wonderfully explicit term is used instead of the vague American "mowing the lawn."

Deaf aid — This phrase reveals British bluntness. Americans say "hearing aid."

Dear — This term is ordinarily used when an American would be likely to say "expensive."

Demolition deposit — Americans more optimistically say "damage deposit."

Deposit account — This is a savings account in America.

Draughts — This is the British word for the game of checkers.

Drawing pin — This word is used instead of thumb tack.

Dressing gown — This is the word for bathrobe.

Dust bin — This mean trash bin or trash receptacle.

Dustman — This is the British term for garbage collector.

Elastic band — Americans say "rubber band" instead.

Finished — This word is used in place of the American

"done," as in "I am all done." In Britain such a phrase may be taken as meaning on the verge of death.

Fortnight — This means two weeks.

Full stop — This is the way the period as a mark of punctuation is expressed in Britain.

Get down — To get down is to get off.

Goods lift — This is a freight elevator.

Goods train — This means freight train.

G.P.O. — This is an abbreviation for General Post Office.

Greengrocer — Shops that sell fruits and vegetables are greengrocers' shops. Usually they do not sell other staples.

Handbag — This means purse. So does "bag" by itself.

Have a go — This is ordinary slang for "try" or "try it."

High street — The high street of a town or a district is the equivalent of "main street" in America.

High tea — This refers to a late afternoon meal.

Hire — To hire means to rent in Britain, as in "car hire."

Hire Purchase — This is the "installment plan" in America. It has sometimes been called the "never-never" in Britain.

Hoover — This is the term that refers to a vacuum cleaner, whether it is a Hoover or any other brand. To "hoover" means to vacuum.

Inverted commas — This is the British expression for quotation marks.

Ironmonger — The ironmonger's store is called the hardware store in America.

Jar — This is slang for a glass of beer, usually containing a pint of it.

Joint — This is a piece of meat for roasting.

Jumble sale — This is the British phrase for a garage sale or a rummage sale.

Kitchen Roll — This is the phrase for paper towels.

Lavatory — This is a proper term for a toilet. "Loo" is a colloquial term for it.

Lead — A lead, pronounced lēd, is a leash.

Left luggage — This is a checkroom.

Lift — This is the term for elevator.

Lip balm — This means chap stick.

Loo — This is a genteel phrase for toilet, but colloquial.

Lot — "The lot" means all of it, or everything. "Your lot" means all of your group. Americans often say "the works."

Mackintosh or Mac — This is the term for a heavy, durable, reliable British raincoat.

Nil — This means zero or nothing.

Nought — This is what the British call a zero.

Off license — This means a liquor store.

"P" — P in slang means pence, as in "Can you lend me ten p please?"

Pack of cards — This is used in place of a deck of cards.

P.C. — This abbreviation means Police Constable, or policeman. In print, the initials P.C. come before the name of the policeman.

Plimsols — These are sports shoes that Americans may call track shoes or, to the amusement of the British, sneakers. They used to be made of canvas. The term "trainers" has come to replace plimsols recently.

Point or Power point — This is the term for an electrical outlet, what Americans call a socket.

Pram — This term, from "perambulator," means baby carriage.

Public convenience — This is the term for an out of doors toilet. Sometimes it is mentioned just as the "convenience."

Queue — This is the classic term for line. It is derived from the French word for tail.

Quid — This is a slang word for pound, just as "buck" is slang for dollar.

Reckon — This verb, which means to figure or calculate, is used in Britain just as regularly as in old Western movies.

Return — This means a round-trip ticket.

Row — Pronounced to rhyme with now, it means an argument or a fight.

Rucksack — This is the word for backpack.

Sellotape — This word is used instead of America's Scotch tape.

Scent — This is what the British say when they mean perfume.

Scrubber — This is a slang word for a person with very poor standards of behavior.

Single — This is a one-way ticket.

Smart — This term usually means "stylish" in Britain, such as in "That is a smart coat."

Sorry — This is the all-purpose word for an apology. It needs to be inserted sharply and crisply. The American "excuse me" is not a good substitute, because British people tend to use it when they want someone to get out of the way.

Stone — A stone is a measurement of weight that comes to 14 pounds. "He weighs ten stone" means that he weighs 140 pounds.

Sticking plaster — This is what a band-aid is called.

Subway — This is an underground passage for a busy road. What we call the subway is the underground or the tube.

Surgery — This is the medical doctor's office. When the doctor is "in his surgery," it means that he or she is in to see the patients, but, if the doctor is "in surgery" he is likely to be operating.

Ta — This is the familiar working class "thank you."

Tea — This is a middle and upper class mid-afternoon snack. For the working class, tea means the meal the working man has when he comes home.

Telly — This is British slang for television, the equivalent of the American "TV." It is also called "the box."

The — (as a missing article) British people leave out "the" and "a " or "an" when discussing such institutions as universities. For instance, a student is "at university" instead of "at the university." The same applies to hospitals: One is "in hospital" in Britain.

Tick — A tick is the notation that Americans would call a check mark, as when we check something off.

Tin — One meaning of this word in Britain is tin can or, as Americans usually just say, can. Therefore "tinned" means "canned" in America.

Tipping — Tipping means dumping in America. So the familiar signs saying "no tipping" mean "no dumping."

Ton — This is 2,240 pounds in Britain. An American ton of 2,000 lbs. is often called a short ton.

Top of the street — This means the end of the street.

Torch — This means flashlight.

Trainers — This is the word for tennis shoes or any sports shoes with treads.

Tube — This is slang for the underground railway, what we would call the subway.

Turf accountant — This is a bookmaker in Britain.

Underground — This is the shortened and universally used form for Underground Railway, what Americans would call a subway.

Utility — This means something that is simple and cheap. The American term is "generic."

V.A.T. — This is the Value Added Tax, which functions like a sales tax. It is often wise to ask whether it is included when prices are quoted. This is a very substantial addition to all purchases in Britain. See p. 57

Washing up — This ritual chore in Britain is what Americans call "doing the dishes."

Week — When this word is put after a day, as in "Monday week" or "Tuesday week," it means next Monday or next Tuesday.

Well done — This is what is said to congratulate any striking accomplishment, such as a feat in sports or a good speech.

Wellingtons or Wellies — This refers to those high, reliable, waterproof British boots, which are similar to galoshes.

Wire — This is the word for telegram. An overseas telegram is called a cable.

Zed — This is what the British call "Z."

Potentially Embarrassing Terms

Inability to translate between British English and American English can sometimes lead to awkward or embarrassing interpretations, as the following list indicates:

Arse — This is an anatomical term that is rendered as

"ass" in America. Nowadays the American word is replacing the traditional British word, and "ass" no longer means what it used to in that country — donkey.

Artsy-tartsy — This is a derogatory description of a certain appearance, wherein a female conveys the impression of being artistic and cheaply fashionable and sexually available at the same time.

Bathroom — Americans who want to go to the toilet should not ask for the bathroom because it has traditionally been the room where people have a bath, usually without toilet facilities. Sometimes Americans who ask for the bathroom are forced to endure a very tired and very old British joke: "Why, do you want to bathe?" Ask for a "lavatory" or a "toilet" in a house; the "cloakroom" in a restaurant; and for the "public convenience" if out of doors.

Bill — This is used in place of our word "check" in places such as restaurants.

Bloke — This means fellow or guy. It may not sound as innocuous to Americans as it does to Britons.

Bloody — This is a strong adjective term of exasperation or annoyance. Its origin was in the curse "God's Blood." A euphemism for it is "ruddy."

Braces — This is the British word for suspenders. In Britain, "suspenders" mean garters.

Bum — This term does not mean hobo or worthless person in Britain. It is a slang word for the portion of one's anatomy sat upon, often euphemistically called the "behind" in America. For reasons that seem inexplicable to Americans, the word is curiously laughable in Britain.

Check — Unlike us, the British do not use this word for bill in restaurants and such places. They say bill.

Common — This word does not mean ordinary in Britain. It means lower class, or cheap, or worthless and is often used pejoratively. The term is used without prejudice in America, where the "common" man or woman is held in high esteem.

Daft — To say a person is daft is to say that a person is crazy.

Fag — This means cigarette and sometimes a dreary task. It is not, as in America, a slang word for homosexual.

First floor — It is really the second floor in America. What Americans call the first floor is the ground floor in Britain.

Fanny — This is a harmless euphemism for buttocks in America, but in Britain it is a rude reference to female genitalia. Americans should consequently avoid the name "fanny pack" for the small packs worn by bicyclers.

Homely — In Britain this word means homey, or domestic, pertaining to comfort by the warm fireside, etc., while in America it means at best plain; at worst, ugly.

Ill — The word is used instead of the American word "sick." "Sick" in Britain means nauseous, and to "be sick" means to vomit.

John Thomas — This is an expression for penis. So if an American is asked, in the middle of an exasperating situation, "Is your name John Thomas?" a strong insult is being given.

Keep your pecker up — This is a classic phrase. It means "keep your spirits up" in Britain and quite another thing in America.

Knickers — This is an archaic term for underpants, something like "bloomers" in America. This is another one of those curious words that becomes very amusing to the British. The phrase "Don't get your knickers in a twist!" translates as "Don't get upset."

Knock up — This is another classic term. In Britain it means to look someone up or wake someone up instead of slang for impregnating someone.

Knotted — The phrase "get knotted" has the American equivalent of "get lost" or "drop dead."

Mad — The usual first meaning of this word in Britain is insane, whereas the first meaning in America is usually angry. The second meaning in Britain is angry and the second meaning in the United States is insane.

Mate — This is a word meaning friend or pal. It is a very ordinary working class colloquialism.

Mean — This word is apt to mean "stingy" in Britain

rather than cruel, nasty or vicious, which are its first meanings in America.

Mick — This is a colloquial and often derogatory phrase for Irishman. It is never advisable to use it.

Mickey — There is a slang phrase "taking the mickey out of someone," which means to say something rude or derogatory, what Americans would call a 'put down,' in a sarcastically funny way.

Mind — When this is used in a British phrase, it means "be careful of" instead of obey or follow what someone requests. In America, "Mind your sister," would mean do what she says. "Mind your head" or "Mind the stairs" are frequently heard in Britain, meaning look out.

Mr. — Oddly enough, higher ranking doctors and dentists in Britain have the title of Mr. instead of Dr. Americans often mistakenly think that they are lower ranking professionals than those bearing the title of doctor. They are not.

Nancy or *Nancy Boy* — These are British slang terms for male homosexuals.

Nappy — This is the British word for diaper.

Nick — This is slang for jail. "In the nick" is the equivalent of the American "in the slammer."

Nipple — In Britain, this term is used just for part of the breast. The word "teat" refers to the nipple on a baby's bottle.

Paddy — This is a colloquial word for an Irishman that is more acceptable than "Mick," but it is best for Americans to avoid using it.

Pants — These are underpants in Britain. The word "trousers" is used for our word "pants."

Pissed — This is slang for being drunk.

Piss off — In Britain this slang phrase means "go away," but to be "pissed off" in America means to be quite angry.

Popped his or her clogs — Slang for having died.

Pouf — This is British slang for homosexual.

Public Bar — This is the part of the bar used by ordinary people. Where public houses still have a slightly costlier saloon bar, it is supposed to be used by visitors and ladies.

Queer — This means feeling unwell or queasy. It can also be slang for homosexual, as in the United States.

Rubber — This refers to an eraser and not, as in America, slang for a condom.

Ruddy — This is a polite euphemism for bloody. It can be used as an adjective for nearly everything.

Saloon bar — This is the section of a bar that is somewhat better furnished and where drinks cost just a little more. Visitors and women are traditionally expected to be served there instead of the public bar, where ordinary local men drink. The distinction is a thing of the past for many public houses.

Sanitary towel — This is the British expression for sanitary napkin.

Screw — This is slang for salary in Britain.

Sick — This means nauseous and to "be sick" means to vomit. The word "ill" is used in Britain for everything else.

Sticky wicket — This refers to a difficult situation and comes from a sporting expression.

Suspenders — This is the British word for garters. In Britain, braces mean suspenders.

Tart — This is an old, classic euphemism for prostitute.

Teat — This is a nipple on a baby's bottle. The term "nipple" is used exclusively for part of the breast.

Tights — This is the word used for what Americans call panty hose.

Twig it — If someone cannot "twig it," a slang expression, he or she is unable comprehend the matter. The implication is mental dullness.

V for Victory sign, palm inward — This is not a word but a gesture, yet it does need to be included in this list because it is the British equivalent of the American middle finger in the air or the southern European arm gestures. It seems to be used more rarely than its equivalents elsewhere, but when it is used it is intended to be very rude. Note that when Winston Churchill gave the victory gesture his palm was facing outward. When the palm is towards the person making the gesture, it does not mean victory.

Vest — This means undershirt in Britain. The American "vest" is a "waistcoat" in Britain.

Waistcoat — This means "vest" in America.

Wanker — This is slang for a masturbator. Less literally, it means someone who is a shirker, who coasts on a soft job or undeserved reputation.

W.C. — This is an abbreviation for water closet that really means toilet. It is used internationally.

Willie — This is a euphemism for penis. This explains why Prince Charles once declared that he would not have the name of his son, Prince William, taken in the diminutive. Indeed, Prince Willie would not be a flattering nickname in Britain.

Wog — This is a very nasty term for a nonwhite person. It is supposed to come from an acronym for "wiley oriental gentleman." It is a term of prejudice.

EDUCATION

Contrasts with American Education

Education in Britain differs in several significant ways from education in the United States. It tends to be less democratic, more elitist and more demanding. The end result is that a thinner stream of well-educated youth go to the universities and the prestigious careers beyond. A recent estimate by an American national news magazine puts the percentage of Americans who will attend college at least at some point in their lives at 60% The percentage for Britain is only 20%, lower than that for the Germans, French or Japanese.

It is generally stressed in Britain that the teachers are the professionals and that the parents are mere amateurs. Therefore, the teachers are likely to take command and the parents are likely to take advice. The author's children went to a school in London that had a sign near the entrance that read: "No parents beyond this point." The British counterparts to the Parent Teacher Organizations, elected school boards and Parent Advisory Boards are not as prominent nor as powerful.

For a long time in Britain there has been a clear emphasis on hard work in school, which is carried on over a longer school year than in America. Also, elementary school starts at an earlier age. Infant school takes in children five and six and lasts for two years. The British equivalent of kindergarten is far more vigorous, offering far less in the way of fun and games.

Throughout the British system, there has been an emphasis on segregating the academically able into separate streams or into separate schools. Long, grueling tests are the means that are used. The process reaches a culmination at the end of what Americans would call the high school years. At fifteen and sixteen, a battery of tests called the "O Levels" must be faced, and those who wish to go on to college must pass the dreaded "A Levels," usually taken in three subjects. Defenders of the British testing system say that it provides a fair screening because any pupil of whatever socio-economic background can take them. Poor but highly talented youth who do well on tests are given scholarships to the best schools. Detractors of the system say that the tests favor the upper and middle classes because the questions and material have a class bias. While admitting that brilliant working class youngsters can get a free ride to the top in education, critics maintain that the merely good working class pupils are discriminated against. The class issue flares forth in debates over education as much as racial issues have in the United States.

Two parallel systems of education operate in Britain, one public and one private. What invariably confuses Americans is that private schools are usually called "public" schools. At the time they were originally founded, and the oldest schools go back to the thirteenth to the seventeenth centuries, they were open to the general public, which really meant that they were open to the parents who were able and willing to pay the substantial fees. Eton, Harrow,

Winchester and Rugby are examples of these private "public" schools.

In most places in America, the public school gathers in almost all of the students, the good, bad and indifferent. Public schools vary considerably in quality, ranging from first class, well-financed, suburban education palaces to dreary, rundown, underfinanced inner city schools to bucolic, rural schools that draw students from amazing distances. There are some exceptions to the dominance of the public schools in the United States, and the scope of private education may grow in the future. Prep schools, parochial schools, church schools and various academies offer alternatives to some parents. Nevertheless, taken all together they do not come anywhere near matching the prestige and importance of the parallel system of private education in Britain.

Sorting Out the British Educational System

American parents who plan to send their children to British schools, American college students who plan to study in Britain and anyone who will come into contact with British students or graduates should benefit from sorting out the confusing British educational system and understanding the terms they use for it.

At the Elementary Level

Primary School is what we call "grade school," and it goes until age eleven. *infant school* takes up the first two years of primary school, and is attended by pupils five to six years old. This is followed by *junior school*, the part of primary school that educates youngsters from seven to eleven. Parallel to the primary school is the *prep school*, or *preparatory school*, which is a high status private school for the elementary years. Many take both boys and girls up to age thirteen.

At the Junior High and High School Levels

As mentioned, the most prestigious schools, academically and socially, are the so-called *Public Schools*. The most prestigious of these old and famous private boarding schools is probably Eton, with Winchester, Rugby and Harrow not far behind. They take boys from ages thirteen to the time they are ready to enter the universities. Some schools take girls of the same ages, but public schools in Britain are rarely co-educational and rarely non-boarding, at least in the south. Parents of most public school students see their teenagers only on holidays, what Americans call vacations.

The social connections fostered at these ancient, traditional public schools are of considerable importance to the nation's elite. The "old school tie" leads to advantages in politics, business and the professions. From their inception until recently, most "public" school students have been the sons of the wealthy and influential. Thirty years ago, 60% of the "new boys," the entering class, were the sons of "old boys," the alumni. Now it is down to just over 40% Fewer than ten percent of the school-age population go to them, and the cost per year is comparable to sending a young American to a good liberal arts college. Yet parents who put a premium on their youngsters' education see the expense of tuition and room and board much in the same way that similarly disposed American parents regard the costs of college, as heavy but necessary burdens.

Public school students learn much else besides academic subjects. The emphasis on community living and sports provides lessons in sportsmanship, friendship, authority, loyalty and team play. Public school traditions also encourage political skills by having boys stand for various elections regularly and carry on some responsibilities of self-government. In many schools there is an atmosphere of a rather muscular, cold water Christianity. When they graduate, public school boys usually have an unshakable social confidence based on the firm conviction of their own superiority to other young men.

There is a payoff in admissions to the best British universities, namely Oxford and Cambridge. A recent estimate shows that 64% attending these universities came from private schools that only the wealthy could afford.

Recently, the defenders of the public schools have become embattled with members of the left wing of the Labour Party who want to shut them down because they perceive the schools as bastions of perpetuated privilege. There were some reforms of the public schools in the '70s, which abolished beatings and "fagging," a practice wherein the younger boys were ordered about like servants by the older boys.

Public schools are unabashedly elitist. For the overwhelming majority of adolescents, education consists of going to day schools, either public or private in the American sense. Even the state-supported schools tend to segregate the more able from the less able students, sometimes adopting the terminology of a "clever" and "less clever" stream.

Grammar schools are academically oriented, take in high achieving students and have a span equivalent to our sixth to twelfth grades. Grammar school students are given much hard work in preparation for the universities and their careers beyond. Grammar schools have long served as ladders for many people, including Prime Ministers Wilson and Heath. In recent years many grammar schools have either been replaced by *comprehensive schools,* or they have become schools successfully collecting fees.

The *secondary modern school* takes in the less academically talented, in general, and has a span equivalent to the American sixth to twelfth grades. Practical subjects are encouraged, since students are not expected to go to the university. Moreover, many are seen as potential school drop-outs, teenagers who will swell the horde of very young employees seen all over Britain working at low paying jobs that offer little hope for advancement in the future. Youngsters indulging in extreme fashions are likely to come from this group, probably to compensate for their bleak prospects.

From the 1960s onward, there has been an attempt to get away from strict segregation into streams of academically able and less able students. The *comprehensive schools* tried to break the barriers between academic and vocational schools by having a wide variety of students and subjects under one roof. Comprehensive schools mark a strong move towards the typical American high school that offers all kinds of programs to all kinds of students. Recently it was estimated that 70% of secondary schools in Britain are comprehensive.

At the University Level

British universities can be divided into six categories. The foremost universities are Oxford and Cambridge, comparable to Harvard and Yale in prestige and world renown. Both universities were founded in the Middle Ages and display rich architecture dating back over the centuries. The term "Oxbridge" is used to refer to both schools as a single entity, much as Americans would say "Ivy League" to indicate a certain group of prestigious East Coast Universities. Scotland has its equivalent ancient institutions at Edinburgh, Glasgow, and St. Andrews. Next are the "red brick" universities, solid, older universities, many of them founded in the nineteenth century when bricks were the usual building material. Some of them, such as the University of Manchester or the University of Birmingham, are institutions of high reputation, particularly in some of their specialties. Another category is that of the large number of ultra-modern universities sprouted after World War II, sometimes called "cement block and plate glass universities." They resemble many campuses in the American West, and have few traditions in a nation that relishes tradition. The great schools of London are in a category of their own, the huge and prestigious University of London and the much smaller but world famous London School of Economics. Yet another category is that of the *polytechnics* which were created to be practical, down to earth schools of applied technology. They usually do not have a resident student population. The last category is the *open university*, which offers television and correspondence courses to older students who may be teachers, housewives or factory workers. It has been an immense success.

There are some sharp contrasts between British universities and their American counterparts. First of all, the student population is selected from approximately 20% of the population of university age, although strong efforts are now being made to expand this percentage. American universities and colleges draw close to half of the traditional college age group. While Britain has just over 40 universities, there are over two thousand colleges and universities in the United States.

The more select body of British students bring a solid grounding in basic academic subjects with them. This is in part due to the fact that they did not spend much time in what Americans call their high school years with such subjects as driver education, journalism, theater, pop psychology under various labels, gymnastics and band. Therefore university instruction can begin at a more advanced level and continue in a narrower, more specialized and intense manner. By contrast, American university education is broader and more diverse, and American students have more opportunities to pick and choose from a variety of subjects. Another contrast is that most British undergraduate degrees have traditionally taken only three years. Now this is stretching into four as their American counterparts are staying five and six years to finish an undergraduate degree.

In general, British universities emphasize closer relations with junior faculty, called *tutors*, who give *tutorials*, which are small classes where intensive one-on-one instruction occurs. Absent is the great American obsession with regular exams, grades and grade points. In fact, the major examinations come after students have finished their undergraduate courses. A whole battery of exams at the end of college determines whether or not candidates will graduate (and they almost invariably do), and whether or not they will gain first or second class honors, which is similar to graduating *summa* or *magna cum laude* at an American university.

Gaining a *first* in a chosen field is widely regarded as a splendid achievement in Britain.

The internal structure of a typical older British university is different from an American counterpart. The use of the word "college" is at the heart of the difference. At American universities, colleges denote specialized areas of instruction, such as a college of engineering or a college of natural sciences. In Britain, a college is a relatively self-contained unit, offering a wide variety of subjects in various fields, possessing its own varied student body, its own buildings, its own housing, its own administration and its own faculty. In fact, the British universities really are federations of individual colleges. Yet the university will provide what the individual colleges cannot muster themselves, such as a large library or special pieces of expensive equipment. These facilities will be shared by students and faculty of all the colleges. Therefore the advantages of both smallness and largeness are effectively combined in the British university system.

Sometimes the word "college" in Britain is applied to schools unconnected to any university. Usually these institutions are without high status and are able to award only lesser degrees.

Faculty ranks in Britain can be confusing for visiting Americans. American universities are largely staffed by professors. Most have "assistant" or "associate" in their titles to denote lower ranks. Below them are the toiling and untitled instructors. In Britain, people with the title of professor are comparatively rare. It usually distinguishes someone of great achievement in his or her field or an accomplished department chairperson. The usual ranks for academics in Britain are, in descending order, *professor, reader, senior lecturer* and *lecturer*. The plain title of *instructor* in Britain usually means someone who teaches in a technical or vocational institution rather than a university. The dilemmas created by having different titles can be circumvented for visiting Americans by simply calling those with the Ph.D. "doctor."

Many Americans expect stereotypical Oxbridge students

to appear at all British universities. Instead of undergraduates wearing straw hats and sipping champagne as they discuss Plato, they are apt to encounter a horde of loud, shabbily and drably dressed youngsters who are ferociously committed to parties and drink. Some British universities are just as notorious party schools as some American universities in the West which need not be named. Overall, the amount of alcohol and tobacco that British undergraduates consume is remarkable.

Some Additional Words Needing Translation

Here are some words not fitting into the sections on education which might be helpful to know:

Campus — This is not a word heard in Britain, generally. It is an American import.

Direct grant school — This is a private school that receives financial support from the government directly, usually with a provision enabling a number of students from poorer families to attend on scholarships.

Form — The noun is used to designate "grade" in Britain, as in "He is in the fifth form."

Headmaster or *Head* — This is the name of the principal of a British school.

Holidays — This word denotes vacation periods, for school children as well as for everyone else.

Maths — Mathematics is always abbreviated in the plural and not in the American singular, math.

Mature students — This is the quaint British term for what Americans more cumbrously call "non-traditional-age students." If the older students are the mature ones, does the logic of the phrase label the ordinary students as immature?

Old Boys and *Old Girls* — These are the people that Americans speak of as alumni and alumnae.

Rag — A students' rag means a time of high spirits and uproarious behavior, what Americans would call "letting off steam."

Send down — To fail at school for an academic or moral

reason results in the student being sent down, what Americans call being "kicked out."

The — This is a missing article when the university is discussed. People are "at university" instead of "at the university."

TELEVISION AND RADIO

Since an increasing number of bed and breakfast rooms and hotel rooms come equipped with a small color television set and a radio, visiting Americans are likely to spend at least some time watching and listening to British entertainment.

There will be a few surprises. One surprise is that there are comparatively few regular channels, although cable has remedied that situation for those lucky enough to receive cable programming. Another surprise is how many American programs and films are run, a good many of them of dubious quality. Another surprise is the way censorship takes out excessive violence yet allows far more explicit sexual material than the networks would at home.

Probably the greatest surprise of all is the prominence and prevalence of public broadcasting. While Britain does have independent television and radio stations, complete with many, many commercials, the British Broadcasting Corporation, or the BBC, dominates the media. The "Beeb," as it is known colloquially, derives much of its income from taxes paid directly on television sets and radios in the form of licenses for their operation. Its governing board functions independently as a corporation, and every effort is made to ensure that its membership is skilled, professional and nonpolitical. Whenever there are attempts of the government to pressure the BBC, a great outcry results. Its independent governing board is based upon an appreciation that the media must be kept free from the control of whatever Prime Minister or party is in office at the moment.

The BBC tries to maintain a high standard of quality,

since from its inception the BBC has been charged with elevating and educating the whole British public. Critics can point out that this often leads to programming that is overly serious and pretentious, to the extent that comic satirists regard it as a prime target. Indeed, many Americans who see the BBC in action for the first time think that they may be watching a comic skit.

The BBC runs several TV channels at once, which allows lighter entertainment and regional specialties to appear. The blessing of all BBC offerings is that they are free from commercials and the pressures that sponsors might impose.

Public broadcasting in the United States is crippled by being underfinanced. Some of its best programs are actually from the comparatively well-financed BBC. Americans who watch such productions as "Masterpiece Theater" in the United States may be deluded into thinking that British programming is that good across the board. This is not the case. A viewer without cable can be left with four bad and mediocre choices at a given time during an evening. For the careful observer, however, TV watching in Britain can be a remarkably rewarding experience.

Radio is interesting also. It is never difficult to pull in all sorts of popular music, classical music, jazz, comedies or mysteries on the radio, particularly on the BBC stations. There is also an amazing array of freewheeling private radio including outrageous talk shows that seem to violate all of those generalizations about British politeness and respect for privacy. Americans are surprised at how the old tunes of yesterday never cease to be played at random on the airwaves in Britain today, interspersed with the latest sounds from those who fancy themselves to be on the cutting edge of musical creativity.

RELIGION

Why You Should Go to Church in Britain

Great spires pointing heavenward all over the island attest to Britain's magnificent religious history. But cold statistics demonstrate that most British people do not get near churches or chapels on Sundays. Nominal members, inactive members, agnostics and atheists are found in greater proportion than in the United States. The British pattern is similar to the rest of Europe, whereas the United States is noted for a high percentage of the middle class going to church. Even so, devout Britons are not hard to find, and each of the major denominations has a vigorous core operating.

No matter what a visitor's religion or lack of it, going to church in Britain is a valuable cultural experience. The music alone is generally of a high standard. In many churches, boys' choirs provide angelic sounds. Great organs are grand in old churches and congregations have a tendency to sing not only with vigor but with sharp and distinct pronunciation.

Sermons and readings are also in distinct, precise English, although the presentation might be too restrained, orderly, rational and cold for those Americans who are used to loud, emotional sermons on Sunday. But the point is to get out and sample some of what goes on in British churches, where the visitor can feel the past in a real, tangible way. It can be a thrill to be inside a chilly old church or cathedral, hearing an elegant service echoing off ancient stone. Do not pass up such an opportunity.

Sorting out the Vocabulary for Churches

The various names used for religious groups and officials can be confusing. The following list should be helpful in sorting them out, and the key definitions will be reinforced by their reappearance in the text which follows.

Anglican — The Anglican Church is the Church of England. It is similar to the Episcopalian Church in America, but it is the established, official state church in England.

Archbishop — An archbishop is the highest ranking official in the Anglican Church. There are two of them, one at York and one at Canterbury. The latter has precedence over the former.

Bishop — Both the Anglican and the Roman Catholic churches have bishops. Each presides over a diocese or see, an area where the bishop is in charge of the church and its priests.

C. of E. — These initials refer to the Church of England, the Anglican Church, which is established as the official state church. In worship, it is similar to the Episcopalian Church in America.

Chapel — This term refers to a religious meetinghouse or church for members of Nonconformist or Non-Anglican Protestant denominations.

Church of England — This is the established official state church, otherwise known as the Anglican Church. It is similar to the Episcopalian Church in America and is sometimes known as the C. of E.

Dissenter — This term can be used interchangeably with Nonconformist. It means a Protestant who dissented from the Anglican Church and refused to conform to it. Baptists and Congregationalists would be examples of dissenters.

Free churches — This is another name for the Nonconformist Churches, those that are Protestant but do not conform to the established Church of England.

High church — A tendency in the Anglican Church to stress liturgy, communion and the rich history of the church has been called the *High Church* Movement. Its opposite is the *Low Church* Movement, described below.

Kirk — This is the name that the Scots have used for church.

Low church — In the Anglican Church, low church places emphasis on simplicity, piety and the Bible rather than on the rich historical traditions of the church.

Nonconformist — This term refers to Protestant denominations which do not conform to the Church of England, including Baptists, Congregationalists and Methodists. This term can be used interchangeably with Dissenter.

Rural dean — This is a Church of England clergyman with authority over several parishes.

Vicar — This is the name for a Church of England parish clergyman.

The Established Church

The established church, or official church of the state is the church of England, also called the C. of E., or the Anglican Church. Since Henry VIII's break with Rome in the early sixteenth century, the Church of England is usually considered to be a Protestant church. Yet many of its leaders and members today choose to describe it as a catholic church with a small "c." They take the meaning of catholic as "universal," and their church as a church for everyone everywhere. Anglicans describe their church as "apostolic," meaning that they see a direct, unbroken historic line reaching all the way back to the apostles. The Pope's role as leader of the Roman Catholic Church is regarded as a late medieval growth of power that was not present in the early church. From their point of view, the Church of England goes all the way back to the time St. Augustine arrived in 597 to convert the heathen Anglo-Saxons.

Outside of England, the church takes on other names. In Wales, it is the Church of Wales and in Ireland the Church of Ireland. Neither of these churches is established as an official state church, but at one time they were, much to the chagrin of the majority of the population in Wales and Ireland. By the way, the sparsely attended Church of Ireland's main cathedral in Dublin is named St. Patrick's, and it often confuses tourists who expect it to be Roman Catholic.

The sister church of the Church of England in America is the Episcopal Church. The name "episcopal" simply means having bishops. This name was chosen after the American Revolution because attending the overseas branch of the established church of the recently defeated imperial power was not popular.

Episcopalians are best prepared, of course, to appreciate the Anglican Church. They are familiar with its liturgy, meaning the patterns of worship presented in a prayer book. They also accept the emphasis placed upon a version of the Mass called Communion or the Eucharist. Dignity, style and beauty in art and music are features of this denomination.

The Church of England and its sister churches have an informal diversity within. There is a distinction between the so-called "high" churches and the so-called "low" churches. The former put emphasis on historical ceremonies, featuring color, costumes, chants, bells and incense. The latter are much simpler and plainer, stressing the Bible, old English hymns and straightforward sermons. "Broad" churches attempt to incorporate the best of both emphases, although it seems that some low churches shelter behind the designation. Parallels to these high, low and broad styles flourish in the Episcopal Church in the United States, and provide no end of discussion and controversy for Episcopalians.

It is necessary to understand something of the sixteenth century Reformation in England in order to understand the Anglican Church. It came about suddenly, for almost overnight the Roman Catholic Church became the Anglican Church. The same buildings, the same priests, bishops and archbishops carried on as the Church of England thereafter. There were a few noted exceptions; some Roman Catholics became martyrs because they were either too principled or too old-fashioned or too rigid, depending upon one's point of view. The most dramatic change from the English Reformation, something that marked the English landscape forever, was the dissolution of the monasteries and convents. Rich church land was sold by the crown to private individuals; monastic buildings were left empty to become ruins, and monks and nuns were pensioned off. The other changes of a Protestant nature were less dramatic, and most of them were introduced gradually, changes such as allowing the marriage of priests, the reduction of the number of sacraments from seven to two (baptism and communion), the end of private confession, the circulation of the Bible in English and greater emphasis upon sermons.

The Church of England was left with a mixture of Protestant and Catholic practices. Architecture reflects this mix. On the one hand, the stark and often strikingly beautiful ruins of the monasteries are all over Britain. They were used as quarries for stone and their roofs supplied lead. These ruins testify to the force of Henry VIII's Reformation as well as to the greed of the landowners. But the cathedrals, churches, hospitals, alms houses and other church properties were kept much as they were before the Reformation. Even when the Puritans were active in the seventeenth century, destroying whatever they deemed "Popish," or Roman Catholic in the Church of England, the Anglican artistic heritage was largely saved from their depredations. Therefore, the long, deep medieval past of Christianity in England can still be sensed by the reflective observer despite the Protestant Reformation.

The Church of Scotland

The Church of Scotland is a Presbyterian Church which has had a very special role in Scottish history. Scots rallied around this church for their early assertions of nationalism. In fact, the civil wars of the seventeenth century were triggered by Scottish resistance to having Anglicanism foisted upon their "kirk" or church.

Today when the British monarch is in Scotland, she attends the Church of Scotland and functions as its leader. American Presbyterians will be interested in contrasting the Church of Scotland practices with their churches at home. They may be left with the conviction that Scottish practices are very "high" compared to American Presbyterian worship, particularly if they attend St. Giles Cathedral on the Royal Mile of Edinburgh. Ironically, St. Giles was the place where violent resistance to Anglicanism first took place. The story is that one parishioner, upon hearing of the "Papist" nature of the new prayer book imposed by England, flung a stool at the pulpit. Pandemonium followed. Today a bronze plaque marks the spot on the floor where it all began. Friendly people at St. Giles will be very happy to point out this spot to visitors.

Other Protestants: Dissenters and Nonconformists

The Dissenters and Nonconformists are the Protestants who, historically, dissented from the Anglican Church and refused to conform to it. Together they comprise a very substantial minority of Protestants in Britain. Something over half of the British population is officially Anglican. The various denominations of the Dissenters and Nonconformists make up the rest of the population that is officially Protestant.

In America, Baptists, Presbyterians, Methodists, Quakers and Congregationalists correspond to dissenting Protestants in Britain, with English, but not Scottish, Presbyterians counted as Dissenters. American Congregationalists have a bewildering variety of names besides Congregationalist. In general, they have unattached churches wherein the congregations themselves are in control. For all of these churches which have descended from British nonconformity, whether they are in Britain or in America today, their considerable Puritan influence can be perceived in their emphasis upon the Bible and upon the importance of preaching.

The Nonconformists began in the seventeenth century as radical Protestants within the Anglican Church who wished to "purify" it, or make it less like the Roman Catholic Church. They gained the name "Puritans" as a result. Puritans broke away into several distinct groups and were no longer contained within the Anglican Church. A century later, in the middle of the eighteenth century, the Methodists broke away from the Anglicans. After Puritan leadership in the seventeenth century under Cromwell came to an end, these Protestants were discriminated against in employment, education and in society in general. Nevertheless, their freedom to believe what they wanted, or their "liberty of conscience," was tolerated. Despite the flagrant discrimination against them, this limited toleration can be seen as a major step forward in human history. Dissenters who could not hold jobs in government or graduate from Oxford or Cambridge because of their religion could worship in peace in their churches, which were officially called chapels.

Puritans from Britain gave American Protestantism a decided emphasis. All through the seventeenth century they left England in numbers that were to multiply greatly in the open lands of the New World. The influence of Puritanism has been felt many times in American history, through such movements as temperance, prohibition and laws concerning sexual behavior. The old-fashioned, strict, sober work ethic, so quickly eroding in many places today, can also be attributed to the Puritan heritage.

What about the Puritans who stayed in England? Shut out from politics and many government careers, many Presbyterians, Baptists, Congregationalists and Methodists turned to making money in business. Given their religious discipline that inculcated habits of thrift, industry and sobriety, businessmen from these groups tended to become very prosperous. When the Industrial Revolution began, Dissenters were on hand with substantial capital, business expertise and a willingness to work hard. Many built up tremendous fortunes at the time of industrialization. A number of their richer descendants converted to Anglicanism in order to become part of the establishment, but many remained in old Puritan denominations. The last vestiges of legal discrimination against them were lifted while the Industrial Revolution was in progress.

Visitors should observe how the descendants of the Puritans carry on their worship. Some of their chapels are stark and bare, enabling the worshipers to concentrate on the sermon and Bible readings. Almost everything from the rich medieval traditions of religious symbolism and art is absent. The contrast between a simple Congregational chapel and a high Anglican Church should be noted because this contrast reveals the range of Protestantism in England.

Roman Catholicism in Britain

A very substantial minority of the British population adheres to the Roman Catholic Church. Here is another striking similarity with the United States. Of all the countries of the Western world, only Britain, Germany and the United States have a Protestant majority and a Roman Catholic minority in these proportions. The other countries of the world having a Protestant majority all have relatively small populations. Sweden, Denmark and Australia can serve as examples.

Roman Catholics in Britain today come from two historical streams. "Old" English Catholics are those who resisted the Reformation and preserved the faith even in those desperate days when Henry VIII, Elizabeth I and Oliver Cromwell hounded their priests. Old English Catholics have traditions of private masses held in secret, of priests hidden away in unlikely places and of unflinching resistance to attempts to convert them to Protestantism. Many of these old English Catholics were in prominent families living in conservative rural areas far from London.

The other stream of Roman Catholics emanated from Ireland, particularly after the British Industrial Revolution created a great demand for unskilled labor. The major industrial cities of Britain today, including Liverpool, Manchester, Glasgow and London, have substantial populations of Irish ancestry. In the nineteenth century, the Irish came to work as "navvies," construction workers on the railroads, or as factory hands. They took jobs as Mexicans take many jobs in the United States today, accepting low pay for doing tasks that the native-born shun. Emigration to Britain and America became a flood as a result of the dreadful Irish potato famine at mid-century. In the twentieth century, drift out of Ireland to jobs in Britain has continued, but on a much smaller scale.

The rough proletarian Roman Catholics who came to

Britain from Ireland turned out to be much stauncher Catholics in their adopted country than they had been at home, and the same can be said for Irish Catholics in America. The Roman Catholic Church became a means to preserve their identity and culture in their new Protestant environments.

Jews in Britain

Like the United States, Britain has long had a reputation as being a good environment for Jews. As a result, substantial numbers of people of the Jewish faith comprise an important if small component of the population in both countries. This reputation does not go all the way back in England, however, because there were brutal medieval persecutions. Perhaps the most famous of them occurred at Clifford's Tower in York, where Jews who were threatened and surrounded chose mass suicide. For a long time, Jews were officially banned from England, although many continued to live in the country surreptitiously. Jews were welcomed back to England in the seventeenth century by Oliver Cromwell and the Puritans who, ironically, were noted for persecuting Roman Catholics. Puritans appreciated Jews because they were living witnesses to the Old Testament. Other English people did not share the Puritans' appreciation, and Jew-baiting continued into the nineteenth century.

Over the centuries, groups of Jews came to Britain to escape the pogroms, persecutions and ghettoes of Continental Europe. The last great influx was in the era of World War II, when refugees from Nazi persecution followed the old emigration routes. Here again Britain and the United States share an aspect of history.

There is a sweeping generalization about the assimilation of Jews in Western society that makes sense geographically: the further east one goes in Europe, the less the assimilation; the further west, the greater the assimilation. Most Jews in Poland and Russia were locked in their own communities, either in separate Jewish small towns or in ghettos or districts in the cities. In Germany, father west, Jews underwent greater assimilation, experiencing the cultural stresses of becoming less distinctly Jewish and more German. In Britain, the westernmost country in Europe, Jews became the most assimilated, and often very British.

This is not to say that anti-Semitism has been absent from Britain in recent times. Much of it has been subtle, and hard to pin down, particularly the anti-Semitism of the upper classes. Benjamin Disraeli, who was Prime Minister in the latter nineteenth century and the converted son of a Jewish man of letters, had to endure more blatant anti-Semitism. When he rose in the House of Commons to give his first speech, members drowned out his voice with shouts of "Old Clothes!", a reference to a trade that many Jewish immigrants had made their specialty when they came to Britain.

Today a much more low key anti-Semitism still exists, and it is probably connected to the high degree of class consciousness in Britain. But over against this is an enduring tradition of British liberalism and commitment to democracy that despises anti-Semitism in any form.

CHAPTER FIVE

Understanding British Politics
Americans are Disconcerted When They Discuss Politics in Britain

AMERICAN visitors do not have to be in Britain very long before they learn that comparable British people know much more about American politics than they know about British politics. It does not stop there. British people seem to know much more about the political affairs of the whole world. Perhaps they are so keen to understand global politics because of their long tradition of political achievements in Britain. Perhaps it is also because they were at the center of a worldwide empire for so long, and perhaps it is also because they have been, in recent decades, a small state highly dependent upon developments in foreign places. The pervasive influence of the sober, serious, high quality British Broadcasting Corporation newscasts is undoubtedly a contributing factor as well. Another factor is the penchant of British people to read a great deal in newspapers, magazines and books.

The upshot is that many Britons will invariably have many clever and insightful things to say about American political leaders and situations. Ordinary Britons will have some sharp remark about whomever is President and over whatever subject is at the forefront of news in America. Despite their sharpness, British people are likely to be murky about some topics, particularly concerning America's regionalism, or about the powers of the states in the federal system, or about the great diversity of the American people. The British emphasis in discussing American politics does tend to focus on personalities who are well known throughout the world.

Most American visitors are not likely to have similar comments to make about British politics or politicians. While he or she might have a glowing memory of Winston Churchill as a great hero, or an opinion about the remarkable Mrs. Thatcher, and be at least able to recognize the current Prime Minister on television, all of the other major British politicians, such as Wilson, Heath, Foot, Callaghan and many more, are blurred, little known or unknown to them. Americans cannot comment on these leaders the way so many Britons can speak in some detail about Reagan, Carter, Ford, Nixon and Johnson.

Even worse, the workings of the British parliamentary system may be a partial or entire mystery to visiting Americans. They should know how this system works not only to enhance their visit but also in recognition of the fact that the British system has been utilized all over the world in countries where democracy truly flourishes, including modern Europe. While the British and American systems of government have many similarities, there are also many contrasts. The following account strives to be brief and clear on the subject.

UNDERSTANDING THE BRITISH PARLIAMENTARY SYSTEM

Basic Differences from the American System

The British parliamentary system has been a celebrated success for a long time at home and in the vigorous "daughter" nations, Canada, New Zealand and Australia. This goes a long way in explaining why nearly all the new representative governments that have come into existence in recent decades have adopted one variation or another of this system. Almost no nations have sought to adopt the American system with a presidential executive, Congress as the legislature and the courts in a judicial branch. All of these branches are supposed to operate under the sacred principles of the separation of powers and the application of checks and balances.

High school American social studies or civics classes that extol the virtues of our Constitution would be uncomfortable making a comparative study of the British parliamentary system. Why? Because Britain is a free country without checks and balances, without separation of powers, without federalism and without a written constitution.

All actual power resides in the House of Commons. So, in effect, the British system is unicameral, having only one chamber that really counts. The all-powerful executive is the Cabinet, otherwise known as the Government, and the Prime Minister presides over it. The Prime Minister is at the same time the leader of the party in the House of Commons that has a majority in that body.

What a contrast this makes to the American system! Our cabinet members are required not to hold seats in the Congress in order to ensure the separation of powers. British Cabinet members almost invariably must be strong leaders in the House of Commons.

Other Differences: The Constitution

British people never have to worry about whether a proposed piece of legislation is constitutional or unconstitutional. If it passes into law in the House of Commons, it becomes part of the constitution immediately. All of the laws on the books, called statutes, make up the British Constitution. There are also some hoary documents which we as Americans are entitled to share, namely, Magna Carta of 1215, the Petition of Right of 1628 and the Bill of Rights of 1689.

Despite the existence of these documents and all of the unrepealed statutes, the British constitution is declared to be "unwritten." Indeed, part of the constitution involves operating on long-entrenched customs and precedents, much in the same way, for example, that the United States Constitution does not specify how the political parties operate to produce candidates. Nowhere does one read about national party conventions in our Constitution.

Since the British constitution can be changed by the vote of a simple majority in the House of Commons, the British constitution can be extremely flexible and responsive to new needs. By contrast, an elaborate procedure must be followed to change the American Constitution, or the Supreme Court must interpret aspects of it at the end of an elaborate judicial process. The long struggle for the Equal Rights Amendment is an apt example of something that would not have to happen in Britain.

Other Differences: Political Style

Interruptions, heckling, shouts and even tumult often break out in the House, usually in the middle of somebody's attempt to make a speech. It is not the usual style for the better politicians in the United States, but the rough-and-tumble at the top has been the style in Britain for a long time.

The same style operates in local campaigns, especially when candidates "stand," not "run," for office, and show up at "the hustings," or election meetings. ("Hustings" is always used in the plural, by the way.) Candidates must stand on their own two feet and fend off the attacks that come from random constituents on the floor. Sometimes these attacks take the form of crude interruptions and nasty heckling, and the only way to face up to them is head on. With skill, the audience can be turned on the heckler in derision, but it is always up to the candidate to defend himself or herself. Here is another example of how highly regarded verbal skills are in Britain.

Other Differences: When a Government Falls

Ordinarily presidents cannot be dislodged for four years, senators for six years and members of the House of Representatives for two years. British Members of Parliament, or M.P.s, as they are invariably known, can be dislodged when the whole government tumbles down, which can happen on any day.

The Prime Minister, known as the P.M., has what baseball fans would call a fielder's choice. The P.M. can either serve out a full five year term and then hold election, or the P.M. can call for elections at any time. Theoretically, any Prime Minister and his or her Cabinet can also be overthrown by an adverse vote on a major piece of legislation on the floor of the House of Commons. But party discipline prevents this situation from developing as it did in the last century, when Prime Ministers were expected to resign under such circumstances. Party discipline imposes upon members of the majority party the imperative to vote with the Prime Minister and the Cabinet. Disloyalty can be severely punished at the next election time. Even so, a scandal as grave as Watergate would have toppled a British Prime Minister much more quickly than Nixon. An issue of that magnitude would bring M.P.s to vote on the basis of conscience alone.

So today it is really a question of taking the full five years or calling for fresh elections before that period is up. Prime Ministers usually wait for a time when a tide of public support seems to be running in their favor before calling for an election. The aim is to add to the majority already existing and to prolong the length of time that the party controls the government.

Sometimes Prime Ministers miscalculate in calling an early election — "early" meaning before the term is up — and find themselves out of office because a majority of the opposition party members of Parliament have been elected. Then, too, some governments last the whole five years without ever perceiving the tide running strongly for them and decide to fight it out at the end of the term instead. Regardless of what option the Prime Minister takes, the unpredictability of election contests adds a note of excitement to British politics absent from our own.

The formalities observed in calling an election are colorful. The Prime Minister must seek out the Queen and ask that the sovereign grant a dissolution of Parliament. It is theoretically the Queen's Parliament and the Queen's Cabinet and the Queen's Prime Minister, and she can call Parliament into session or dismiss it at will. In actuality, she dutifully does what the politicians request.

When Parliament is dissolved, all the members run for office in their individual constituencies. After the returns are in, the leader of the party with a majority in the House of Commons is summoned by the Queen and asked to form a government. This means that the leader of the victorious party can pick a Cabinet and serve as Prime Minister.

Long ago, the choice of ministers was the sovereign's alone, as these rituals testify. Today the Queen has no real choice because she is a constitutional sovereign who must act as a ceremonial figurehead only. That is why she must summon whoever has the backing of a majority in the House of Commons.

Other Differences: The Loyal Opposition

The Prime Minister and other Cabinet members sit on one of the two "front benches" of the House of Commons, either the one to the left or the one to the right of the impartial Speaker who presides. People of lesser importance sit farther back, and are called "backbenchers," which is another term for "rank and file."

There is another front bench right across the way, with only a table in between. This is a unique seating arrangement for legislatures, unmatched anywhere in Europe. The people who occupy this other "front bench" in the House of Commons, shortened in most uses simply to "House," are the leaders of the opposition. They form a "shadow cabinet," a group of leaders ready to form a government when their opponents lose an election and become a minority instead of a majority. Until that happens, they sit a few feet from their opponents' front bench and at eye level with them. During debate and questioning periods, the opposition is capable of mounting direct attacks on the Prime Minister and the other ministers unlike anything that the American president or cabinet members have to face. The closest our leaders come to it is during heated news conferences, where their questioners are journalists rather than opposing politicians, or when members of our cabinet are brought before Congressional hearings.

The adjective "loyal" has historical significance. Once it was thought that those who opposed the monarch's ministers opposed the monarch. This was often the case, certainly, but as the monarchs were increasingly removed from the fulcrum of political power, the concept that politicians could oppose the monarch's ministers and still be loyal to the crown and state began to be accepted. They could oppose and yet be loyal. How different this is from all of those governments in the world today which cannot tolerate any opposition, where those who oppose are automatically regarded as enemies. These places confirm that the concept of a "loyal opposition," first developed in Britain, is essential for true political freedom to flourish.

Other Differences: Efficiency in Government

The British are freed from the elaborate procedures required to keep the American presidency, Senate and House of Representatives functioning together. All of the negotiating, arm-twisting, threats and compromises between these bodies are not needed in Britain because everything emanates from the House of Commons where all of the real power resides. The phenomenon of "divided government" which has caused such trouble in America in recent years cannot exist in Britain. "Divided government" manifests itself when the president is of one party and the majority of the Congress of another party and the two branches do not get along very well.

The House of Commons is the only organ of the central government in which all the elected members sit together, the ministers as well as their opponents. This brings a speed and an efficiency in government that the American system simply cannot muster, except in a time of dire emergency. Political maneuvering certainly preoccupies British politicians also, but it usually goes on within the respective parties, rather than between organs of government.

Other Differences: Efficient Elections

No subject more clearly reveals the efficiency of the British system in comparison to ours than the nature of elections. Our campaigns seem to stretch on endlessly. For example, our presidential contests get underway years in advance of the actual election date. Since members of Congress must stand for reelection every two years and senators every six, and since each state has a governor and a legislature that also seek reelection, the American political scene is one of almost constant electioneering and fund raising. Campaigns never seem to end, so there never seems to be any freedom from all of the fund-raisers, sloganeering, hoopla and sound bites.

By contrast, British campaigns are kept short and relatively inexpensive. Why? One reason is that a whole layer of election activity does not exist because the federal system does not exist in Britain. More important is the fact that the time for campaigning is strictly demarcated as a period of a few weeks. The amount of money that can be spent by each candidate is also limited.

Another Difference: The Tone of Elections

Individual candidates on each side of the Atlantic will provide strong exceptions to the generalization that the tone of British election campaigns is pitched higher. Moreover, it cannot be denied that repetitious slogans, slick TV ads and glib half-truths are used in Britain as well as in America. Nevertheless, the British do seem to put more emphasis on debate and intelligent arguments over substantial issues. British candidates seem to aim more at their voters' minds and common sense than at their apprehensions, fears, greed and preoccupation with scandals.

Understanding The House of Lords

Americans in Britain who discuss politics are likely to be "joshed" about the U.S. Senate. No matter how populous or how empty, each state produces two senators. How can this be in a democracy? How can Nevada have the same representation as California?

Strangely enough, the U.S. Senate is based upon the British upper house, the House of Lords. The Duke of this or the Earl of that or the Baron of the other were all territorially based, often having a shire as their name. Together, the House of Lords represented vast sections of the British countryside. The Senate represents territories also, the states.

An obvious major difference between Senators and members of the House of Lords is that the former are elected and most of the latter inherit their positions. The first-born son inherits the title and the seat upon the death of his father. His siblings are in law non-noble, although they sometimes have courtesy titles. Since 1958, "life peers" have been selected to recognize the achievements of distinguished individuals, but they cannot pass on their titles. In addition, women have taken seats in the House of Lords in recent years.

Everyone in this aristocratic house is supposed to be in a special noble caste, but they are assumed to be peers, meaning equals, to each other. The term "peer" is preferred to lord, which is ordinarily used as part of a specific name.

All of the members of the House of Lords either had ancestors appointed to that body by a monarch or were appointed themselves. Distinguished persons would receive an elaborate declaration called a letter patent, ennobling them, and, until recent years, their first-born male heirs. Historically, only great landholders in the realm who had rendered outstanding service to the crown, usually through holding important offices or providing wartime leadership, were recipients of letters patent. For similar service, lesser folk might gain a knighthood, a non-noble title in Britain.

In recent centuries, patronage over appointing peers has been taken over by the leading politicians, along with nearly all of the other honors that the crown can dispense. Political contributions have been paid off with titles and seats in the House of Lords, a practice that has drawn criticism for debasing the upper house. The charge has been made that politicians such as David Lloyd George sold seats. Furthermore, those becoming peers were no longer from established, landed families. Many were from business. In fact, the peerage was once called the "beerage" after a number of beer manufacturers who were heavy political contributors gained the scarlet and ermine robes, the uniform for the House of Lords.

While the U.S. Senate is still as powerful as ever, the British House of Lords has been deprived of nearly every bit of power. Powerlessness was arrived at early in this century, as a result of some very complex political history. Since then, all that the House of Lords can do is delay legislation briefly, talk and fulfill colorful ceremonial purposes.

Much of what the peers do talk about informally concerns medicine and doctors, because a good many of them are very old men. Even so, the formal debates in the House of Lords are often quite worthwhile, since the members are entirely independent of the electorate and incapable of influencing the House of Commons in any way except by persuasion.

Politicians on the extreme left call for the abolition of the House of Lords, declaring it to be a useless and expensive anachronism. For most British people, however, it is like the crown in being one of those priceless links with the past, present and future.

UNDERSTANDING THE BRITISH MONARCHY

Why Americans Are Closet Royalists

Like the House of Lords, the monarchy exists in the modern world in order to carry on ceremonial functions. Although powerless in politics, the monarchy is the greatest of all the ancient institutions linking the generations of the past, the present and the future. Somewhat surprisingly, it also links countless members of the American democratic republic with the royal past. Americans have always been fascinated by the kings and queens of Britain, as demonstrated by the enthusiasm brought forth by every royal visit to the United States. No place outside of the Commonwealth is more willing to go all out celebrating a royal arrival. Moreover, popular magazines in America dwell on the lives of the members of the royal family almost as much as some popular magazines and newspapers in Britain. Indeed, the wit who described Americans as closet royalists was probably correct.

How can this be in a nation that has always appeared to be so staunchly small "r" republican? Perhaps it is because the British monarchy is a link with our own historic past, a past often thin and barely recognizable in the newer America of rootless, wheeled suburbia. Queen Elizabeth I, Henry VIII, Henry V, Richard the Lionhearted and even King Arthur were monarchs of all the English-speaking people, and so until 1776 they were also the monarchs of the ancestors of what has been up until now the recognizably dominant American ethnic component. After all, the British flag flew over the American English speaking frontier for 169 years, from the first English settlement at Jamestown in 1607 to the Declaration of Independence in 1776. In short, Americans have their own legitimate claim to a long stretch of the history of the British monarchy.

There is something more. Why do housewives in Cheyenne, Wyoming, keep up with the royal behavior of Prince Charles, Prince Andrew, Princess Anne and Princess Diana more than 200 years after British sovereigns ceased to be American sovereigns? Shouldn't this go against the grain in the American Republic, considering its heroic images of self-made men and women and the vigorous, emphatic denial of inherited class distinctions all through its history? Perhaps the answer lies in the realm of romance, fantasy, glamour and magic. Perhaps the repression of such feelings in our uncompromising republicanism leads to a heightened preoccupation with the British monarchy by certain Americans. Childhood stories about princes and princesses may have much to do with the phenomenon also.

Regardless of the exact psychological origin, it is undeniable that the British monarchy is one of the great lures for American tourists. For their part, the British are brilliantly adept at heightening and perpetuating the drama surrounding the throne. As one young Briton explained to visiting Americans, the crown is "Show Biz" today. Yet it has been show business since it started, since the first Anglo-Saxon monarchs put on their shinier and fancier armor. It will remain one of the most magnificent shows on earth so long as Britain remains a kingdom, a situation which looks as if it will continue forever. After all, could the bands play and the red-coated soldiers march to change the guard at Buckingham Palace if there were no monarchy?

The Value of Monarchy to Britain

The monarchy is simply wonderful for tourism. Despite criticisms of it from the far left over the whopping salaries paid to individual members of the royal family and the enormous untaxed fortune of the Queen herself, the royal establishment undoubtedly pays for itself many times over through the lure for tourists provided by royalty's color, traditions and enhancements of history.

There are other payoffs for British subjects, who never have more than a small minority of republicans among them. No matter what shocking changes might occur, such as the collapse of the known international order, or the arrival of a thoroughgoing socialist regime or the collapse of the pound, the monarchy will always be there as an indissoluble link between past and present and a living assurance of continuity.

Generations are bound together by the living institution of the monarchy. Parents of toddlers can anticipate that their offspring will be ruled some day by a contemporary royal toddler. In an era of adverse effects from what has been called "future shock," or the inability to adjust to a plethora of changes that come along too fast, there is undoubtedly a very beneficial psychological payoff for British subjects through their strong bond of continuity through the crown.

Royal Ribbon-Cutting

Another benefit of the monarchy to Britain is that there is always someone of dignity and importance to cut ribbons, launch ships, lay cornerstones, pass out awards, undertake ground breakings and attend various other kinds of important ceremonies. Such activity is one of the most important functions of the royal family, and they know how to do these things with style. The family is, in a way, a big public relations firm, and none of the leading royals can ever retire from it. Meanwhile the Prime Minister and other important Cabinet members are free to carry on with the truly important business of governing the nation.

By contrast, our harried presidents must steal time from vital affairs of state so that they can nip out into the Rose Garden for a ceremony and a photo opportunity. Often the first lady must must leave the White House and her husband in order to fly somewhere for a ribbon-cutting or a dedication. The vice president can be sent, of course, but most vice-presidents come without the aura of power and importance that a president can lend to an occasion. Even the Boy Scouts can experience a let-down when the vice president substitutes for the chief of state.

Other democracies that do not have a crowned head of state, such as Germany for example, have a high ceremonial office above the real power center. The German Chancellor exercises day-to-day political power, but the President of the Federal Republic of Germany, ceremonially above the chancellor, has the stature to take the load of ceremonial duties away from the more powerful lower office. So the German president frees up the time of the chancellor just as the Queen does for the Prime Minister.

The Royal Family as a Sponge for the Media

The royals are like birds exposed in a gilded cage. Since the tabloids and gossip mills go overboard to relate their real and imagined activities, cabinet members are more free from media interference. Leading politicians, their wives and children are all shielded to a very considerable extent from the glare and annoyance of excessive journalistic zeal by the royal family acting as a sponge for this attention. In a way, the royal family is an ongoing soap opera that rivets the attention of not only British subjects.

For example, in the beginning of the spring of 1992 Britain was in one of its worst economic slumps since World War II and just weeks before a national election. Even so, the news about the angry separation of Prince Andrew and the Duchess of York, Sarah Ferguson, completely overshadowed these graver concerns. After the election of 1992, the press exploded with inside stories of how princess Diana was faring in her marriage and how there was a real possibility of divorce. Media coverage reached a pitch of frenzy and critics of such coverage became enraged at these violations of privacy.

Surely British politics would lose much of its efficiency if this distraction for the media were not operating. Undoubtedly American presidents and their families must wish that they could escape the focus of the media the way British politicians can, thanks to the royal family.

The Royal Family as a Model for Deportment

Still another benefit of the monarchy, at least for most of the time since Queen Victoria, has been that it has displayed a standard of behavior, dress and propriety to guide subjects who wish to appear correct but who may be unsure of themselves. This explains why the social behavior, general deportment and even the clothes of the entire royal family, from the queen downwards, are subject to such intense observation.

For some Britons, who may range from sophisticated intellectuals to poorly paid workers and who share a political position on the left, monarchy appears to be a stuffy, expensive, showy and even a dull extravaganza carried on at taxpayers' expense.

Since Victoria, who reigned from 1837 to 1901, a high standard of proper behavior has been expected from the members of the royal family. All of the celebrated virtues of the wellborn and well raised are supposed to find their noblest expression in the royal palaces. Indeed, if the hallmark of a British lady or gentleman is in making other people feel at ease, certain members of the royal family are masters of the art. They have style, magnificent style, and no matter how staunchly republican a visitor to a palace might be, he or she is more than likely to leave with a keen appreciation of royal grace in action.

The Fascination of Royal Scandals

Beneath all of their glittering trappings, members of the royal family remain human beings, so it is not surprising that the strict standards of behavior expected of them have not always been maintained, particularly in the troubled area of sexual expression.

To be sure, many royal figures from the past were quite debauched, including proper Victoria's wicked old uncles. Victoria herself made a mark on social history by trying throughout her reign to set a standard for sexual propriety, a standard much admired by the middle classes. Even though it often drew ribald humor from some aristocrats on one end of the scale and from many British workers on the other, the middle class standard dominated the nineteenth century, declaring that all sexual activity be confined to marriage alone.

Ever since it was established, the Victorian standard for sexual propriety has been violated by royal scandals. Victoria's own son, Edward VII, was a notorious adulterer, and the next King Edward had to abdicate and become the mere Duke of Windsor when he insisted upon marriage to a twice-divorced American woman, Wallis Simpson. This scandal riveted the attention of Britons in the 1930's at the very time that Hitler was moving to swallow central Europe.

Recently there has been more trouble for the royals, leading some journalists to go so far as to say that the royal family has become dysfunctional. Princess Margaret, sister to the reigning Queen, suffered from marriage and divorce problems. Princess Anne, the Queen's daughter, recently filed for divorce after a long separation. On top of this, the celebrated marriage of Prince Andrew, who was nicknamed by some as "Randy Andy" because of his amorous proclivities before marriage, to Sarah Ferguson, nicknamed "Fergie" and regarded as rambunctious for a royal, has come apart. Meanwhile the media keeps an eagle eye on the seperated heirs to the throne, Prince Charles and Princess Diana, just as they had watched for years for the slightest hint of any domestic stress or strain between the royal couple.

Such pursuit of royal sexual peccadilloes and problems borders upon insensitivity and, of course, goes far over the line of common decency and good taste. It is the kind of coverage reminiscent of that which has been meted out to American presidential candidates recently. Dealing with harassment of this sort is one of the more unfortunate aspects of the job of being royal.

Regardless of recent marital difficulties, real and imagined, the royal family is no different from millions of other British families, where the divorce rate now stands at more than one for every three marriages. Meanwhile, the unshakable marriage of the Queen and Prince Philip remains as a model to be emulated, and not only by other royals.

The Unreality of Royal Power

Scholars of the medieval period have long carried on spirited debates over how powerful the British monarchy was at this or that period of history. There is no debate about royal power today: The real power of the crown has dried up.

In theory, the Queen has all kinds of power, but these powers are entirely imaginary. For instance, only the Queen can call Parliament and dismiss Parliament, acts that can be carried out whenever she wishes. She can appoint anybody to any post, from the Prime Minister to an admiral to office clerk. She can also veto any and all legislation to come from the House of Commons and the House of Lords, and do so absolutely. This, by the way, was the origin of the American presidential veto. No monarch has ever tried to veto any bill since the early eighteenth century.

As head of the Church of England, she can appoint and dismiss all archbishops, bishops, deans and priests. As the fountainhead of all honors, she can theoretically create new peers, hand out memberships in chivalric orders, such as the Order of the Garter, create knights and dispense various other distinctions.

What sometimes mystifies American tourists is that the monarch seems to be carrying out at least some of these powers. Nevertheless, it is all show. Her power is hollow, and what she does is carefully orchestrated by the duly-elected government. She passes out the honors they tell her to pass out; she appoints and dismisses whomever they tell her to appoint or dismiss; she calls and dissolves Parliament when they tell her to do it.

These are the functions of the constitutional monarchy as it has evolved to the present day and, should any ruler be so silly as to try to transmute imaginary power to real power, a resolution would probably be passed in the House of Commons declaring that the monarch has abdicated and that a long life is wished to the heir as the new monarch. Since all know the rules, they all perform the way they should.

The monarch's imaginary power is displayed whenever the Queen dutifully reads her speech from the throne to her assembled Parliament. Her words are literally chosen by the Prime Minister of the day, so that under one government Her Majesty will make a Conservative speech and under another she will make a speech for the Labour Party. The sovereign simply says what the politicians in power request her to say.

The ancient ceremony of opening Parliament is perhaps the most magnificent display of imaginary power. The bejeweled and dazzling monarch sits in elevated majesty facing the costumed peers, the great churchmen and all the members of the House of Commons. The scene looks much the way it did centuries ago and serves as another dramatic example of how the past still lives in Britain.

The Prince Consort and the Crown Prince

The distinguished looking man often seen walking just behind the Queen during many ceremonial occasions is her husband, Prince Philip, the Prince Consort. Sometimes people wonder why he has that title instead of king. Traditionally, the crown has passed by heredity to the first-born sons of the royal family. Should the first-born die, the second-born son inherits it. The crown is passed to a female only when no direct male heirs exist. The last king of England, George VI, Elizabeth's father, had two daughters, Elizabeth and Margaret, and no sons. Since Elizabeth then inherited the crown, her husband could not have a similarly exalted status, unless she married a foreign king, which would be very difficult to do constitutionally. Therefore, her husband has the title of prince consort, which confers a special status close to but below that of the monarch. Queen Victoria also had a prince consort, Prince Albert, whose image still adorns certain tobacco cans ("tins" in Britain) to this very day.

The son of Queen Elizabeth and Prince Philip, Prince Charles, is heir to the throne. He will likely become King Charles III when Elizabeth II dies or if she abdicates in his favor so that he can have her job while he is still young and vigorous. The next in line to the throne after Charles is his first-born son, Prince William.

In Continental European royal families, the heir apparent

is often called the crown prince, while in Britain he is referred to as the Prince of Wales. This comes from no particular Welsh ancestry, but from the fact that royal heirs have traditionally been given the title in a special ceremony at Caernarvon Castle in Wales in order to strengthen the tie between England and Wales.

The German Background of the Royal Family

While not very Welsh, the royal family is very German in ancestry. It is descended from German princelings who ruled in the northern German state of Hanover. Queen Victoria's marriage strengthened the German connection, as did the marriages of several of her children to German dynasts. In fact, when Victoria died in 1901, Kaiser William, the future leader of Germany in World War I, marched behind her funeral cortege in a British uniform. The Kaiser was her nephew, so when World War I broke out, royal cousins fought on opposite sides.

It was only in the first half of this century, when Germany loomed as a united, powerful, threatening rival, that the royal family's German connection became an embarrassment. During the superpatriotic days of World War I, there was such pervasive Germanophobia that even lowly sauerkraut became "liberty cabbage." Reacting to this atmosphere, the royal family changed its name from Saxe-Coburg-Gotha to Windsor, a thoroughly English name.

The Ultimate Justification for Monarchy and Heredity: God

In an age of democratic egalitarianism in America and Western Europe, how can the existence of this old, feudal, hereditary right to rule by kings and queens be justified by anyone? There is an old explanation that used to justify all kinds of unequal situations in the European world. To put it simply: Since the truth for the Christian world is found in the Bible, what model of government is found in its pages? Monarchy: powerful, glorious, magnificent and absolute, because God is a king in the Bible. There are no presidents, congresses, parliaments or city councils in heaven. If we on earth are supposed to model our fallen and sinful world as best we can upon the heavenly model revealed in the Bible, then the only possible form of government that there can be is monarchy.

This argument leads to another. Because the Bible describes a hierarchy in heaven, involving several ranks composed of archangels, angels, seraphim, etc., the early imitation in feudal Europe justified a set of noble ranks from dukes at the top to barons at the bottom. For the rest of society in general, heredity justified nearly everyone's status or lack of it. Social mobility was not acknowledged and hardly known for centuries, so if your father was a peasant, you were supposed to be a peasant or married to one because God chose you to be a peasant's son or daughter. Similarly, God chose who would be the knights, the noblewomen, the shopkeepers and the craftsmen. This divine choice permeating all of society went right up to the top, to the royal family. Today, royalty is the only role remaining that depends solely on hereditary choice.

According to the contemporary outlook in the developed world, heredity is only given credit for a few phenomena in our lives. Everyone agrees that it at least determines how tall we are and what basic skin color we have. Yet today, even eye color and hair color can be artificially modified. In traditional Europe, heredity determined so much more than physical attributes. It determined work roles, status and most aspects of what we lump together as "lifestyle" today. This was because the belief prevailed that your particular soul was determined by God to reside in a particular body at a particular time, in order to fulfill a particular role in God's great organization of the universe.

Today only royalty continues to obey such divine command. Therefore, Queen Elizabeth II is justified in having her exalted position, but she is also required to shoulder the responsibilities that this unique position entails. The minute she ceases to be Queen, the heir to the throne by hereditary right, Prince Charles, should assume these awesome burdens.

The Unique Limited Nature of the British Crown

Every so often the Queen, in full regalia, meets the Lord Mayor of London, also in full regalia, in order to ask his permission to enter the City of London, that special and oldest section of metropolitan London where financial centers predominate today. The ceremony points up an old right of the City, namely to be free from royal visits unless the permission of the City's authorities is gained beforehand.

Quaint and strange as it seems today, this ceremony displays the fact that the English crown was limited in ancient days. Many other nations can recall a period in their respective histories when a king or an emperor or a tsar ruled with absolute power, at least in theory. This never occurred in Britain. While one or two inept English monarchs speculated over the right of theoretical absolutism, no British monarch could ever come near to putting autocracy into effect. Those who ruled arbitrarily were abruptly checked: King John by the barons through Magna Carta in 1215; King Charles I, who lost his head to Parliament in 1649; and King James II, who had to flee his throne in disarray in 1688.

A strong and clear lesson of British history thus repeated itself: English monarchs were limited by being beneath the law. This meant that there were certain things that sovereigns could not do, and certain rights possessed by subjects which could not be violated by the state. By the late seventeenth century, such an understanding of the English constitution was stated in a clear, attractive and sophisticated manner by John Locke, whose writings were eagerly read by Jefferson, Madison, Washington and many other founders of the United States, all of whom were profoundly influenced by this concept of British freedom.

Belief in limited, constitutional government that respects

individual rights is one of the grandest achievements to emerge from the long, troubled and sometimes bloody history of the monarchy in England, an achievement enjoyed by many of the nations where English is spoken today. In the United States this achievement is enshrined in the Constitution and the Bill of Rights. So when presidents or their agents are chastised for breaking the law by the Congress and the courts, it can be said that they are being treated according to the principles worked out to limit English kings long ago.

UNDERSTANDING BRITISH POLITICAL PARTIES

The Two-Party System

As a result of complicated historical circumstances, English-speaking societies have been blessed with the prevalence of the two-party system. It is in operation most of the time in Britain, the United States, Canada, Australia and New Zealand. Many other nations of the Western world, such as France and Italy, have a multiple party system functioning in their legislatures, often bringing forth weaker and less stable coalition governments.

Two parties emerged in Britain as early as the 1670s, the Whigs and the Tories. In the nineteenth century, the Whigs became the Liberals and the Tories became the Conservatives. Although the Liberal Party dominated in the nineteenth century, it lost its steam in the twentieth, and was replaced as a contender for victory at elections by the Labour party. Ever since World War II, the Conservatives and Labourites have rotated in office. Presently the Conservative party has enjoyed four consecutive election victories, an unprecedented feat that no party has been able to achieve in this century. Meanwhile, in contrast to the dominance and relative cohesiveness of the Conservatives, the Labour Party has shown signs of internal divisiveness and ideological conflict. In fact, in recent years some Labourites split off to form a new but unsuccessful party, the Social Democrats, which has recently merged with the Liberals to become the Liberal Democrats.

The Conservative Party

In some ways, the Conservative Party in Britain is comparable to the Republican Party in the United States, except that British Conservatives accept most of the provisions of the welfare state. Conservatives are strongly in favor of maintaining the American alliance, which meant, in the decades of the Cold War, reliance upon the nuclear deterrent and acceptance of American bases in Britain. Conservatives generally display more old-fashioned nationalism and patriotism than their opponents, and rely more upon the private sector of the economy for votes and campaign funds. Businessmen, various other kinds of middle-class people, from professionals to shopkeepers, and many skilled workers regularly support the Conservatives. The old aristocratic and gentry families that used to be so closely associated with the Conservative Party are far less influential and numerous than might be expected.

Conservatives tend to praise individual initiative and characteristics of the old Puritan work ethic and put great faith in the workings of the free market in economics. Often they champion the private sector as a replacement for certain parts of the public sector. Sometimes they are still called by their old name, the Tories.

Conservatives are not reactionaries devoted to bringing back the long gone "good old days." In fact, some political commentators have regarded the modern British Conservative Party as more leftward in its outlook than American Democrats, largely because the Conservatives accept a substantial component of socialism in British life to provide such things as the National Health Service and basic maintenance of the less fortunate.

Conservatives have been dynamic ever since they were led in the nineteenth century by the brilliant Benjamin

Disraeli, a novelist son of a Jewish book dealer. It was he who modernized the old Tory Party and gained lasting recognition as the founder of the modern Conservative Party. Since Disraeli, Conservatives have come up with creative legislation that has broadened the franchise and brought about popular social reforms. Such progressive programs have enabled the Conservative Party to appeal to a broad spectrum of the electorate. It should also be pointed out that it was the Conservative Party that produced the first female political leader of an important Western nation, Margaret Thatcher.

The Labour Party

The Labour Party is a phenomenon of the twentieth century. Today it represents a broad spectrum of voters and interests, from the center to the left, and not just the interests of organized labor. The party was organized at the turn of the century and first came to power, although weakened by coalitions, in the 1920s. It was only after World War II that the Labour Party gained solid majorities in Parliament and vigorous cabinets. In the period from 1945 to 1950, Clement Attlee's Labour government ushered in the so-called "quiet revolution" that socialized a substantial sector of the British economy.

Many Labour Party members do call themselves socialists, but they are very British socialists, meaning that they are wedded to using the democratic ballot box for enacting change. Bloodcurdling cries for violent class struggle and volcanic revolution are simply not British. Most British socialists had also distanced themselves from communism and Marxist interpretations of history long before eastern Europe's communist regimes collapsed. Perhaps the best example of the nature of Labour Party socialism can be seen in the way successive Labour governments stood with the American alliance when the Soviet Union was being confronted in the Cold War.

In many ways the Labour Party can be compared to the Democratic Party in the United States. Just as Democrats were supposed to pick up the bulk of their votes from what we have called "blue collar" workers, Labour is expected to have its strength in the British working classes and their unions. Even so, just as substantial numbers of American workers have voted Republican in recent years, large numbers of British workers have opted for the Conservatives. Moreover, the traditional "smokestack" manufacturing industries have become less significant in both countries, as all sorts of service and high technology occupations have opened up, thereby confronting all of the parties with new groups of potential voters.

Another similarity between Labour and the Democrats is that both parties have usually favored deeper and faster change than their respective opponents. Each party has also had a far left that has been the ideological home for many discontented intellectuals. In Britain, the outraged intellectuals come from all classes and share anger over the continuation of class privilege and what they perceive as economic exploitation.

The Labour Party has long had a strong alliance with the organized trade unions, which wield considerable power in Britain, particularly through their Trade Union Congress, or T.U.C., an abbreviation that shows up in British newspapers very frequently. The trade unions organize Labour campaign contributions, and their members participate in various political activities from the grass roots right up to sitting in the Labour government's cabinet. Unlike their American counterparts, Union leaders have been prone to enter politics and take seats in the legislature. There is a marked tendency for the trade unions to be very conservative about arrangements over wages and working conditions, which they guard jealously.

The Third Party Movements

One other characteristic that the Labour Party shares with American Democrats is that both parties have a tendency to become badly divided between moderates and leftists. Splinter groups or minority parties do form in the

United States from time to time, but they are usually absorbed into one of the two major parties. In Britain it has not always worked out this way. Early in the twentieth century the Labour Party replaced the Liberal Party, and it is conceivable that another third party can come along to eventually replace one of the two existing major parties in the future.

Recently third party advocates have endured some sharp disappointments. Several prominent dissident Labourites broke with their party to form a moderate new party called the Social Democrats. To gain strength at the polls they allied themselves with the remnants of the Liberal Party to become the Liberal Democrats. They have fared badly in gaining seats, largely because Britain does not have proportional representation, and the alliance has proven to be rather unstable.

Civil Servants: Esteemed British Bureaucrats

Bureaucrats, whether they deserve it or not, receive a bad press in the United States. They are the butt of countless jokes, usually depicting them as dull, overpaid, insensitive and utterly bogged down in red tape. American politicians regularly target them as the cause of waste and mismanagement in government.

The stereotype is different in Britain, where government workers are called civil servants. Working for the government in managerial positions has long had high status and professional dignity associated with it, to the extent that many of the best graduates of Oxford and Cambridge regularly aspire to careers as civil servants.

In Britain civil servants actually have a higher status than lawyers or doctors. The best British stereotype for the bureaucrat is that of a dedicated, intelligent, impartial, hard working, self-effacing professional denied by choice all hope of fame and wealth while toiling for the good of all. The worst British stereotype of the civil servant is that of a "mandarin," someone privileged by having a secure and well-paying job, a good pension during retirement to look forward to, and considerable power. They are least esteemed when they go on strike, which causes chaos while detracting from their image as dedicated public servants.

British civil servants take a stand above politics, and the chiefs of departments, called permanent secretaries, serve whatever cabinet minister is appointed to be responsible for that department. At one time the minister may be a Conservative, and at another time a Labourite. The temporary chief, the minister from the cabinet, and the permanent secretary and his staff, from the civil service, may differ over how to implement programs and may have other disagreements. Nevertheless, the democratically elected cabinet has the right to direct the civil service to accomplish its ends.

Perhaps some government workers at higher levels in the United States enjoy some of the prestige that is ordinarily associated with British civil servants. For example, among Washington's executive agencies, the State Department has had a strong reputation for professionalism. Yet overall, a sharp contrast remains between the stereotype of the bumbling American bureaucrat and that of the dedicated British civil servant and Americans traveling in Britain ought to be aware of it.

SENSITIVE AREAS IN POLITICS

All countries have certain sensitive political subjects, and visitors from abroad should know at least something about them to avoid awkward blunders. Just as the traveler in Germany should know something about the Nazi era, and the visitor to South Africa should be familiar with apartheid and the meaning of "majority rule," the American visitor in Britain is at a decided advantage if he or she has some knowledge of certain highly sensitive areas in that country today.

Ireland and Britain

Anyone who has gone through a divorce has an understanding of Anglo-Irish relations. The exaggerated outpourings of resentments, the inability to see both sides, the resolute, even ferocious determination to be separate that occur in so many divorces often can be observed when people in Ireland or people in Britain talk about the other island. The visitor can be put into a difficult situation similar to that of the friend of a divorcing couple: If you are not entirely for one side, you are likely to be immediately suspected of being for the other side. Sometimes visitors are confronted with the choice of seeing either the "Irish problem in English history" or the "English problem in Irish history."

Whatever it is called, a deep problem exists in the history of each country, going all the way back to the conquest of Ireland by the Anglo-Normans in the twelfth century. Thereafter, old Gaelic or Celtic Irish culture was overcome by English culture, century after century, district after district, spreading out from the most Anglicized area right around Dublin. The replacement of the native Irish language by English is indicative of this cultural imposition. Today only the more remote and rural parts of Ireland, basically the western fringe of the island, speak Gaelic as the first language within the home. Yet when the Reformation changed the religion of most of the English in Ireland, the native population generally continued to adhere to the Roman Catholic Church. Later on, Irish nationalism would rise from this religious base.

In a way, Ireland was a colony supporting an alien Protestant English aristocracy, but in another way it was an outlying British area, just as Wales or Scotland were. Certainly wave after wave of exploiters from England produced descendants who became very Irish with the passage of time.

By the nineteenth century, it became clear that Ireland suffered from a unique dilemma. It was too close to Britain physically and too connected to Britain economically to develop in the autonomous way in which New Zealand, Canada and Australia advanced through the nineteenth century. These former British colonies became dominions which evolved into *de facto* independent nations. On the other hand, the Roman Catholic religion, Celtic culture and the Irish nationalism made it too difficult for Ireland to subside into an unequal union with England. Protestant Scotland and Protestant Wales had been able to do this, although nationalists from these places are apt to disagree with this characterization.

Many concessions and would-be solutions for this "Irish problem" were put forth by the British Parliament, but none of them came soon enough or went far enough for some Irish patriots who would settle for nothing short of independence. "Home Rule" was the solution put forth by more moderate Irish nationalists in conjunction with British liberals in Parliament. This was a solution granting Ireland control over internal affairs, much the same way that self-governing dominions operated. Under Home Rule, Britain would retain control over foreign relations, defence and the currency. Just before World War I, when it seemed near fruition, this solution crashed on the adamant resistance of the Protestants in Northern Ireland.

The "Orangemen," Protestants who were thickly settled in the northern province of Ulster, wanted no part of an Irish dominion that would have a Roman Catholic majority rule Ireland. Orangemen were descended from Scottish settlers who arrived in the seventeenth century, and were Presbyterian or Anglican. In the American colonial period, these people provided hardy frontier pioneers who became known as the Scots-Irish.

While the war clouds darkened over Europe in 1914, Orangemen prepared to fight a civil war against Home Rule. Two years later, while the First World War was grinding along, Irish republicans rose in a futile but highly inspirational manner in the Easter Rising of 1916. The brutal British overreaction fanned the flames for an independent Irish republic instead of the more moderate achievement of Home Rule.

A nasty civil war followed between the British and the republicans, and after that, among the republicans themselves. In order to achieve an independent "Irish Free State" some republicans signed a treaty that partitioned Ireland by separating six counties from Ulster, which were allowed to continue on as Northern Ireland, and are still a part of Great Britain today.

The Orangemen in the six counties of Northern Ireland often see themselves as a nationality sharply distinct from the Catholic Irish. While they regard themselves as "British," which is something of an umbrella term, they do not see themselves as merely transplanted Scots. To many of them, being Northern Irish connotes a distinct nationality, thereby granting the right of national self-determination. To many Irish Catholics, in the north and the south, this is nonsense. For them, the Protestant Northern Irish are just a peculiar and stubborn variety of the Irish nationality.

The fatal hitch in the scheme to separate the Orangemen from the rest of Ireland was the existence of a very substantial minority of Roman Catholics in the six counties of Ulster. Recent estimates put this minority up to 40% of the total population. Nearly all of these Catholics identify with the nationality of the Republic of Ireland to the south and would like to see the six counties link up with the rest of the island again. To make matters worse, the Orange majority has a long history of flagrantly discriminating against the Roman Catholics in housing, jobs and social services. Such discrimination led to a Roman Catholic civil rights movement, originally led by Bernadotte Devlin, and when this movement met brutal repression, the area exploded with sectarian violence. The struggle became something of a civil war, and it goes on to the present day, having claimed thousands of victims from both sides in a spate of brutal killings.

The British role in this conflict is extremely sensitive, costly and painful, so visitors are cautioned against offering snap judgments or simple solutions. For example, the most infuriating of simple solutions can be seen spray-painted all over Ireland and Britain: "Brits out." It implies that if the British would only withdraw from all of Ireland, the situation would subside and peace would finally come. It is the favorite solution of many Irish-American patriots who do not really understand the situation.

Certainly all the British taxpayers and those British parents, siblings and wives who have loved ones serving in the British army in Northern Ireland earnestly wish that the British could get out. Should British forces withdraw at this stage, a civil war on a much grander scale would probably flare, causing horrible suffering for the innocent on both sides. Moreover, Britain has a legitimate commitment to Northern Ireland, no matter how difficult and stubborn some of their leaders have turned out to be. The Northern Irish contributed heroically in blood and toil to the British war effort in the twentieth century. Can the British desert these people who call themselves British now, especially in the light of treaty arrangements pledging the British to underwrite the maintenance of peace and order in the area?

There are no simple solutions. The Orangemen in the North are dead set against joining the republic to the South, fearing that the Roman Catholic Church would impose control over personal lives in matters such as birth control, divorce, other family matters and education. What it comes down to in the end is that four million Catholic Irish cannot force one million unwilling Protestant Irish into a union they will not accept, a union that many of them will resist with all the violent strength that they can muster.

Recently the British have been able to bring the government of the Irish Republic into the picture as one of the parties working to ameliorate the situation, much to the chagrin of the Orangemen. The intransigence of the parties in the north have clearly exasperated the British, who are likely to push harder to have the north's more moderate people of both sides gain greater control and replace the hitherto dominant extremists of both sides.

Meanwhile two sharply contradictory developments have been taking place. First of all, Britain and Ireland are closer together than ever, thanks to one-hour cheap plane travel between London and Dublin. Jobs in Britain have led to a mass exodus of the unemployed from Ireland, many of them young and talented. They have joined the large number of Irish immigrants already located all over Britain, and in thick clusters in key areas. Whenever a citizen of the Republic of Ireland settles in the United Kingdom, he or she is automatically regarded as a British subject with all the rights pertaining to British subjects. Intermarriage in Britain has proceeded unabated. The net upshot is that just about everyone on the island of Ireland has relatives and friends on the island of Britain.

The other development is the attempt of the outlawed Irish Republican Army to bring the war in the north to Britain itself. The I.R.A. has launched a series of terrorist attacks that have included bombs that have gone off at important locations in London, killing innocent victims randomly and disrupting the lives of ordinary Britons. They have blown up a patrol of the Queen's Horse Guards, attempted to blow up Mrs. Thatcher at a party conference in Brighton, and even sent mortar shells towards the residence of the Prime Minister at Number 10 Downing Street. These atrocities have outraged nearly all of the Irish living in Britain, of course, but this violence has nonetheless created awkward situations for them in dealing with some of their angry British co-workers and neighbors. It is sad to reflect that the people setting the bombs off are a tiny minority of Irish fanatics who are despised not only by the British but by the overwhelming majority of their fellow nationals and also by the Roman Catholic Church.

Unfortunately, both the Orange and the Roman Catholic Irish have terribly long memories, and both sides will conjure horror tale after horror tale about what the other side has done. Militants on both sides champion the use of violence. Of course, they always plead that they are merely responding to violence, defending themselves, etc., but the fact is that many conclude that the only way to deal with the people on the other side is with force and violence. Until these brutal, primitive feelings change, British, Protestant Irish and Roman Catholic Irish will continue to bury their dead in vain.

The Irish situation today is the latest chapter in a tragedy that has gone on for centuries. Americans in Britain are well advised to treat it with restraint. Be very careful about responding to discussion about the situation. Snap judgments, flip assumptions, jolly partisanship can all label the visitor as a boor quite quickly. Instead, listen, ask questions, try to savor the complexities, try to measure the depth of the passions invoked and try to empathize with the grief expressed. In other words, play the kindly listener to a party in a painful divorce.

The Falkland Islands War

In world history, the Falkland Islands War can be considered a brief, remote and insignificant contest between Britain and Argentina over bleak islands inhabited by less than two thousand wind-blown settlers whose main preoccupation was and is sheep farming. American visitors had best not make light of this struggle, however, because most Britons hold a serious regard for what they perceived to be at stake.

From a British point of view, a democracy went to war because a military dictatorship had ruthlessly invaded small islands against the wishes of their inhabitants. Britain went to war over a principle, namely that the Falkland Islanders had a right to be British if they wanted to be British. Americans must be cautious in not jumping to the conclusion that Britain was a colonial power violating the Monroe Doctrine. Regardless of the geographical location of the Falkland Islands, only a handful of Argentineans or Chileans were on the islands. Well over 90% of the population was British and wanted to continue to be nothing but British.

There are good reasons why Americans should take pains to treat the British victory with respect. The British have a tendency to hark back to their most glorious days of this century, the time when they stood in defiance of a ring of fascist military dictatorships during World War II.

It was easy for them to identify the Argentine invaders of 1982 with their fascist foes of 1940.

It had been a long time since the British fought a war in legendary fashion, that is, by supporting right over might, by sending the fleet, by hanging on with bulldog tenacity and, finally, seeing the foe collapse and run up white flags. When the bands thundered down Whitehall in celebration to the tune of "The British Grenadiers," any Anglophile could agree that the British really needed that victory, if only to reaffirm their glorious past.

The Anglo-American Alliance

The Falkland Islands War was won with considerable American cooperation, particularly in supplying military intelligence. This was but one of many examples of how these two nations have helped each other ever since their alliance was forged in the two world wars. Often called a "special relationship," the Anglo-American alliance stands as a keystone of the foreign policy of both nations. No nation is apt to support the United States more vigorously than Britain, either at the United Nations or when the United States is embroiled overseas. British support during the Iranian hostage crisis, during the 1986 conflict with Libya, and in the recent campaign against Iraq are cases in point. We can count on them and they can count on us.

Limits to the alliance show up from time to time, naturally. For example, there was a disagreement over the precipitous American invasion of Grenada. More serious was the American denial of support for the British and French invasion of the Suez area in 1956, and American pressure to get them to withdraw. British Conservatives have been more keen to maintain the alliance than the Labour Party. Recently the Labour left took a strong stand against allowing American nuclear weapons to be based in Britain. Yet even when these limitations are taken into account, the Anglo-American alliance still remains the most solid voluntary international arrangement of this type in the world today.

There are a good many reasons for this solidarity, although it is ironic that American nationalism originated from fighting Great Britain in the Revolutionary War and in the War of 1812. A shared language is an obvious reason. So is the strong ethnic connection. Somewhat less than half of the American population can trace most of its ancestors to the British Isles. The ancestors of the rest of the American population come from everywhere else, from Africa to Asia and from Continental Europe to Latin America. More significantly, the truly important values and ideals of Britain and the United States are very similar. Citizens of both nations think along parallel lines about such topics as right and wrong, justice, individual rights and liberties, limitations on government's encroachment on personal freedoms and how people should live under government by laws and not government by individuals. All sorts of legal safeguards for personal freedom, specifically the Bill of Rights, trial by jury and habeas corpus, evolved out of the English experience in history and were taken up by British Americans once the Atlantic colonies were established. To put it succinctly, both societies are supposed to adhere to due process rather than to the naked use of power. Both societies, ideally at least, shun the Machiavellian view that the ends justify the means.

After 1945, the United States began to take over the historic role of Britain throughout the world. Today we have bases everywhere, fleets in all oceans and aircraft on patrol on the vast periphery of the Eurasian land mass. Large numbers of Americans work overseas, some in American businesses and some in programs to aid and develop countries. American products and influence are just as ubiquitous as American people. Should a serious crisis erupt somewhere in the world, some sort of American involvement seems to manifest itself.

Such American activity may be seen as something of a twentieth century version of the British Empire. Whether or not a person agrees or disagrees with the deployment of United States power and influence overseas, the role of a great world power has been taken on, just as Britain assumed this role in the Victorian era. Britain was a very small island to command a quarter of the world's people, a quarter of the earth's land surface and most of its salt water regions. Yet such was the British achievement in the 19th century. While America is much larger than Britain, Americans still make up only approximately 5% of the world's population, so our far-flung role can also be regarded as a prodigious effort in the style of the British Victorians. Moreover, it can be argued that just as the British Empire went into decline in the early part of this century, the American empire seems to be contracting at the end of it.

The British are still adept at diplomacy, banking and foreign affairs and help us play the role of preeminent world power in countless subtle and direct ways. They are to us now what the Greeks were to the Romans: the suppliers of brains and expertise to a powerful imperial people.

The American Revolution and the War of 1812

How might the American wars against Britain commencing in 1776 and 1812 be reconciled with the existence of the strong Anglo-American alliance of the 20th century? This subject may very well come up for Americans in Britain, therefore some understanding of these struggles based on modern scholarship may be helpful.

First of all, it should be pointed out that when the bicentennial was being celebrated the British put on a lavish display celebrating the American Revolution. For them, as well as for Anglophile Americans, the American Revolution was really a civil war, with a pro-revolutionary and an anti-revolutionary faction on both sides of the Atlantic. Besides, Americans fought for traditional English freedoms that had been assured to Englishmen through their own heroic seventeenth century civil war struggles against Charles I, an arbitrary Stuart king. The cry of "no taxation without representation" was voiced against this king long before Americans took it up. For pro-revolutionaries,

George III assumed the role of Charles I in the American Revolution, although it is known through historical hindsight that a majority in a rather corrupt British Parliament was equally responsible for handling the colonists arbitrarily.

Famous Britons such as William Pitt the elder, Edmund Burke and John Wilkes championed the colonists' struggles in that same House of Commons, while in America at least a third of the population was what the British still choose to call "United Empire Loyalists." We have called them Tories. Estimates have it that another third in America was either neutral or would side with whichever force was in power locally. So what it comes down to is that the active revolutionaries were really a minority of the population in America.

The War of 1812 was a different matter. Americans can trace a good deal of their early nationalism to this struggle. It was, after all, the occasion to write our national anthem. For the British it was merely a minor sideshow in the larger, desperate struggle to defeat Napoleon's France. They see it as a victory for themselves, or at least a draw. From their perspective the War of 1812 featured a successful defense of Canada from Yankee greed and had a highlight in the capture and burning of the American capital. The most stinging British defeat, Andrew Jackson's celebrated victory at New Orleans, was tragically fought after the war had been concluded by diplomats in Europe.

It was fortunate for the later relations of Britain and America that both of these wars were not marred by the brutality and ferocity that have come to mark civil wars in the 20th century. There were hardly any atrocities against men in uniform or against civilians. The leaders on both sides behaved like gentlemen because they were gentlemen. To be sure, tarring and feathering is most unpleasant, but it is far milder than the punishment meted out to most suspected traitors or collaborators in our century. When the British were defeated in the American Revolution, the losers' friends were not lined up against walls and shot. Defeated Tories could go to Canada, Bermuda, or back to

Britain. Most actually located elsewhere in America, perhaps closer to the frontier, where they could cover up their past loyalty to Britain. Who knows how many Daughters of the American Revolution are actually descended from these former Tories?

When visiting Britain, it is best to be generous when the topic of the American Revolution comes up. Treat it as a civil war. Do not stress how the British lost the war. Instead, point out that they, too, were winners because the best elements of British society, the reformers, were on the side of the Americans. After 1783, these reformers were eventually able to correct many abuses and glaring corruptions of the old parliamentary system. Therefore, in the long run the American Revolution can be seen as a victory for representative government on both sides of the Atlantic. By the way, if the American visitor can pull off this interpretation of the American Revolution, he or she will be a practitioner of the British art of diplomacy.

Race and Racial Disturbances

Americans are highly sensitive to racial issues. One important reason is that one out of eight descends, at least in part, from slaves whose status was denigrated by the concept that people have called 'race' historically. Older Americans remember the struggle for civil rights firsthand, and the segregation that went on so blatantly before that. Most Americans are aware that some of the saddest topics in American history are about the brutal effects of racism and bigotry.

It therefore comes as something of a shock to learn of racial disturbances in Britain, complete with looting, burning and accusations of police brutality and insensitivity. Some cynics say that whatever comes to the United States will eventually arrive in Britain, and urban racial disturbances are cited as another example of this phenomenon. Bigots blame the heavy post-war immigration of blacks from former British possessions, particularly from the West Indies, for causing these scenes in hitherto peaceful Britain.

Americans should be forearmed with some perspective on this kind of disturbance in Britain. First of all, there have been many periods of ethnically inspired riots and disturbances going all the way back in the country's history. They involved Jews, Germans, Irish, Scots and, going far into the past, even Vikings and Romans. Secondly, in the recent riots, the overall scale of racial violence was much lower than has been the case in the United States. Thirdly, the racial composition of the British rioters was somewhat mixed, and the issues of discrimination protested against did not seem to be as clearly racially based as they have been in the United States.

Behind these differences may be the essentially different history of blacks in Britain. A decision handed down by a British judge in the latter eighteenth century declared that the instant a slave set foot in Britain, he or she was a free person. This is, by the way, just the opposite of the notorious Dred Scott decision in United States history. So blacks who came to Britain during the time that slavery flourished in America were all free regardless of their former status. Groups of blacks who lived in Britain from the eighteenth century onwards tended to be servants and seamen. With the passage of time they simply blended into the British population undramatically.

The blacks seen in many cities in Britain today are from the new immigration of blacks that took place after World War II. They, and millions of Asians, came to Britain from newly independent former colonial areas to seek employment and a better way of life. Their numbers have never put the non-white population of Britain much over 5%, a much smaller percentage than that of the black population of the United States.

Behind American race relations are the tragedies of slavery, segregation and of bloody repressions of civil rights. The American Civil War and the Reconstruction Era were major traumas in American history. There is nothing parallel to this in the British experience, so it is not realistic to predict American patterns for future developments in race relations in Britain. The only major preoccupation that the

British have that can possibly parallel the American preoccupation with so-called "race" is the class system. In other words, what "race" is to Americans, class consciousness is to the British.

Americans are often shocked by blatant, overt racism in Britain, since most bigots in the United States have become closet bigots nowadays. Racism in Britain is often outspoken and crude, whether shouted by poor East London cockneys or smoothly enunciated by Enoch Powell, a student of the classics and member of Parliament. In one way, this racism is an angry reaction against change. In another way, it is a manifestation of age-old British xenophobia, or fear of foreigners. British verbal skills at getting to the point and emphasizing it unambiguously undoubtedly contribute to Americans' frequent dismay at the tone of British racism.

On the other hand, there is an old British tradition which affirms that all people of all backgrounds in race, creed and origin can become British. Being British is hard to define, but it consists of a certain civilized behavior, a certain openness of mind and a certain sense of fair play. Therefore, from this point of view, a population of "Black British" exists, and visiting Americans should not make the mistake, as they very often do, of thinking of the British as whites only. The bigots, cockney or sophisticated, can all be matched by other Britons who are tolerant, accepting and appreciative of superficial physical differences among humans. They appreciate the malleability of cultural backgrounds in a British environment. They know that the great civilizations of history have been world civilizations, capable of inspiring the loyalties of varieties of people. At its best, British civilization is such; at its worst, it is insular and narrow minded. The visitor will undoubtedly see both aspects.

Gun Control

Gun control can become a sensitive issue for Americans in Britain because the British are likely to express interest in the subject to elicit a conversation. They know that opinion in America is bitterly divided over the subject and the easy availability of lethal weapons fascinates them.

Gun control is not an issue in Britain. Laws are strict and severe: Handguns are banished and other guns can only be used for sport. When not in use, sporting guns are to be kept broken down and in a locked receptacle subject to regular police inspection. Very few people in Britain own guns or want to own guns. Even criminals traditionally prefer knives or cudgels because they are less dangerous, although, sadly, this is changing. Moreover, only certain crack units of the British police use guns. The rest do without, relying instead upon the authority of the law, cheerfulness, common sense and a short, heavy truncheon, the equivalent of the nightstick in the United States. They keep it tucked away somewhere in their uniforms. The ordinary London "bobby" stands in sharp contrast to the American police officer whose arsenal of gun, mace, club and handcuffs dangles menacingly from his or her exterior.

If anything truly appalls and frightens the British about America, it is the homicidal carnage brought about through the indiscriminate use of handguns. Indeed, a person's chance of being a homicide victim is something on the order of over 20 times greater in the United States than in Britain.

Some interpretation of this alarming statistic is necessary. While homicides in America are widespread, they cluster most heavily in the inner city areas, where minority citizens are the most common victims and the most common perpetrators. Poverty and the deprived environment in which it festers can be cited as the root cause. The easy availability of handguns and the long American tradition of gun use certainly contribute considerably to the toll of homicides. For the rest of the country, the availability of handguns and cultural traditions of having them handy make murder and accidental shooting commonplace events in all kinds of American neighborhoods. If American hosts want to startle visiting Britons, or, for that matter, any European visitors, all they have to do is take them to a gun shop to see the arsenals on display.

Americans who point to the right to bear arms in the

Constitution will be countered by Britons who declare that this right is also in their constitution. They will insist that they can still bear arms if they want to, but only according to strict rules, rules derived from laws passed by their democratic legislature.

Clearly, American visitors in Britain will be on the defensive if they choose to debate the issue from the pro-gun standpoint of the National Rifle Association. By contrast, those Americans who are for banning handguns will feel that unarmed British life goes a long way to prove their point.

Crime and Violence in America

Another sensitive area for Americans in Britain involves the high incidence of crime and violence in the U.S. Stories circulate all over Britain about such things as the mugging of British tourists in such places as Miami or New York by gun-toting, minority-group adolescents. Fear of violence in America is reinforced by the plethora of bizarre films made in this country featuring disgusting characters who indulge in simply amazing orgies of violence and horror. The more discerning British know that there are certain high risk areas in all American cities, places that have fantastically high crime rates and thereby skew all of the crime statistics for America. It remains up to the American visitor to explain to the less discerning Britons that there are many quiet, peaceful towns and vast stretches of generally law abiding suburbia where crime and violence are much more exceptional events.

Even when all of this is pointed out, it must be admitted that the United States is a far more violent society than Britain and other western European nations. Ghetto crime, family violence, violent thefts, rape, and acts of violence for the sheer sadistic fun of it are all too prevalent. Americans agonize over solutions. Some wish to get tough with criminals and lock them away for as long as possible, often overlooking the fact that we already have a higher percentage of our population in jails than any developed nation.

What is more, it costs just about the same to warehouse a criminal for a year as it does to send someone to a good college for a year. Other Americans call for campaigns of public effort to combat the unemployment, deprivation and neglect that they see as the ultimate causes of violent crime. Some Americans deride and others cheer the "John Wayne" image and the celebration of violent solutions to problems that have been a part of American history, particularly in the legends of the frontier and in the glory derived from victorious wars.

British people will probe the subject of violent crime in America with great interest. They fear that their own society is heading in the direction of America by becoming more violent also. They want to know more about its causes in America so that they can do more to prevent its rise in Britain.

Fears of violent tendencies in the American character also make the British apprehensive over the possibility of irresponsible, trigger-happy American foreign policies. Such penchants are imputed to Americans quite readily. In recent decades, Barry Goldwater, Alexander Haig and Ronald Reagan were each the source of considerable concern in Britain out of fear that their militant nationalism might lead to war.

Awkward Exceptions over Sensitive Areas

Britain has long been a place where freedom of thought and expression have been given free play, so expect to find dazzling nonconformity. Just as some people delight in wearing outrageous fashions, others extol positions that go against the grain of the majority. So the visitor may encounter someone who will give excuses for the Irish Republican Army or take up the position of the Argentineans over the Falkland Islands. What is often engaging about these blatant British mavericks is that they may use wonderfully persuasive English to present weak arguments.

Sometimes they enjoy challenging visitors. The main thing to do in such a confrontation is to stay level headed, be good natured, and keep a sense of humor at play.

Getting angry and shouting will make the situation worse, creating what the British call a "wind up," which is pronounced "wined up," and means that someone has been led to be overly flustered. It is precisely the reaction that many ideological mavericks are looking for because they often get their jollies from winding people up.

CHAPTER SIX

Understanding British History
INTRODUCTION: WHY IT IS IMPORTANT TO GET A GRIP ON BRITISH HISTORY

BRITISH history can overwhelm Americans because it is so rich and complex, and has been going on for so long. This crowded, small island has been populated by dynamic and creative people who have left an intricate legacy. The cumulative effect of all the eras, styles, events and individuals emanating from British history can bewilder. Any visitor to Britain is likely to encounter such historical terms "the Stuart era" or "Jacobean" or "since Lloyd George was Prime Minister" or "Norman keep" or "Anglo-Saxon foundation" or "Wars of the Roses" or a thousand other references to the past. The reason for this is that it is a living past, kept alive in the minds of millions of its living heirs and constantly reinforced by an enormous physical legacy in the form of cathedrals, castles, stately houses, inns, walls, parks, old villages, graves, statues, paintings and memorials. History is also present in customs, institutions, names, costumes, entertainment and there are countless other reminders. It is simply impossible to avoid history in Britain because it is everywhere, and at the very heart and essence of the British experience.

British history is much more important for visiting

Americans than for tourists from Continental Europe or Japan. After all, British history is American history before 1607, the year when Jamestown became the first permanent English speaking settlement in America, or 1776, the year when the American states declared their independence. All of the language, customs, laws, institutions, and beliefs which were brought across the Atlantic to flourish in the New World had evolved from hundreds of years of experience in England. Even the most American of figures in the most American of environments, the sheriff of the frontier, evolved first in the forests of Anglo-Saxon England as the Shire-Reeve. The posse of the American Wild West actually began as the "posse hundredi" of England in the early Middle Ages.

Since American history actually grew right out of English history, it can be said without hesitation that such figures as Henry VIII and Elizabeth I belong to all Americans just as much as they belong to all Britons. Note how many Americans know quite a bit about these monarchs while they know nothing about the rather colorful French dynasts on the throne in the same century. Furthermore, events in English history such as Magna Carta and the Glorious Revolution of 1689 had everything to do with how Americans have come to view the power and obligations of government. Those very familiar American notions that we are a free people enjoying certain rights and liberties first evolved in England.

American history seems very recent when compared to over two thousand years of recorded British history. In some parts of America, particularly in the West, English speakers have settled for only about a hundred years, while on the East Coast, English speaking settlements have flourished for up to four hundred years. As a result, some Americans from the East Coast can sometimes assimilate the historical depth of Britain more readily.

A tendency to despise and destroy the old and to build everything anew has been an American characteristic. In many places wrecking balls and demolition charges destroy part of the American historical heritage regularly. In the name of profit and progress old buildings and famous sites give way so that more gas stations, condominiums or fast food emporiums can spring from their ruins.

Certainly the destruction of the past for the profits of the present occurs in Britain also, and there are similar disagreements between the historical preservationists and the developers. Yet there are differences. In most parts of Britain, there is simply much more from the past remaining almost everywhere. Preservation laws are more stringent and regularly enforced. Above all it is much harder to demolish the past because so many British people maintain such a deep appreciation for it. They treasure their history and what remains of it in physical form. Another factor is that the British, like many European nationalities, master the art of renovation. They can adapt the treasures of the past to function in modern life. For instance, electric lights and modern plumbing can be fitted into a comfortable five-hundred-year-old house that is sure to last for at least another five-hundred years. The result of conscious efforts to preserve the past as well as a disinclination to destroy old objects just to replace them with new objects means that a person who visited Britain decades ago can return now and find most landscapes little changed.

For all of these reasons, any visitor to Britain needs an orientation to this vital topic of British history. What follows is a brief chronological overview of all of British history which presents the most significant epochs, names, dates, and events. There is also an attempt to convey something of the spirit of each particular era. Bear in mind that these topics are as familiar to British people as the Civil War and Thanksgiving are to Americans.

PREHISTORIC BRITAIN

A vast stretch of British history is prehistoric because, according to a traditional definition, history does not begin until there are written records. The Romans were the first to provide them for Britain, beginning around a half century before the Christian era began. By this definition of history, all that came before was prehistoric, just as everything before 1492 is prehistoric in the Americas.

What we know about prehistoric Britain still remains largely shadowy and sketchy. Folklore abounds. It was the time of the Druids, who were mysterious priests, and of great female warriors who went to battle in chariots.

"England before the English" is one description of the era because the English were the Anglo-Saxons, and they did not settle until the period from the 400s to the 600s A.D. Various other people invaded and subdued the island of Britain during prehistoric times. The most famous of them were the Celts. Today considerable numbers of their descendants and Celtic cultural attributes are to be found in Scotland, Wales and the West Country. They are related to the Celts of Ireland and the Celts in the French province of Brittany.

There are several impressive sites in Britain that indicate the profound efforts of what were very thin prehistoric populations. Many are in the form of megaliths, or specially arranged large stones. Stonehenge is the most famous of these sites, standing bold and magnificent on the plains near Salisbury. A recent computerized study has confirmed earlier speculation that Stonehenge was built for the purpose of sun worship. Americans who go to Stonehenge will invariably find some of their fellow countrymen and women wandering about at the site, since it is very popular with visitors from the United States.

ROMAN BRITAIN

It is difficult to conceive of a period when Britain was a remote frontier area rather than a vital center of civilization and empire. Yet this was precisely the case during the surprisingly long period when the far-flung Roman Empire prevailed over Britain. The Romans ruled this wet and cold frontier region far from their sunny Mediterranean center for 400 years, from 43 B.C. to 450 A.D. or so.

Despite the length of time that the Romans occupied Britain, the net effect of the impact of their civilization on Britain was largely negligible. The main reason for this is that the Anglo-Saxons flooded into Roman Britain in such numbers and with such barbaric force from the fifth century onwards that they largely obliterated Roman civilization on the island. The substantial physical remains from the Romans in Britain, mostly ruins and excavated sites, are more significant for understanding Roman history than for understanding British history because no spiritual inheritance from Rome came directly from their long occupation. Even the vital Latin component of the English language came indirectly from Norman French rather than from Roman Latin.

The Romans left testimony to their skills in engineering all over Britain. Stretching across the narrow neck of northern England is Hadrian's Wall, a massive defensive barrier designed to keep the fierce northern peoples out of Roman Britain. Many sections of it remain today in extremely impressive form. Roman villas, temples, baths, floors and statuary have been dug up in many places by archaeologists. In many other locations Roman structures were incorporated right into medieval walls, gates and roads, tributes to how the Romans built things to last.

Two Romanized Britons are famous. Both lived in the shadowy world at the very end of the Roman period when barbarian onslaughts were destroying Rome's hold on Britain. One of them, St. Patrick, is famous for Christianizing Ireland. The other, King Arthur, has wrongly gone down in history as a Christian king who supposedly lived when knighthood was in flower. The stories of his adventures with the Knights of the Round Table have been famous for centuries. In actuality, Arthur upheld Roman Christian civilization against the invading floods of Anglo-Saxon pagans.

ANGLO-SAXON ENGLAND, 450-1066

There is a significant irony about the whole Anglo-Saxon period. Momentous developments occurred, yet very little physical evidence of this long era in English history remains. It began with the truly Dark Ages when masses of barbarians pushed their way onto the island through countless bloody struggles. It included centuries of building a rich civilization which left a profound spiritual, institutional, legal and mental inheritance for subsequent centuries. The era came to an end when the Anglo-Saxons were conquered by the Normans, who nevertheless utilized most of the elements of Anglo-Saxon civilization thereafter.

The ethnic change from the Anglo-Saxon era was profound. Masses of Germanic people migrated to the plains of England from what is now Germany and the Low Countries and drove the Celts into the hills of the West Country and Wales. This new dominant population, generally tall and blond, would become the basic ethnic stock for the rest of English history. Their Germanic language evolved into English, a fact revealed when comparing everyday words in English with everyday words in German. For example, "Fuss" in German is "foot" in English; "Tür" in German is "door" in English and so on. Of course, after 1066 the Normans brought a rich addition of Latin-based French to this Germanic speech.

The Anglo-Saxons are known for many achievements. They mastered the English landscape by felling forests and plowing up heavy clay soils with iron tools. During their long era in English history they underwent a transformation from pagan barbarians to civilized, medieval Christians who developed a remarkable system of common law which operated on the basis of a high degree of community involvement. Modern British subjects and American citizens enjoy legal systems based upon it.

The evolution of several Anglo-Saxon kingdoms was interrupted by ferocious Viking invasions. A Christian hero,

Alfred, King of Wessex, resisted these Scandinavians heroically. Eventually the Vikings and their descendants were Christianized and absorbed into the population. They were particularly numerous in northeastern England, where they controlled an area called Danelaw for a time.

The American connection to Anglo-Saxon England is substantial because our language, our law, important elements of our institutions and a substantial proportion of our ethnic stock are derived from the Anglo-Saxons. Their world was a world of the forest frontier, so when a new frontier beckoned in North America, Anglo-Saxon folkways, customs and laws proved to be immensely adaptable and successful.

Despite their enormous achievements in the 600-year span of English history, relatively few Anglo-Saxon buildings and parts of buildings remain. Naturally, for the first centuries of their occupation of England the Anglo-Saxons were simply absorbed in the process of becoming civilized. At first they lived in wooden structures, which do not survive from so long ago. Later they did develop impressive architecture in stone, but relatively little remains, in large measure because the Normans and their descendants built over Anglo-Saxon edifices. So visitors should relish any "pure" Anglo-Saxon building they find because they are so rare. Never mind that the cathedrals and castles built after 1066 are much larger and magnificent.

MEDIEVAL BRITAIN, 1066-1485

The Setting of the Times

Medieval is the adjective for the Middle Ages, the thousand years stretching from the end of the ancient world to the rebirth of much of the ancient ethos in the Renaissance era, roughly the 400's to the 1400's. The Anglo-Saxon period falls into it, but because this was such a unique era in

British history, it has been treated separately from the rest of medieval Britain.

The medieval era has been called the "Age of Faith," and it can be argued that never before or never since have religious beliefs so dominated the minds of people living in Western civilization. It was an epoch when the great cathedrals were erected; when new religious orders were founded; when friars, monks, nuns, monasteries and convents were prominent everywhere; when all those who taught at the universities were in holy orders; and when the church had the responsibility to run the hospitals and welfare systems.

Works of faith were only one side of the medieval world. Incessant warfare among armed kings, nobles, knights and retainers added notes of violence and instability. Medieval kings tended to be weaker than later on, unless they were particularly able men. The reason for this was that under the feudal system Medieval kings were bound in contractual roles with powerful lords. Because of this baronial strength, civil war was apt to flare up in medieval kingdoms in such circumstances as when a minor would come to the throne, or when a particularly feeble king inherited the throne, or when the succession was disputed. Poor transportation and communication detracted from royal power also.

The size and strength of castles attest to the power that medieval nobles possessed. Some were clearly what were called "over-mighty subjects" whose domains bristled with armed retainers. The basis of noble power rested upon the possession of numerous manors, or medieval estates. Upon them worked masses of impoverished agricultural workers, the peasants and serfs who made up the overwhelming majority of the population. The manor, the nearby local church and their village comprised their entire world. Most were bound to the manor in some form of servile relationship.

Feudalism, the economic, political and social system of the age, allocated these manors and the peasants who went with them to a militaristic elite. The manors produced a usually thin economic surplus that managed to keep this elite of knights and lords well armed and free to pursue war as a profession. The knights were specialists at war who operated, along with the lords above them, in a complex web of rights and obligations, most of which were sanctioned by the Church. At best, feudalism sought to protect the Church and peasants from violence; at worst, it exploited the masses so that the aristocratic sport of war could have full indulgence.

Romantic writers have embellished the Middle Ages. Troubadours, heroic knights, damsels in distress, mysterious prisoners in dungeons and the whole panoply of chivalry have been exalted. In actuality, the medieval period was dark, filthy, dank, nasty and miserable for at least 95% of the population. Death came early to many people of all classes, and sometimes it came in wholesale form, as a plague.

Grim as these times were for most people, there are many striking medieval achievements of a lasting nature. Significant permanent institutions originated and evolved, including Parliament and the great ancient universities, Oxford and Cambridge. Parliament's development has been cited as the greatest achievement of the age because it shaped the development of the rest of English history. "England made a Parliament and her Parliament made England" is how it is put in a popular saying. Other countries had medieval representative bodies also, but what was special about England's Parliament was that two houses developed, one for the lords and the other for knights and burgesses, who were prominent leaders from the countryside and the towns, respectively. Since knights and burgesses were officially non-noble, they were commoners at law, hence the name "House of Commons."

In the Middle Ages, the function of Parliament was usually to help the monarch to govern his realm. With strong kings, the regal voice was amplified by Parliament. It was his tool to disseminate his views and his organ to gather information and petitions from all over the realm. It was only later on, in the seventeenth century, that the House of Commons would challenge monarchs for authority.

The Norman Conquest

European style feudalism was first imposed upon England by the Normans, who carried out a swift, bloody and brutal conquest of England, beginning in 1066. The Normans kept much of the society and institutions of Anglo-Saxon England intact, but they imposed themselves as an alien elite all over the country. Everywhere defeated Anglo-Saxon nobles were replaced by French speaking conquerors. The language still bears evidence of their impact. Words of French origin still predominate for the topics of diplomacy, war, politics, cooking, hunting and in the realm of what Victorians called "courtship" and what now can be called "interpersonal subtleties." By any measure, 1066 was a landmark year in English history — the year when William I of Normandy, known as William the Bastard, defeated the last Anglo-Saxon king, Harold, at the Battle of Hastings. Who were these Normans who so rapidly imposed French feudalism and church organization on England? They came from Normandy, a seacoast province of France, but they were non-French in origin. These seething, restless conquerors were Frenchified Scandinavians, called Northmen originally, who had come south from what is now the region of Norway to conquer Normandy. This was accomplished just over a hundred years before their invasion of England was launched. Only a few came with William at first. A mere 8,000 disembarked to fight the fateful battle of Hastings in the southeastern corner of England.

Once in authority, the Normans energetically transformed the superstructure of England. They left their hallmarks in massive constructions in stone. Many cathedrals, churches and castles today boast of their Norman portions or foundations. Massive Norman arches and columns are unmistakable, and testify to the sheer power of the conquerors.

The Normans were the very last conquerors of England, and they did the job completely and ruthlessly. The richly detailed Domesday Book is a testament to their thoroughness. It was literally a census of all that they had taken. Like many successful conquering minorities in history, they allowed the conquered to keep as much of their old culture as was compatible with their rule. They were never overthrown. Instead, they were absorbed over a few centuries by a two-way cultural and biological diffusion. The Normans and their culture were simply amalgamated with England's Anglo-Saxon base.

Significant Post-Conquest Rulers

Medieval kings after William I varied in quality from the awful to the magnificent. For most people, learning about all of the medieval rulers has little point, so what follows is a list of the most outstanding, along with their main achievements. These are the kings most familiar to the British and the kings that American visitors are apt to hear the most about. Since medieval political history is such a tangled skein, presenting just the minimum number of royal personages might be the most helpful approach.

Henry II (1154-1189) was a vigorous, able monarch who made dramatic improvements in the legal system. He was implicated in the assassination of Thomas à Becket, which left a permanent stain on his reputation. He was married to Eleanor of Aquitaine, and had quarrelsome sons. The play *Lion in Winter* is about his family. Henry II was the king in the film *Becket* which, incidentally, contains some dubious history. Henry II was the first of a line of kings called Plantagenet, a line with strong French connections.

Richard I (1189-1199) is known as Richard the Lionhearted. He spent only a short period of his reign in England because he devoted himself to the Crusades and other adventures abroad. Robin Hood was supposed to have been active when Richard was away. He was one of Henry II's sons.

John (1199-1216), Richard's younger brother, has gone

down in history as a villain. He had to sign Magna Carta in 1215, that great historic document which acknowledged legal limitations to royal power. In it, specific liberties of lords and freemen were spelled out in great detail, and subsequent monarchs acknowledged it when they ascended the throne. Through the centuries, Magna Carta was reinterpreted again and again, so that eventually due process, the right to trial by jury and the right to be represented in a legislature all came to be read into the document. Magna Carta is also cited as a foundation for American freedom, particularly for the limitations placed on executive power.

Henry V (1413-1422) had a short but glorious reign. He fought the numerically superior French in famous campaigns across the Channel with dash and heroism, achievements celebrated by Shakespeare in the ever popular play named after this monarch.

Richard III (1483-1485), thanks to his treatment by Shakespeare, has gone down as one of the worst villains in English history, an ugly vicious and greedy usurper who was responsible for murdering two little princes in the Tower of London. Debate still simmers over just how evil or misjudged this monarch actually was.

Famous English Medieval Struggles

From Henry II on, England's line of Plantagenet kings had extensive holdings in France and claims to the French throne. Their combined English and French holdings were called the Angevin Empire. Holding on to French land and claims was a costly preoccupation for English medieval kings. Long struggles with France, which are collectively called the Hundred Years' War, lasted from around 1388 to 1453. In this struggle England won grand and glorious battles, such as Agincourt, but lost the war. Joan of Arc emerged at one stage to resist them as either a saintly or mad warrior, depending on one's point of view.

In the fifteenth century, the descendants of the Plantagenets fell out among themselves as they sought to capture the throne, aided and abetted by rival factions of powerful nobles. These confusing struggles, involving seven monarchs and lasting from 1399 to 1485, were called the Wars of the Roses. One faction, the house of York, was associated with the white rose, and the red rose was attributed to the House of Lancaster, its rival. The Lancastrians won when Henry VII ascended the throne in 1485, but he smoothed the rivalry over considerably by marrying the heiress of the other side, Elizabeth of York. Therefore in their son, Henry VIII, both factions were united.

THE AGE OF THE TUDORS, 1485-1603

A Magnificent Century for England

The age of faith and feudalism, symbolized by cathedrals and castles, gradually faded into the early modern period in Europe during the sixteenth century. In England, the change is marked by the arrival of the House of Tudor in 1485. The Tudors included some of the most magnificent English rulers of all time, and their resplendent age is appreciated far and wide today for its color and romance, as well as for the rich legacy of Shakespeare and other contributors to English theater and literature. It was also the time when many striking women played major roles in history. It was, to put what went on in this century succinctly, the time when the Renaissance came into full flower in England.

Many courses in American history begin with sixteenth-century England because it was then that English ships laid claim to the New World and English monarchs began to colonize Virginia for the first time.

This magnificent century in English history actually began very inauspiciously as crafty, clever Henry VII barely managed to grasp the crown during the last major round of the Wars of the Roses. He won it at the battle of Bosworth in 1485, defeating Richard III, the last king of the House of

York, a monarch given a very evil image by the pen of Shakespeare, whose plays were enjoyed by the descendants of Richard III's Tudor enemies. Henry was an heir from the rival house of Lancaster, yet he was able to marry the most prominent Yorkist heiress, Elizabeth, which guaranteed that all of the subsequent Tudors would have a blend of the red rose and the white rose in their ancestry.

Henry VIII and His Times

Henry VIII has always been controversial. Who was the real Henry VIII — the charming, talented Renaissance prince or the vicious, egotistical tyrant? The debate will never end. In order to secure a legitimate heir, he married six women. He beheaded two of them; divorced two of them; one died in childbirth and one outlived him. Along the way, he opened the floodgates of the Reformation in England by breaking with the Roman Catholic Church and becoming the leader of the Church of England, which more or less kept the same buildings and personnel. While he did destroy the monasteries, which was a very Protestant thing to do, much else in the church remained similar to Roman Catholic practice.

The American equivalent of the Church of England is the Episcopal Church. Episcopalians sometimes have considerable difficulty in dealing with the significance of Henry VIII's religious innovations. The topic can still elicit sprightly discussions among them.

Henry's first queen, Catherine of Aragon, a serious and devout Spanish princess, produced his daughter Mary, who later ruled as Mary I or "Bloody Mary." No other children were forthcoming, and anxieties rose about the need for a legitimate male heir to prevent a relapse into the bloody civil wars of noble factions that had preceded the Tudors. At this time, the prospect of rule by a queen was deemed dangerous, because it was feared that a female ruler would be dominated by a male faction or be unstable. This was indeed before the time of Elizabeth I!

Henry's desperate need for a legitimate male heir coincided with the eruption of his great passion for Anne Boleyn, who was a woman at court from a not particularly high ranking family. The relationship between Henry and Anne become one of the most remarkable romances of all history. Because of Henry's unbounded passion for her, he divorced Catherine of Aragon and made Anne queen. Because of a complicated international situation the Pope did not cooperate when Henry sought an annulment of his marriage to Catherine. The net result was a breach with Rome and the sacking of Henry's colorful right hand man, the notorious Cardinal Wolsey. Incidentally, Wolsey built Hampton Court Palace, just outside of London, a place that seems to be haunted by these colorful Tudors.

Henry's great passion for Anne Boleyn soon changed from love to hate, however, and Anne was executed, leaving a daughter who would become Elizabeth I. Henry's next wife, Jane Seymour, died in childbirth, but the child was the long-awaited male heir, who became Edward VI. Henry had no other children by his other wives, Anne of Cleves, Catherine Howard and Catherine Parr. The fate of these ladies can be recalled by the schoolboy's rhyme: "Divorced, beheaded, died; divorced, beheaded, survived." They made up a total of three Catherines, two Annes, and one Jane.

After Henry VIII died in 1547, he was succeeded by his only son, Edward VI, who was still a child, and a sickly one at that. He died at sixteen after being a manipulated child king for only six years. Henry's two daughters followed, the eldest first. Mary I was a tragic figure, a pious Roman Catholic like her mother, a woman who put her religious principles above prudence and all else. She became notorious for burning Protestants at the stake at the notorious "Smithfield Fires." While personally kind when not motivated by religious fanaticism, Mary has gone down in history as "Bloody Mary." She is sometimes confused with Mary, Queen of Scots, who was also a Catholic, but a member of the Stuart family instead of the Tudor dynasty. Mary, Queen of Scots, played her role in history during the reign of Elizabeth I.

The Elizabethan Age, 1588-1603

Most Americans are familiar to some degree with Elizabeth I because her reign marked the full blossoming of the Renaissance in England and the nation's first efforts at colonization in the New World. As Henry VIII's second daughter, her early years were traumatic because her mother, Anne Boleyn, had been beheaded not long after her birth, and she was in an extremely precarious position at court until the death of her half-sister, Mary I. Elizabeth ruled thereafter for one of the most colorful and dramatic half centuries in English history, from 1558 to 1603. This was truly a golden age: a time of spiritual, cultural and economic expansion and achievement.

Like other golden ages, it was also a time of immense international tension, as the Catholic Counter-Reformation gained strength on the continent. English sea dogs, who were really semi-pirates, found adventure on all the oceans, particularly against the Spanish. Assassination was a constant threat for Elizabeth because Mary, Queen of Scots, who was emotional, flamboyant and attractive, was the Catholic heir to Elizabeth's throne waiting in the wings. When Mary fled from factions in Scotland to England, Elizabeth made her a captive and finally, when Mary was implicated in plots against Elizabeth's life, the English monarch reluctantly allowed her execution.

Tudor Architecture

Part of the Tudor heritage is in an unmistakable physical form that impresses all visitors. Tudor architecture was unique, and fortunately much of it has been preserved. In later centuries it continued to inspire English and American architects. In fact, even today recently built townhouses and housing developments in America sometimes feature fake black and white timbering reminiscent of Tudor buildings.

Although expensive, bricks were esteemed by Tudor architects who built the great mansions of the era. Elaborate brickwork patterns and numerous and highly decorated chimneys were characteristic of their handiwork. Less imposing structures, such as inns, farmhouses and merchants' houses, were frequently made of "half timber." These buildings are striking because the timbers were usually painted black and framed by white plaster and lath panels, so that a "zebra effect" was often achieved. All of the very old towns of Britain have at least some of these treasured Tudor originals. Unfortunately, the Great Fire of London in 1666 and the many fires of World War II claimed all too many of these highly combustible buildings.

Interestingly, at least some Americans do not like the black and white patterns, complaining that the stark contrasts are too glaring for their eyes. For most Americans, however, these Tudor half-timber buildings are ineffably charming.

In Tudor times, architecture again reveals something of history. The buildings are transitional, just as the times were transitional from medieval to modern. The great houses of the nobility were no longer castles because castles could no longer hold out against artillery. Architecture, therefore, shows that the time when great nobles could resist the crown effectively were over. Even so, the sixteenth-century gatehouses and notched tops of turrets, called crenelations, were decorations reminiscent of the medieval castles.

THE STUART ERA, 1603-1714

The Chronology of the Seventeenth Century

It is fairly easy to arrange the Stuart era chronologically. It covers roughly the seventeenth century, and the kings can be remembered by this string of letters: J-C-O-C-J, for the reigns of James I (1603-1625); Charles I (1625-1649); Charles II (1660-1685); and James II (1685-1688). Remember that the Js are on the outside and the Cs are on the inside and that two Is come first, followed by two IIs. The "O" in the middle stands for Oliver Cromwell, who ruled most of the time during the interregnum, or times without kings, which lasted from 1649 until the Restoration of 1660. During the interregnum, there were two republican forms of government, which were called the "Commonwealth" and the "Protectorate." In actuality, both were dependent upon Cromwell's military power.

The Civil Wars and the Gentry

The central dramatic event in the Stuart century was the English Civil War, a struggle which pitted royalists, called Cavaliers, against Parliamentarians, who were often called Roundheads because of the shape of their helmets. These struggles for and against the policies of the Stuart king Charles I were fought out from 1642 to 1648. While these times can be regarded as romantic and colorful, they also ushered in important changes in English society. The rise of capitalism and the appearance of varieties of radical and powerful Protestant religions, generally put under the label of Puritanism, were strong factors underlying the contest.

Who actually fought whom in the English Civil Wars is actually a complex problem. Families often divided over the issue, as they so often did in border states during the American Civil War. Royalists and Parliamentarians fought hard for control of England. The battles of Edgehill, Naseby and Marston Moor are among the bloodiest ever beheld on English soil. In the end, the wealth and numbers from the southern part of England, London especially, defeated the royalists, whose strongholds were in the west and north, the more traditional regions of England and Wales.

The ineffective rule of the first two Stuart kings contributed significantly to the outbreak. James I, for whom the King James version of the Bible is named, was a pretentious Scot. He was the son of Mary, Queen of Scots, but he was raised as a Protestant. He was reasonably successful as King James VI in Scotland, but when he came to rule in England as James I, he proved to be arrogant and ineffective. Elizabeth I was certainly a hard act to follow, but James made matters worse by becoming overly attached to male favorites. At least he did unite the two nations in his personal rule.

The term "Jacobean" refers to the period of the reign of James VI and I, as he is often referred to, because it is derived from the Hebrew name for James, which is Jacob. He also gave his name to the first permanent English settlement in America, Jamestown, which was founded in 1607, just a few years after he ascended the throne.

His son, Charles I, has gone down in history as a saint and martyr in the view of some people and as a would-be autocratic tyrant in the eyes of others. He was one of those royal figures whose temperament simply did not lend itself well to the task of ruling. He was often incompetent or irresolute and at other times he was blind and stubborn. What he wanted to do was to strive for strong royal government in England along the lines of the kinds of royal absolutism appearing at that time on the continent. His attempts to raise money by dubious means so that he could dispense with Parliament led to one conflict after another. Charles' policies simply went against the grain of a long tradition of Parliamentary government and the exercise of the common law.

The group that presented the most forceful and effective opposition to these Stuart kings was a class unique to England and highly represented in the House of Commons — the gentry. These were the proud, well-educated, active and public spirited landowners who were just below the aristocracy and, therefore, non-noble, although they did fashion coats of arms for themselves. As a group, they descended from the medieval knights. Yet the gentry was constantly reinforced by incorporating landowners with more questionable pedigrees. Many wealthy merchants, lawyers, doctors or prosperous yeomen held hopes that their sons or their grandsons, installed on purchased estates, could eventually be regarded as country gentlemen. Country gentlemen were called "Sir" and usually had "Esquire" tacked after their names. Great Virginia families, such as the Madison or Washington families, lived lives that were similar to those of the English gentry.

In the early seventeenth century significant numbers of the gentry became radicals in religion as Puritans and then radicals in politics as rebels against the crown. From their bastion of power in the House of Commons, they were able to break the power of the Stuart kings and limit the power of the British monarchy for all time to come. Thereafter the gentry in general turned away from revolutionary excesses and became rather conservative. Their role before and after the Civil Wars was to hold power on the land and in local government all over England. They continued to dominate the House of Commons until the end of the nineteenth century, and even today their influence is far from negligible.

Oliver Cromwell and Puritanism, 1649-1660

Once Charles I was beheaded by a so-called "Rump Parliament," consisting of the radical members, a remarkable and formerly rather obscure Puritan country gentleman, Oliver Cromwell, took over the state. Although he sought to rule with Parliament, the times were so chaotic that for the first and only time in English history, a virtual military dictatorship prevailed. So a rebellion against arbitrary rule by a king ended with arbitrary rule by a general.

Arbitrary rule did preside during a time of social upheaval when many men and women emerged from the lower and middle ranks of society to assume new responsibilities. All sorts of political experimentation took place. For a time, aristocratic power in England was crushed, as attested to by the abolition of the House of Lords. What is more, the upper classes could no longer enjoy control over an established church, because the Puritans disestablished it while they were in power. They also practiced new innovations in taxation and law.

Ever after Cromwell, militarism has had a bad reputation in Britain. Ever since, except during the World Wars, British standing armies have been small, professional and nonpolitical.

Religious fanaticism was another aspect to gain widespread and lasting disrepute due to its nature during the period between royal reigns, 1649-1660, which is called the interregnum. During these years all sorts of raving fanatics came out of the shadows, as sects multiplied with amazing speed. Some were so radical in social behavior that Cromwell's soldiers were required to suppress them. Puritanism itself, which can be considered a general tendency towards simpler or more extreme Protestantism, fell into lasting disrepute after the interregnum was over because in those years it was associated with Cromwell and military rule. After Cromwell died the Puritans found themselves a despised minority in England.

As a result, many English Puritans gave up on their home country and left for America, where the strong legacy of Puritanism can still be found, particularly in New England. American Presbyterians, Baptists, Congregationalists and a number of independent denominations can all trace their origins back to England during the Puritan revolution. Their Puritan heritage is indicated by their emphasis on sermons, simplicity and the Bible.

Many of the defeated and despised English Puritans stayed on in old England, where they were tolerated and called Nonconformists or Dissenters because they did not conform to the reestablished Anglican Church. Toleration of them did not mean, however, that they were free from discrimination. Religious toleration, which was new in European history, began in England where it operated with a rather narrow scope. It merely meant that they were allowed to believe whatever they wanted to without persecution. Social and political discrimination against the Puritan sects lasted for over a century. For example, non-Anglicans were not supposed to hold public office or earn degrees from Oxford or Cambridge. Barred from the centers of power, many Nonconformists turned to careers in business and industry, where many of them became famous as successful capitalists noted for their strict attention to detail, sobriety, and honesty.

Cromwell has remained a controversial figure. It is difficult to be impartial about this important figure in British history. For some he is a hero and for others he is a villain, particularly in Ireland, where his rule was noted for brutality and destructiveness. So English Baptists, Presbyterians, and Congregationalists, among others, including many left wing politicians, think that he is something of a knight in shining armor. To most Anglicans and certainly to Irish Roman Catholics, Cromwell was a scourge.

This controversial man died in bed and bequeathed his power to his son, who was incompetent. Soon some of the army generals were negotiating with the Stuart heir to the throne to restore the monarchy in a new, limited and constitutional form.

The Restoration of 1660 and the Glorious Revolution of 1688

For Americans, it seems curious that a republic would be replaced with a restored monarchy in 1660. The Stuarts came back to the throne in large measure because royal governance was deemed normal for seventeenth century society. Charles II made it all easier by promising to be a limited and constitutional monarch who would obey the laws of the realm and guarantee all Englishmen their freedoms as well as most of the property they had expropriated during the Civil Wars. Another reason for the Restoration was that the gentry had been soured against radical experimentation in church and state by the excesses of the interregnum. This powerful landed class was, therefore, quite willing to welcome back a Stuart monarch and reestablish the Anglican Church along with the monarchy. They were also willing to see the House of Lords reappear.

Charles II turned out to be a skillful, genial lecher devoted to getting as much pleasure out of life as possible. He played skillful games with Parliamentarians and thereby retained a fair amount of royal power. During his reign some disasters befell England: the plague broke out again; most of London burned down in the Great Fire; and the Dutch were able to inflict some defeats on Britain at sea.

Since Charles had no legitimate children, although he acknowledged a swarm of illegitimate ones, his brother succeeded him as James II. Soon constitutional troubles came to the fore again. James II was a devout Roman Catholic who tried to fill offices in the state and the army with his co-religionists, despite laws which were designed to keep the government of England in Protestant control and despite the small number of able Catholics who were available to serve him. He simply declared the laws to be suspended.

Opposition to James' brash pro-Catholic policies grew among the great landowners of England. Yet most decided to wait out his reign, since he was in his late fifties, which was regarded as a much more advanced age then than it is now. James' first wife had been a Protestant, and he had two Protestant daughters, Mary and Anne, who seemed to be destined to succeed him. Then an event occured which was regarded by Catholics as something of a miracle and by Protestants as a probable fraud: His new wife, a Catholic, gave birth to a healthy male child, who, if he lived to maturity, might guarantee a long line of Catholic monarchs for England, a country which, by that time, was solidly Protestant and only had a small Catholic minority.

The influential portions of the landed classes decided to act. They invited his eldest Protestant daughter, Mary, who was married to William of Orange of the Netherlands, to come to England to reign. They sailed from the Netherlands, were welcomed by their supporters and turned to face the Catholic-led armies of James which seemed to dissolve before them. James fled, and was declared to have abdicated.

This set of events, actually a coup d'état, was the much celebrated "Glorious Revolution" of 1688, which reaffirmed the limited nature of the English monarchy. It demonstrated the principle that monarchs who broke their contracts could be fired. Americans subsequently made use of this principle in dealing with George III. The very language used to accuse James II of misdeeds against the constitution was borrowed for the Declaration of Independence. Americans also adopted almost all of the Bill of Rights that was promulgated immediately after the Glorious Revolution. These rights are fundamental to the constitution of both countries, and demonstrate how similar both counties are in cherishing liberties and specific freedoms.

The Last Stuarts and the Wars with France

William and Mary were followed by another of James II's Protestant daughters, Queen Anne (1702-1714). Anne had the sad distinction of begetting seventeen children, all of whom died.

From the time of the Glorious Revolution onward, it was clear that powerful France, dominant on the Continent, had become a national enemy much as Spain had been in the sixteenth century. As Britain arranged coalitions of Continental states to fight French expansion, the Churchill family rose to prominence. John Churchill, Winston Churchill's ancestor, became the first Duke of Marlborough as a reward for winning military glory against the French on the Continent.

Cultural Achievements in the Later Stuart Period

English literature and theater maintained a high reputation for creativity and richness from the Restoration to the end of the Stuart era. In architecture, the genius of Christopher Wren was at work. Not only did he design St. Paul's Cathedral and dozens of churches, but he also supervised the rebuilding of London after the disastrous Great Fire of 1666, which left the older parts of the city a smoldering ruin. Wren employed classical features, such as domes and columns, on structures which were strongly influenced by the Renaissance in France and Italy. This Renaissance impulse sought to incorporate the restraint, discipline and order of ancient times in a graceful, moderate style.

Some of the greatest achievements in British science belong to the latter seventeenth century, and are perhaps in part attributable to the inclination of many talented people to turn away from the vexed topics of religion and spend their energies on the exploration of the natural world. The giant among these scientists was Sir Isaac Newton, whose world view of physics lasted until the time of Einstein, and which still has many practical applications today. Newton shares with Charles Darwin the distinction of being one of the two greatest British scientists of all time.

THE GEORGIAN ERA, 1714-1789

The Dominance of the Landed Classes

This period takes its name from the four Georges who ruled England in the logical order of George I, II, III and IV. The last George in this series died in 1830, but the eruption of the French Revolution in 1789 can be used to mark the coming of a new era. In addition, the Industrial Revolution, which was beginning to get underway by the 1770s, would transform Britain for all time. Therefore, there is some logic in curtailing the Georgian period in 1789.

For the last time in British history, the landed classes, the aristocracy and the gentry, clearly dominated society and politics. Towards the end of the century, the middle class had grown considerably in both in numbers and importance due in large measure to the expansion of trade and of urban areas. By the nineteenth century, the middle class would seek to break the dominance of the landed classes in politics and society. Yet in the eighteenth century the landed classes enjoyed an unchallenged exercise of their power and relished the display of their style of life.

Government Under the Hanoverians

The four Georges were called Hanoverians because their dynasty came from the small German province of that name. They were the closest Protestant heirs to the English throne, and ascended it only because a law passed in the early eighteenth century permanently disqualified Roman Catholics from being crowned as rulers of England. Therefore the Stuart line, then exiled in France, remained disqualified even though their line had a better claim by heredity. Fortunately for the development of the English constitution, the first two Georges were foreign, homesick, and rather limited intellectually. This meant that great English statesmen who sat in the House of Commons and the House of Lords took over much of the function of the executive branch of government. They passed out honors and offices in the king's name, arranged for appointments to ministries and jockeyed among themselves for political prominence.

Because the Hanoverians were such weak executives, organs to manage the state evolved which became highly significant in the modern constitution. In a quiet, generally informal manner, the British politicians of Georgian England worked out the practice of cabinet government. Operating together, a small group of key ministers formed the first cabinets, and the most important minister gained the title of Prime Minister, ironically a term of derision at first. Almost invariably, all of these politicians had to command substantial followings in the legislature to be at the center of things. A minister with a following would have support for legislation from his friends on the floor of the House of Commons and in the House of Lords. If the whole cabinet was made up of influential men with many supporters the Prime Minister had a good chance of governing effectively.

The first Prime Minister was Sir Robert Walpole, a skilled manipulator of patronage and influence. Later in the century, two Prime Ministers named Pitt, father and son, were outstanding Prime Ministers. William Pitt the Elder was a great war leader who was in charge during the French and

Indian War, which is usually called the Seven Years' War in Europe. Pittsburgh, Pennsylvania, was named after him. He was sympathetic to the American cause in the era of the American Revolution. William Pitt the Elder became the Earl of Chatham late in life and is therefore sometimes known as Chatham. His son, William Pitt the Younger, picked up the pieces for King George III after the American Revolution and continued in office until he died while the wars with Napoleon were still going on. William Pitt the Younger is noted for becoming Prime Minister while only in his early twenties.

Eighteenth-Century Lifestyles

The big country houses, town houses, elegant clothes, rich furnishings and frequent travel clearly indicated the unchallenged economic and social dominance of the upper landed classes.

For part of the year most stayed on their vast estates where they lived in large, luxurious stately homes staffed by small armies of servants. All around were the fields of the estate, worked on by much larger armies of agricultural laborers. Another part of the year was spent in London where they lived in town houses in order to enjoy the political and social season. The town houses of the Georgian upper classes were substantial, expensive buildings, usually grouped around London squares. Today most of them have been converted for use as hotels and expensive flats, but at least some of their grandeur remains. Town houses certainly did not have the American connotation of often less expensive, undetached row housing. Members of this landed elite were also likely to go to a spa for part of the year. Bath was particularly popular, as its great crescents of Georgian buildings testify.

The upper classes rode hard, drank hard and fancied themselves the new Romans of the world, a concept fostered by their classical education. Restraint, discipline, proportion and moderation were the ideals of the ancient Greeks and Romans that eighteenth century Englishmen admired, although many found it impossible to live up to them. They did not lack confidence or self-assurance. It was God's will that they should live in grand style and be placed over millions of poor and toiling agricultural laborers, each of whom worked for a mere pittance. Extremely wealthy contemporary Americans have similar attitudes about the contrast of their riches to the poverty faced by most people living in the world, quite a few of whom are also Americans.

The upper crust of society was an extremely thin crust. Below them eighteenth century English society had a vital and growing middle class. Middle class numbers and importance had been growing since the late Middle Ages, and in the next century, after the tremendous enlargement of their numbers from the Industrial Revolution, they were strong enough to challenge the landed classes and question the very legitimacy of aristocratic power. In the eighteenth century they plied their trades and professions in all British cities and prospered. They became known as England's "shopocracy."

Naturally London had the greatest concentration of them. The London of Dr. Johnson and his biographer Boswell reached out to the world of trade to become the clear world leader. Countless merchants, bankers, insurance agents and retailers, all clearly middle class types according to the contemporary understanding of class structure, enriched themselves and multiplied.

Below the middle classes were the masses who often experienced cruelty, wretchedness and misery, whether they lived in urban or rural environments. In one way, eighteenth century England was similar to third world countries in Latin America or Africa today, where the very rich and the very poor live in close proximity, but are worlds apart in lifestyles. Debtors' prisons, infanticide, widespread crime, an epidemic of alcoholism from cheap gin, widespread venereal disease and chronic malnutrition and all of the illnesses it fostered blighted the lives of the British poor in the eighteenth century.

Misery had always been the lot of the submerged masses

of the world, but what made the eighteenth century different was an incipient humanitarian movement that expressed a new social criticism and made efforts to provide remedies. Many hospitals and various charitable organizations originated in this century.

In religion the most notable development was Methodism. It was an offshoot of the established Anglican Church which Methodism's founder, John Wesley, thought too cold, distant, unemotional and impersonal for the needs of ordinary people. Wesley began to preach outdoors to the poor, sending a warm message the stressed personal salvation. While he did not aim to break away from the Anglicans, a breach did result, and Protestantism gained a new denomination.

BRITAIN IN AN AGE OF REVOLUTION

The Era of the French Revolution, Napoleon and Romanticism: 1789-1815

Since the American Revolution is a very special topic that bears directly on Anglo-American relations, it appears in the chapter on politics, under Sensitive Areas.

The years of the French Revolution and Napoleon were exciting and heroic, as great monuments all over Britain commemorating events in this era attest. For a time, Britain faced invasion alone, a situation that was repeated again in 1940, when the Nazis threatened the island. France, Britain's historic enemy, was inspired by a new, revolutionary ideology in this era which was eventually thrust forward on Europe by the bayonets of Napoleon's armies. Britain's class structure, property and religion, in short, its way of life, were all menaced by it.

Two great heroes emerged to stop the French. Horatio Nelson, one-armed, one-eyed and just over five feet tall, stopped the French at Trafalgar in 1805 and died at the battle's close. The Duke of Wellington stopped Napoleon's forces at Waterloo in 1815.

Times of tension and change often bring on a burst of cultural creativity. In this era the great romantic poets and writers flourished: Keats, Shelley, Wordsworth, Coleridge and Sir Walter Scott. Romanticism stressed the overwhelming forces of nature, religion and emotion. It celebrated the glories of the Middle Ages and distant, exotic cultures. Romanticism left its impress upon architecture, art and music in addition to literature, as classical restraints and proportions were broken through by surges of feeling.

The Era of the Industrial Revolution

The world's very first Industrial Revolution came about in Britain, and all the subsequent industrializations which have swept the world have copied its pioneering techniques and methods to some extent. This makes the first Industrial Revolution an extremely important topic in world history as well as British history.

Britain's unprecedented leap into industrial production came from a spontaneous breakthrough. Several factors came to bear simultaneously, and the concentrated economic energies released by them brought about what were regarded as amazing innovations. Britain had been favored by an extensive preexisting worldwide network of capitalistic trade, the existence of ample resources in coal and iron ore, a spirit of inventiveness, a skilled workforce in carpentry and metal trades, an elaborate financial infrastructure, good transportation facilities, an accumulation of capital to invest and last, but hardly least, a government friendly to enterprise.

Both population and food resources rose in the eighteenth century and contributed to industrialization. Abundant labor, paid low wages, enabled some entrepreneurs to experiment with machinery in order to meet massive demands for certain goods. Skilled workmen fashioned them and eventually became the world's first modern engineers. Contraptions that worked in one industry inspired other entrepreneurs to fashion them in other industries. Cotton textile production became the pioneering industry for many techniques of mass production, replacing hand spinning first and then hand weaving with mechanical production. The most effective new machines relied on the steam engine, which was developed in Britain somewhat earlier in order to pump water out of the coal mines. These mines would never have been dug so deeply had there not been a shortage of wood for burning that had developed over many centuries because of an expanding population and an expanding number of acres given over to agriculture.

These few interacting factors give some indication of the complexity of this spontaneous explosion of innovation in Britain that occurred between 1770 and 1840. During these years, the cumulative effect of so much new production enabled the economy to take off and become airborne, an economist's phrase signifying permanent, self-sustaining growth and development. Changes came fast, were massive and irreversible, and often dramatic, as when the world's first railway grid was constructed. Much labor changed from hand to machine; more and more consumer goods were produced at generally decreasing cost per item; fortunes were made quickly, often by mass producing ordinary household goods.

All of this had a profound effect on the structure of British society. Industrialization led to rapid urban growth, the creation of an urban factory proletariat, and a broadening of the middle class strata. Rapidly growing towns and cities needed more lawyers, doctors, teachers, bankers and managers. Eventually, Britain had the world's first society with an urban majority and the first society where the middle classes were so numerous and influential that they came to play a dominant role in important aspects of politics and culture. This was a key feature underlying the society of the nineteenth century.

For the generations undergoing these changes for the first time, the costs in human suffering were staggering, as any reader of Dickens or Marx knows. But once industrial production was well under way, widespread prosperity and comfort were the results. Britain was the first place in the world where the majority of the population came to enjoy what we have come to call the affluent society. Since then, most of Europe, America and Japan have followed Britain's model to become modern, industrially developed areas.

Britain still celebrates its special role in the Industrial Revolution. Museums display old machinery as treasures; huge railway museums have been erected; and places in the industrial northern part of England have been set aside to commemorate the origin of the factory system.

There is also a psychological inheritance from this era. For roughly a century, Britain led the whole world in technology. British goods were produced faster, better and with a higher technology than anywhere else in the world. By contrast, American industrial development in the nineteenth century was still in its early stages in the North, at least until the great stimulation of the American Civil War. In general America was regarded as a vast agrarian area noted for producing raw materials and foodstuffs. American food, cotton and timber were regularly exchanged for the wonderful cheap goods from Britain's booming factories.

In the present age, when Japan, Germany and the United States all lead Britain in most, but not all, advances in what are called "high tech" and also "post-industrial" developments, Britons remember their long span of superiority in the nineteenth century with remorse mixed with pride. Perhaps Americans may feel the same way in the next century. If so, the British may have given us an example of how to accept economic change with dignity.

THE EARLY NINETEENTH CENTURY

The Regency Era

The Regency era began in 1811, the year that the future King George IV came to rule in place of George III, who had become mentally incapacitated, or, as he was described, "sad and mad." The term "Regency" comes from the title "Prince Regent" that the future George IV took until his father died in 1820. In style and outlook, the Regency era can be said to have continued until 1830, when George IV himself died.

In art and architecture, Regency style was powerful. Buildings tended to be massive and neoclassical, meaning that regularity, order and discipline were imposed. Greek and Roman motifs, such as bas-reliefs and Doric columns, prevailed. Many imposing structures in London date from this era, especially along Regent's Street, also in the Trafalgar Square area and near Regent's Park.

The Era of the Reform Bill, 1830-1837

For Europe in general, the early nineteenth century became a revolutionary era, as impulses from the French Revolution toward equality convulsed Europe in waves of upheavals which occurred in 1820, 1830 and 1848. Britain was singularly unique in avoiding revolution. Why was this so? How were the British able to transform their ancient, political institutions to accommodate the needs and demands of that ever growing urban and industrial sector without violence? The answer is complex. A key factor was that the deeply rooted and somewhat representative Parliamentary system was able to operate through a set of compromises in a gradual manner to reform itself. This satisfied enough people for the time being, thereby thwarting the drive for violent revolutionary change.

The British Parliament actually passed a number of Reform Bills in the nineteenth century, in 1832, 1867 and 1884, each of which broadened the franchise to give more males the opportunity to vote. Yet the first of them was the greatest because it showed the way to the gradual achievement of democracy in the future. What the Reform Bill of 1832 did was to give the vote to those in the middle class who did not have it already; create new electoral districts for the new industrial towns; and eliminate small and corrupt electoral districts called "rotten" or "pocket" boroughs from which the landed classes had traditionally drawn much of their political power. The bill did not go far enough for the British working classes, who had agitated for democracy. Even so, the Reform Bill of 1832 marked the successful inclusion of the new industrial society into the political process. It also indicated that evolution, not revolution was to be the mode of change for the British constitution.

By contrast, on the continent of Europe middle class types were apt to be ardent revolutionaries, at least up until 1848. In Britain, the middle classes came to believe that their limited, constitutional monarchy was moving towards greater and greater liberalism. Hence they supported the system against any would-be revolutionaries. So the Reform Bill of 1832 guaranteed that 1688 would be the last year of revolution in British history.

THE MAGNIFICENT VICTORIAN ERA, 1837-1901

The Spirit of the Times

The long and happy reign of Queen Victoria, from 1837 to 1901, has left its undeniable stamp on the Britain of today, materially and psychologically. It was the time of Britain's apogee, or high point, when Britain led the world in science, technology, politics, power and influence. Never before and never since the Victorian era has Britain been so important to the whole world. Britain's role in the nineteenth century can be compared to that of the United States in much of the twentieth century, except that Britain did not face an international rivalry as America had with the former Soviet Union for several decades. *Pax Britannica*, or the peace of Britain, was imposed and usually welcomed on all of the oceans of the globe and many of the lands that they touched. Britain's large and unchallenged navy served as the nation's instrument of supremacy.

Progress was the all-important word for the Victorian era. Victorians believed in it fervently and saw themselves as the most progressive people in the world. Invention following invention and science advancing on a broad front, seeking to control nature for the apparent benefit of humankind, all confirmed this conviction. Victorians could measure progress in many tangible ways: production was dramatically up in coal, iron, textiles, shipbuilding and in a wide range of consumer goods. Railroads transformed the landscape, and everywhere efficiency and speed became British hallmarks.

Victorians could also measure progress in politics. Old bastions of special hereditary privilege and discrimination were removed one by one in a free Parliament where reason, discussion, debate and voting determined decisions. Happily, literacy and education advanced simultaneously with the increase in the number of voters.

Victorians were free from many worries of the twentieth century. Pollution was not as serious a concern as it is today; science did not appear as a dangerous genie, and modern totalitarianism, either fascism or communism, had not yet emerged. It was a time when Britain had the most envied and admired state in the world, and upper and middle class British people had the most envied and admired lifestyles. The whole world seemed to want to develop along British lines.

The Victorians exhibited unique psychological characteristics that directly influenced American great-grandparents or grandparents and may continue to influence us all indirectly today. Ideally, Victorians were strict in their morality, pious and committed to the work ethic. Thrift, discipline, honesty, temperance, hard work, earnestness, obedience to God's Word and cleanliness were all solid Victorian virtues. Sex was only to be expressed in marriage and repressed otherwise. While contemporary life for many Americans has departed far from Victorian virtues, it can be argued that the Victorian inheritance is still at work, contributing to frequent guilt feelings, the penchant for cleanliness and the phenomenon of the workaholic.

Some Victorian Achievements

Famous Victorians are legion. This was the world of Charles Dickens, Rudyard Kipling, Thomas Hardy, Keats, Shelley, Sir Walter Scott and Alfred, Lord Tennyson, to name but a few in literature. It was the world of Gilbert and Sullivan on stage. In politics, two great figures dominated the later years of Victoria's reign: Benjamin Disraeli, a novelist of Jewish background, and William Gladstone, the embodiment of open-minded liberalism and pious leadership. In foreign policy, the irascible and dashing Lord Palmerston celebrated and fostered British interests throughout the world.

The British Empire grew in all directions in Victoria's heyday, stretching over "palm and pine." "The sun never sets on the British Empire" was a true cliché in Victorian times. It meant that the sun had to be shining on some part of it somewhere on the globe during all 24 hours. Eventually, one-fourth of the earth's surface and one-fourth of its people came to live under the Union Jack, a remarkable achievement for such a small island. Beyond this, there was an informal empire of trade, wherein British goods, ships, money and services operated profitably almost everywhere.

The Victorians were great builders, inventors, developers and producers since they were the first people to harness machines to their economy. Goods of all sorts from the Victorian era can be found everywhere in Britain today as well as in many other parts of the world. Much of the clutter of furniture and mass produced items that they created goes under the rubric of "antiques" today. In addition, there are acres of Victorian buildings, great Victorian bridges and aqueducts, and an essentially Victorian railway system to testify to the energy of these people.

Victorian Arts

Victorians did not produce great visual arts by anyone's standards, but today younger people tend to appreciate the "charm" of Victoriana more than many older people who had to grow up with it in their parents' or grandparents' homes. Furniture was overstuffed. There was too much clutter, too many fancy little details to catch dust and too much sentimental coyness. Nonfunctional decoration ran riot. Perhaps the most familiar example of it known to Americans is in the form of "gingerbread" decoration on buildings. But all kinds of structures, even structures as functional as railway bridges, received typical Victorian superfluous decoration.

It can be argued that the Victorians really had no true style of their own. Instead, their arts were what is called eclectic, meaning that they borrowed from here and there. The Middle Ages provided their favorite source of inspiration, and reveals the Victorians' essential romanticism. The medieval castles, cathedrals and knights in shining armor were highly romantic in the eyes of Victorians, and they celebrated the medieval world in their literature and arts.

Victorian appreciation for the medieval era has often served to confuse contemporary American visitors. Many seemingly medieval creations turn out to be just over a hundred years old. So the visitor may go into a grim, brooding, turreted hulk of an Anglican church building in suburban London and think it to be the very essence of a medieval edifice until he or she discovers that the Victorians erected it in the 1880s.

A Victorian Paradox: Romanticism and Materialism

One of several Victorian paradoxes is that they were so

romantic in the midst of their intense material preoccupations. They were obsessed with making things and making money. The Victorian world of business was a hard world of facts, figures and balances. Yet at the same time their paintings celebrate sentimental dogs and children, medieval heroes and imaginative fairies. Their authors, many of whom are still avidly read today, used comparable themes. The romanticism of Victorian art and literature seems to have functioned as an escape, or a change of pace, from the harsh, practical and prosaic realities Victorians faced.

Many contemporary Americans still curl up with Sherlock Homes or a Dickens novel and transport themselves back to foggy nights in Victorian London. The fogs are no longer there, thanks to strict air ordinances, but American visitors can find rich deposits of Victoriana everywhere. When we come to think of it, contemporary Americans might have something of their own version of the Victorian paradox: the nation that builds so many interstate highways, computers, cars and aircraft carriers is also responsible for the world of Walt Disney and countless imaginary sagas of travel in space.

THE EDWARDIAN ERA, 1901-1914

Although the king for whom the era is named died in 1910, the Edwardian era is generally regarded as the period from 1901, the year Victoria died, to 1914, the year that World War I broke out. Impressions of the quality of life in Britain during this time span vary considerably. The wealthy and well born usually remember the Edwardian era as a glorious sunset on a world where the empire, capitalism, social life and British influence throughout the world were all splendid. On the other hand, the humbly born might recall the huge disparities between rich and poor, the long hours of work for low pay, the slums and the lack of all but the beginnings of welfare provisions. All might agree that it was a brassier, more strident age than the Victorian era. The popular song of the times, "Ta-Ra-Ra-Boom-De-Ay" captures something of its essence.

The Edwardian era began at the conclusion of a nasty little imperialistic war in South Africa, the Boer War, which the British won at considerable cost. The war revealed the widespread unpopularity of the British in Europe. The Afrikaners, the Dutch descendants who had lived in South Africa since the seventeenth century, had the sympathy of the Europeans because they appeared to be the underdogs who were heroically resisting aggressive British imperialism led by Cecil Rhodes, a diamond and gold magnate. The British made matters worse by terminating Afrikaner guerrilla resistance by means of a scorched earth policy and the use of concentration camps. British recognition of their isolation in Europe and a sense of the hostility directed against them led to attempts to engage in *ententes*, or loose alliances, with European powers thereafter. This, in turn, helped bring Britain into World War I.

No matter how high the status of British capitalism in the Edwardian era, the period also marked the beginnings of the modern welfare state. Old age pensions and national health insurance were inaugurated during this time. While Britain lagged behind Germany and other European states in this, Britain was far ahead of the United States in making such provisions.

Socialist theory also made headway in the Edwardian period. One very characteristically British kind of socialism to emerge was that of the Fabian Socialists, who included George Bernard Shaw and Sidney and Beatrice Webb in their membership. The former was the greatest English playwright since Shakespeare, and the latter were a team of social scientists whose works are still important. The Fabian Socialists were intellectuals who sought to convince influential people of the rational and just nature of socialism brought about by democratic means. At first they worked to prove the practical nature of socialism at the local level by taking over such things as gas and water services, which gave them the nickname of "gas and water socialists."

About the same time, masses of unskilled workers enrolled in large, militant unions. These unions and several groups of socialists came together in the Edwardian era to form the Labour Party. While it was only a minor party in the period before World War I, its influence and the influence of the Fabians who inspired it would come to the fore later, particularly after World War II.

In all of this, Marxists played a very small role. In general British Labour politics did not accept the Marxist view of the inevitability of class warfare.

Another movement of the Edwardian era that was to have a major bearing upon the future was the Suffragette Movement aimed at gaining votes for women. The right to vote was viewed as the key to ending male dominance and discrimination in many fields. The more militant suffragettes deliberately broke the law by doing highly visible and outrageous deeds, such as setting fires and destroying private property, in order to draw attention to their movement and its unmet goals.

Yet another source of tension was Ireland, where Home Rule was destined to occur. Home Rule was what was called "dominion status" elsewhere, an arrangement that would allow the Irish to run their own domestic affairs by themselves the way Canadians or Australians did by the late nineteenth century. A major act had passed Parliament in 1911 which severely limited the power of the House of Lords. Henceforth this ancient body could only delay legislation for a limited period of time and could not block it the way the United States Senate can block legislation passed in the House of Representatives. For Ireland, this meant that self-rule would be passed. Nevertheless, in Ulster militant Protestants declared that they would fight rather than be dominated by a Roman Catholic majority ruling from Dublin. Then as now, the British were faced with a seemingly insoluble Irish situation. Civil war loomed in Ireland. It was only prevented by the outbreak of World War I. Soon Protestant and Catholic energies poured into the war effort. So did the efforts of militant union members and militant suffragettes. World War I absorbed whole currents of tension and potential violence stemming from Edwardian times into its own great vortex of conflict.

For the rich who were not interested in women's rights, socialism, poverty or Ireland, the Edwardian era could be delightful. The monarch, Edward VII, personified so much of the tastes of the rich in his time. Queen Victoria's eldest son had always been something of a hedonist and Francophile, at odds with his strict and Germanophile upbringing. Edward and much of upper class society indulged themselves in wine, women, song and gargantuan, spectacular consumption in a style that parallels the Gilded Age in America, when American millionaires reveled in garish materialism.

THE ERA OF WORLD WAR I

Contrasts With American Experience in the War

The joys of Edwardian Britain came to an abrupt end with the outbreak of World War I in the summer of 1914. Britain and Europe were never the same again, as a deep trauma settled upon civilization. Americans seldom appreciate the depth of the impact of this tragic war upon Europe. Perhaps this is because American participation was far less than the scale of British participation. The United States entered the war late, in 1917, and most of the American forces never got to the front lines. While America suffered 50,000 deaths, Britain endured 750,000 deaths. In fact, Britain lost twice as many of its people in World War I than in World War II, a longer contest, which took place from 1939 to 1945 and featured heavy bombing of civilian areas from the air.

In addition to all of those who were killed or wounded, as well as all of those who lost husbands, fathers, sons, brothers, sweethearts and potential mates, the war brought psychological ramifications that are extremely strong and complex, and included such phenomena as individuals' alienation from Western civilization and disgust with what was formerly held in high esteem, such as nationalism and patriotism. On the Continent, the war led to a new, sick kind of violent nationalism called fascism. Perhaps one way for Americans to come to grips with the impact of World War I on Europe is to contemplate the varied reactions and difficulties expressed by returning Vietnam veterans. Interesting parallels can be drawn between them and the returning survivors of World War I.

Causes of the War

In Britain, one frequently hears the name "the First German War" for World War I, and, indeed, many still choose to blame the war upon the Kaiser and German militarism. Yet historians have shown that all of the major participants and some of the minor ones were to a degree guilty and to a degree innocent regarding the outbreak of the war. Seen this way, the ruthless sacrifice of the blood and treasure of European civilization from 1914 to 1918 was simply a tragedy on a monumental scale.

When the Archduke Franz Ferdinand of Austria-Hungary was assassinated by a Serbian nationalist or terrorist in the streets of Sarajevo in Bosnia Herzegovina, a diplomatic crisis ensued. To British people, the situation seemed to be just one more crisis in a long series of Balkan troubles. They were as used to them as contemporary Americans are used to Middle Eastern crises. Unfortunately, this Balkan crisis got out of hand and escalated into a small war between Austria and Serbia. This in turn escalated into a world war as the major powers lined up to support their allies.

Britain had an *entente,* or loose alliance, with France and Russia, two nations with whom Britain was able to smooth out imperial rivalries around the globe. Anglo-German amity was ruined by the headlong effort of the Germans to build a great fleet. The German fleet was a direct threat to Britain because the island nation had to import a substantial amount of its food and raw materials from over the oceans. What decided those British who wavered about going to war in 1914 was the German invasion of Belgium, a country whose neutrality was guaranteed by Britain and several other powers. Belgium had a particular strategic significance because it was the logical place from which to launch an invasion of the British Isles.

British Participation in World War I

British participation in World War I was similar to that of France and Germany in that it involved costly, dreadful campaigns that seemed to go nowhere. The Western Front consisted of a maze of trenches stretching from Switzerland's border across France and across Belgium to the sea. The British fought on the western portion of the Western Front, in the flat portion of Belgium for the most part. The most tragic losses "in Flanders' fields" came along the Somme River. Up to 60,000 British casualties were recorded there in a single day of fighting. Year after year, armies on both sides hurled masses of foot soldiers against barbed wire, machine guns and artillery without breaking the stalemate. Defensive weapons had the advantages. The offensive weapons of the next war, the plane and the tank, were in early and experimental stages during World War I.

Gallipoli was an ill-fated campaign that sought to open a way through to Russia via the Turkish-controlled Dardanelles. Winston Churchill, at the Admiralty, was wrongfully blamed for the costly British failure at Gallipoli.

At sea, there was only one major battle on the surface, Jutland, which was something of a draw. The much feared German fleet stayed in port thereafter. The submarine fleet kept active, however, and mounted a very serious threat to the British war effort by threatening to cut off vital supplies. Convoy tactics eventually turned the tide.

The great British leader of World War I was David Lloyd George, a Welshman who rose from obscurity to become a leading Liberal minister in the Edwardian era. When the war began, he displayed his ability by meeting the challenge of a munitions shortage. Then he engineered the overthrow of the Prime Minister so he could take the office himself. David Lloyd George was a dynamo of a leader, and a magnificent orator. In many ways he played the role in World War I that Winston Churchill would come to play in World War II. He certainly had the will to victory. Yet he had a negative side as well, and suffered accusations of corruption, craftiness and guile and resentment at his domineering style and political ruthlessness. He remains a controversial figure and is best loved to this day in Wales.

Britain did win a few clear victories on the periphery of the main effort of the war. Palestine was wrested away from the Ottoman Turks, and the Germans were defeated in Africa. But the war was finally decided by attrition on the Western Front. Russia dropped out of the war the same year that the United States came into it, putting the whole focus on fighting in France and Belgium. After coming close to winning in a last surge in 1918, the Germans called for an armistice and the war was over. Shortly thereafter the Germans had the harsh Peace of Versailles imposed upon them, a peace that became one of the causes of the next world war.

THE INTERWAR ERA, 1918-1939

After the ferocious destruction of World War I, there was an attempt to get back to normal times. But the Edwardian assurance and opulence did not return for Britain in general. The image of the interwar era is that of being gray, grim and depressed. Unemployment was high throughout nearly the whole era, with some families living on the "dole," or welfare payments, decade after decade. Britain's most notable but aged industries, shipbuilding, coal mining, steel and textiles, were hardest hit by chronic depression. Meanwhile, light industries, such as the manufacture of electrical appliances, developed considerably, providing British consumers with all sorts of new products including tinned (canned) goods and various synthetics. On the one hand, there was considerable material progress for many consumers, but on the other there was bare subsistence for the unemployed millions. Hunger marches, strikes and lockouts signified the rancor of the times. An attempted general strike, aimed at bringing out all the workers in key industries, thereby paralyzing the state, failed ingloriously in 1926. One way to appreciate the more dismal aspects of the period is to read George Orwell's *The Road to Wigan Pier*.

The dominant political figure of the period was Stanley Baldwin, a solid, stolid, businesslike and rather dull Conservative. Sometimes the twenties and early thirties are called the "Age of Baldwin." Labour mustered its first and rather brief governments in the interwar period as well. These were governments formed in coalition. Labour never had a clear-cut majority until after World War II. The first Labour Prime Minister was J. Ramsay McDonald, who is still disparaged by many Labourites today for having sold out to the establishment once he got into power. His defenders point to his need to compromise in the particular circumstances he had to face.

The interwar period marked the beginning of the dissolution of the British Empire. Ireland was the first to go. A small but violent rebellion had occurred in 1916. The British overreacted to this "Easter Rebellion" by executing many of its leaders, who became martyrs and thereby made the movement for Irish independence much stronger. Home Rule would no longer be enough for the increasing number of those who sympathized with the rebellion. An independent republic was now desired by Irishmen who were willing to fight a civil war to get it. Britain sought to repress them, sending in the hated "Black and Tans," a voluntary and mercenary paramilitary force. Eventually, Lloyd George signed a peace treaty in 1923 which granted sovereignty to all of Ireland except six of the counties in the province of Ulster. The ongoing tragedy of Ireland today can be traced back to this settlement. (See the section on Ireland under Sensitive Areas in the chapter on politics.)

Royalty became the focus of romantic drama in the 1930s. George V died in 1936, after having reigned since 1910 as a dutiful and appreciated monarch. His eldest son succeeded him as Edward VIII. He only lasted for less than a year because of a dramatic set of events that captured headlines in 1936. The king fell hopelessly in love with Wallis Simpson, a twice-divorced American. Given the standards of the time, she and their liaison and his plan to marry her were all scandalous. As a consequence, the king of England abdicated his throne so that he could, in his words, marry the woman he loved. Thereafter he became an exile, with the title Duke of Windsor, and Mrs. Simpson became his duchess. Together they dedicated their lives to frivolous social life in various elegant places abroad. Edward's brother came to reign in his place from 1936 to 1952 as George VI. He was the father of Queen Elizabeth II.

Britain had its equivalent of America's roaring twenties, complete with flappers and jazz, but the dominant notes of life in interwar Britain for all too many people were those of depression. Talking with old-timers about the interwar period is an interesting pastime. Their bitter memories of hard times after World War I serve to explain why the electorate was so willing to go along with the seemingly radical proposals offered by Labour candidates in the election right at the close of World War II.

Appeasement, 1934-1939

The shadow of World War I haunted the foreign policy of the interwar period. Britain and other nations made numerous attempts to achieve disarmament or at least prevent arms races. All of these efforts proved futile when the rise of fascist dictatorships in Germany, Italy and several lesser countries produced regimes committed to extreme nationalism and militarism. Only armed force could block their chronic, endemic aggression, but before this lesson had been learned, Britain endured grave humiliations in foreign policy.

Prime Minister Neville Chamberlain, always impeccably

dressed, conveyed the impression of being a most reasonable and sensible British gentleman. Since the Treaty of Versailles was more discredited with each passing year, Chamberlain believed that he could appease or soothe the grievances of Nazi Germany by making sensible, reasonable and timely concessions. This policy of appeasement reached its greatest intensity when the national sovereignty of Czechoslovakia was virtually surrendered to the bullying of Hitler at Munich in 1938.

When Nazi aggression continued, Chamberlain and his followers realized how futile appeasement had been as a policy in dealing with fascist dictators. Thereafter, the British government began to rearm as fast as possible, while British diplomacy changed course and confronted aggression by announcing agreements to go to war if other states were violated. Britain therefore went to war in September, 1939, when Germany attacked Poland.

The word "appeasement" passed into English usage as a pejorative term, meaning giving in to aggression. Its original meaning had been much more neutral, betokening attempts at conciliation. One outstanding British politician had warned against appeasement all along. Events proved Winston Churchill right, and when the war against Germany floundered in 1939 and 1940, Churchill became Prime Minister for the first time in his life, at age 64, when most men either look forward to retirement or are retired.

THE ERA OF WORLD WAR II, 1939-1945

Contrasts Between American and British Recollections of World War II

After the Japanese attack on Pearl Harbor, December 7, 1941, brought the United States into the war, a flood of men and material from North America poured into Britain and then leapt across the English Channel in the D-Day invasion of June 1944. Both in Europe and the Pacific, the United States was clearly the dominant partner in the Anglo-American alliance. Therefore it is natural that British memories of World War II should stress those aspects in which Britain fought alone, rather than when Britain functioned as a junior partner in the Anglo-American alliance. These aspects include Dunkirk, the Battle of Britain, the North African campaign before the Americans invaded that theater, and the campaign in Burma. What follows is a brief account of these particular topics rather than an overview of the whole war.

Interesting cultural exchanges took place between the millions of Americans who came to Britain in uniform and their British hosts. Many marriages resulted, and there was also some generally friendly rivalry. Americans always complained about the beer being warm. One Briton, exasperated at the deluge of Americans, made the famous declaration that American troops were "overpaid, oversexed and over here." The famous American riposte was that Britons were "underpaid, undersexed and under Eisenhower."

Dunkirk

In 1940 the British army on the continent of Europe was rescued by a vast and varied flotilla of ships hastily thrown together and sent to the port of Dunkirk in France. When France was overwhelmed, the British army had retreated to this port, where their prospects were bleak until all of those ships, great and small, arrived from England to take them home. They sailed home defeated and without their heavy equipment, but Dunkirk was nevertheless seen as a great and heroic event. British soldiers had faced adversity and overwhelming forces with stoic heroism, and were rescued by their fellow countrymen who themselves risked their lives at sea to save them. The heroic retreat has always been a favorite motif of British patriotism, so Dunkirk was admirable.

The Battle of Britain, June to September 1940

Britain stood alone against the ferocious and undefeated might of Nazi Germany during the summer of 1940. While France was defeated, Russia continued to collaborate with Germany at this stage of the war. All the other states of Europe were either conquered, frightened neutrals or German allies. The United States was not to enter the war until the end of 1941, so Britain and her far-flung dominions were the only forces in the whole world fighting against Nazi tyranny in the summer of 1940.

The Battle of Britain was unique in that it was fought almost entirely in the air. The German *Luftwaffe*, or air force, had the task of destroying the RAF, the Royal Air Force, in preparation for an invasion, whose planning name was Operation Sea Lion. In order to carry out this risky invasion, the Germans had to have dominance in the air, which would compensate for their naval inferiority. Eliminating the RAF was therefore absolutely essential as the first step of the planned invasion.

The task proved impossible for the Nazis. Armed with beautiful, powerful and swift Spitfires, as well as with the solid, reliable, slower and less glamorous Hurricanes, the RAF shot down many more German planes than they themselves lost. Except for one desperate period, replacements of men and planes came along just quickly enough to keep the RAF on top.

During the Battle of Britain, Prime Minister Winston Churchill produced some of his finest war oratory as he led his nation in steely defiance of the Nazis. He called that dangerous time in history the British people's "finest hour," and long has it been celebrated as such. He also paid tribute to that small group of RAF pilots who held the Nazis at bay when he declared that never before in history was "so much owed by so many to so few." Pride in these times and in what Churchill's oratory celebrated is very special for British people, and American visitors are well advised to show appropriate respect for the Battle of Britain.

One good way to strike up a conversation with elderly British people is to ask them what they remember of the Battle of Britain. Nearly everyone has at least one good tale to tell.

The Blitz

Once they were forced to give up their plans to invade England, the Nazis sought to pound the country into submission or a negotiated peace by launching massive bombing raids on London. The *Luftwaffe* came over nearly every night, sending down a rain of death and destruction. London, however, was simply too huge to demolish from the air, given the limited payloads of German bombers. Londoners themselves adjusted to the "Blitz" surprisingly well, inspiring the world with their good humor. Hundreds of thousands of them took to sleeping in the underground (subway) stations, where a vibrant community life often developed. Londoners who survived the Blitz usually have a fund of great stories to tell.

North Africa and Burma

Both the North African and Burmese campaigns receive fuller attention in Britain than in the United States. General Montgomery was the hero in North Africa, noted for stopping General Rommel at El Alamein in 1942, in a rather bleak stretch of the war where the British needed some victories. Lord Mountbatten was the supreme commander in Southeast Asia whose primary role was to protect India from the Japanese and eventually to clear them out of Burma. Lord Mounbatten's distinguished career was ended a few years ago by a terrorist's bomb in Ireland.

Montgomery is controversial. Many claim that he was a brilliant general and others maintain that he was phlegmatic and would never give battle unless he had overwhelming superiority in men and equipment. Montgomery's failing attempt to force a crossing of the Rhine in the Netherlands in 1944 is often held against him.

Many critics, most of them Americans, have alleged that the materials lavished on Montgomery's campaign should have been allocated to General Patton because he might have had a chance to end the war sooner, perhaps by reaching Berlin before the Russians.

Despite such controversy, Montgomery, Patton and several other noted generals pulled together under Eisenhower to bring British and American forces to the heart of what was supposed to have been Hitler's thousand-year Reich. It was a time of great men doing great deeds for great principles.

THE POSTWAR ERA, 1945 TO THE PRESENT

Many of the concerns of postwar Britain are of such an ongoing nature that they have already been taken up in the chapters on politics and economics. What follows here is a summation of the main historical developments.

The Quiet Revolution and the Age of Austerity

In between V-E Day, Victory in Europe Day in May 1945, and V-J Day, Victory over Japan Day in August, Winston Churchill and his Conservative Party were given the sack, or, as Americans say, fired, by the electorate despite his soaring world reputation as a great war leader. This dramatic and unexpected defeat did not stem from any lack of gratitude for the way Churchill had resolutely prosecuted the war. It came instead from a realization by the majority that the Labour Party had a program for social improvement while the conservatives' plans were extremely vague. Too many recalled the grim circumstances of depression, unemployment and economic dislocation that greeted the veterans returning home after World War I. The electorate wanted a program designed to avoid such hardship.

Labour planned to inaugurate the welfare state by building up the public sector of the economy and by carefully regulating the private sector. Under the calm, unassuming and rather colorless Clement Attlee as Prime Minister, changes came so fast in the period between 1945 and 1950 that it was called the "Quiet Revolution." Numerous industries were nationalized, including railroads, gas, electricity, airways, docking facilities, the mines, the iron industry and the steel industry. Extensive social services for health, housing and the less fortunate were set up or expanded.

All of this required an enormous investment. The British economy was exhausted from its wartime sacrifices but, nevertheless, a period of continued "austerity," or hard times of scarcity, was imposed on the patriotic, generally cooperative population until the new economy could be shaped. This monumental effort of self-sacrifice was substantially aided by the generous Marshall Plan grants of the United States, a fact that has not been forgotten by many Britons.

The End of Empire and the Birth of the Commonwealth

The British Empire came apart after World War II. New Zealand, Australia and Canada, where transplanted Britons comprised the dominant ethnic stock, had already attained sovereignty and self-government. South Africa was also self-governing. After World War II, almost all of the so-called black, brown and yellow colonies asserted their independence from the mother country. The largest piece of the Empire to go was India, which became independent in 1947, an event involving much bloodshed between Moslem and Hindu before the new states of India and Pakistan were established out of what had been British India.

Some violence accompanied the coming of independence elsewhere. Kenya, in East Africa, had the Mau-Mau uprising. Malaya was the scene of a vigorous spate of British counter-insurgency effort. Britain also joined France and Israel to try to regain control of the Suez Canal. America did not cooperate in the Suez crisis of 1956, and without U.S. backing, this attempt to renew British influence in the Middle East collapsed.

Despite these examples of conflict, the dismantling of the largest empire that the world had ever seen generally involved a peaceful transition to independence. The British had the good sense to realize that the days of a colonial empire were over, and that it was time to surrender power before it would be seized from them by their former subjects. So they sought an orderly retreat from empire. By contrast, the French in Indochina and Algeria did not come to this realization and disasters resulted.

Several British governments put this principle into practice with considerable style and grace. Splendid flag-lowering ceremonies, handshakes, good wishes and sentimental band concerts marked the British surrender of their Empire. They acted like benign parents sending off their adolescent children. In most places, it was a good show, well carried off. Rhodesia was a difficult case, however. White Rhodesians resisted majority rule to the extent of fighting a civil war against groups of black Rhodesians and by formally breaking ties with Britain. Finally, pressure from Britain and many other countries led the white Rhodesians to accept majority rule in the new nation of Zimbabwe. South Africa, just below Zimbabwe, opted out of formal connections with the British long before decolonialization.

Like parents of adolescents sent off into the world, the British hoped to maintain subtle ties with their offspring. The Commonwealth of Nations has been described as a body created to ameliorate the loss of an empire. It is a vague, amorphous body, a shadow of an international body in some respects, but it does promote discussions, international understanding and educational ties. It has its place in a world that needs more contacts between affluent nations and poor nations.

There is much more than the Commonwealth to stand for the British heritage in that vast portion of the globe once included in the Empire. Wherever English is spoken, at least something of British ideas of fair play, public honesty, government by law and due process survive. While critics of imperialism may rightly point out many examples of exploitation and disregard for native ways of life, British people still have good reason for looking back upon their Empire with pride. Compared to all of the great imperial peoples in history, from the Mongols and Romans to the Germans and Russians, the British were overall the mildest in their rule of subject peoples.

The loss of this empire was cushioned by the fact that the average Briton was better off economically in the postwar years than ever before in history.

Swinging Britain: Postwar Affluence Arrives in a New Elizabethan Era

Many observers expected Europe to take decades to emerge from the ashes of World War II. This was not to be the case. The Continent bounded back with an amazing vitality, producing goods, services and babies in vast and unexpected quantities. A few years later, affluence came to Europe as it had come to the United States in the 1950s. Britain was somewhat behind West Germany, France and Italy, where wartime destruction necessitated starting from scratch with fresh plants and new techniques. Many of Britain's tired old industries used the same tired, old machines and techniques left over from before the war. Nevertheless, unprecedented affluence managed to come to Britain as well by the 1960s.

Imagine what the late sixties and early seventies would have been for America without the war in Vietnam and the civil disturbances associated with it. Britain had all of the dynamic change and growth of the period without war abroad and without civil discord at home, although many people were restive and rebellious also. The Conservative Prime Minister, Harold Macmillan, coined an apt phrase which stuck: "You never had it so good!" Indeed, it was true. The welfare state had raised the level of life and expectations for the poor, and a surge of economic and cultural achievement pushed the middle classes into the new lifestyle of abundance. For a while, it seemed that things would get better and better as time went on.

All Americans know something about this era in Britain because it was the time of the Beatles, the Rolling Stones and all of those exciting and strange fashions coming out of places like Carnaby Street before Carnaby Street became another tourist attraction. Long hair, huge beards and moustaches and colorful clothes appeared everywhere. Who can forget the mini-skirt and one of its variations that appeared to be nothing more than a large belt? Everywhere it seemed that a new and youthful British culture was flowering. There was an exuberance, a sense of humor, a sense of liberation and a sense of delirious happiness that anyone who lived and enjoyed that era can never forget. Britain was, in the realm of music, color and style at least, once again the center of the world.

The 1960s became a time of permissiveness, experimentation and hedonism in Britain. Gambling became legal. Homosexual relations between consenting adults became legal by Parliamentary statute. Divorce was made easy. Censorship of the theaters was abandoned, and soon nude people appeared on the stages of London. Capital punishment was ended in 1969, and physical punishment by birching, that is, whipping with a stick, was ended in trade schools and reformatories. More mental patients were released and successful experiments with probation shortened jail sentences for criminals. All sorts of illegal drugs became available and popular, particularly among the young. To treat the scourge of heroin addiction, free shots of another drug and counseling were provided by the government.

In politics during the sixties and seventies there were no dramatic shifts to match the excitement in the cultural domain. Labour governments traded places with Conservative governments without sharp shifts in policy from either party. Various Prime Ministers, including Macmillan, Douglas-Home, Wilson, Heath and Callaghan, carried out relatively minor adjustments in a system that seemed to be working well in general.

The heady years of the swinging 60s did lead to a national hangover in the '70s, which was marked by higher unemployment and high inflation, an economic condition described aptly by the term "stagflation," which denotes recession combined with higher and higher prices. Rashes of strikes broke out, including those of public servants. Less was invested by the government in health and educational services at the very time that a higher percentage of the population became elderly and therefore put greater strains on the available social services.

One major issue to arise was whether or not Britain should join the European Community, what used to be called the European Economic Community or the Common Market. It became an extremely divisive issue within both parties and within the country in general. The Labour government joined in 1972 and held a referendum on the move in 1975. Although the referendum passed, controversy about the E.C. continues. Critics argue that an unrepresentative bureaucracy somewhere on the Continent should not be setting rules and regulations in Britain. Others cannot abide the prospect of replacing the pound by a common European currency.

Meanwhile, the Chunnel, or tunnel under the English Channel, will produce yet another link with the Continent and further diminish the age old psychological comfort that British people have derived from their separateness from Europe.

The Thatcher Era, 1979-1990

Like many imposing figures in history, Margaret Thatcher, Britain's first female Prime Minister, is highly controversial, and not only in Britain. To her admirers, she is the "Iron Lady," the very reincarnation of Winston Churchill or the first Queen Elizabeth; to her detractors, she is a harsh ruler who pandered to the well off and scorned the plight of the poor.

One matter beyond controversy is her importance. Nearly everyone concedes that she was a powerful leader whose efforts were aimed at redressing the post-war pull to the left by fostering private enterprise and the market economy. She was an outspoken critic of big government, high taxes, deficit financing, public ownership of large corporations and many specific aspects of the welfare state. She was also a patriot who was able to invoke considerable old-fashioned nationalism, particularly when she led a war against the Argentineans over their invasion of the Falkland Islands. She was always staunchly anti-communist, yet she was able to realize that in Gorbachev she found someone she could "do business with" as she put it.

Her style was confrontational: She knew where to draw the line and take a stand. She stood up to the unions, to the socialists, to her critics in the House and to the members of her own party who wanted to moderate her staunch stands. These she labeled the "wets." She was an acerbic workaholic as Prime Minister who would get up in the very early hours of the morning after just a few hours sleep and breakfast on black coffee and vitamins while she pored over government documents and reports.

Margaret Thatcher's background is an interesting indication of the evolution of the Conservative Party in recent decades. She was the daughter of a solidly middle class greengrocer from the provinces who played a minor role in local politics. She was university educated as a chemist, which was a particularly unusual field for a woman at the time. Thereafter she was drawn to law and politics. Her background led her to appreciate the virtues of hard work, discipline, thrift, honesty, and, above all, individual effort. Together these are the classic middle class virtues, and it is significant that she would champion them from within the Conservative Party. In the past Tory principles were more closely associated with the outlook of the upper classes.

At first, she was not a particularly successful Prime Minister, according to many observers. High interest rates, rising unemployment, cutbacks in social services and continued budget deficits seemed to point to the failure of her policies. Nevertheless, she persevered, allowing unemployment to rise as she applied strict monetarist pressures to the economy.

The Falkland Islands war was a turning point in her career as Prime Minister. Until then she was the most unpopular Prime Minister since modern polls were devised. Her resolute determination to fight and win was widely admired, and on the high tide of victory over the Argentineans, the Conservatives called for elections in 1983 and won handsomely, producing a large majority for the Iron Lady in the House of Commons. Thereupon the high tide of Thatcherism commenced.

The economy did turn around. It grew rapidly as unemployment stopped rising, nationalized industries were sold off, taxes were cut, and budgets were balanced. Many Britons who lived in public housing, called council housing, were encouraged to buy their homes from the government. When large, nationalized corporations were sold off, or "privatized," stocks in them were so widely sold that up to a fifth of the Queen's subjects became stockholders.

These successes led to yet another Conservative victory in 1987. Then Britain, along with the United States and other developed countries, slid into another recession. "Stagflation," inflation in a stagnant economy, and rising unemployment indicated that the freer market economy and strict monetarist policies fostered by the Prime Minister did not provide immunization from recession and hard times.

Meanwhile a large number of her fellow Conservatives came around to the view that they had enough of the confrontational leadership of the Iron Lady. They were particularly irritated by the difficulties cropping up from her negotiations over the impending closer union with Europe. To many, she had simply been in office too long and was therefore showing signs of a growing imperiousness that was increasingly intolerable to more and more party members. In the end, the party itself overthrew her, not the Labourites, not the electorate, not the majority in the House of Commons. Many of her ardent supporters throughout the country were furious at how this had been done without consulting the electorate or their representatives democratically. Nevertheless, the deed was done and Mrs. Thatcher retired to the House of Lords with a title and with an undiminished desire to speak her mind.

For a time the Tories struggled to see who would replace her. The choice finally rested on John Major, who was Mrs. Thatcher's favorite candidate. He had a similar background as a middle class Tory of humble origins with solid business experience behind him, particularly in banking. His style, however, is quite different. Major is calm and smooth, and therefore much more apt to bring about compromises and conciliation than his predecessor.

Most people did not think he would be Prime Minister for very long, because an election was called for in 1992. Since the Conservatives had won three times in a row, it was assumed that Labour would win this time, especially because voters would go to the polls in the midst of a recession. Surprisingly, the Conservatives won again, their fourth victory in a row, the first time that any party had mustered such a string of triumphs since the early nineteenth century. Once again, Labour was thrown into disarray, as a party still needing to come to terms with the vast changes in technology, society and psychology which have come about in the last decades of the 20th century.

Into the 90s

There is a great paradox about Britain as the 20th century comes to a close. Never before have so many people been so wealthy and so free. They live longer, have more toys, know more about the world and have the opportunity to study, enjoy and experience more of life than any previous generation. Yet the discontent of contemporary Britons, as well as Americans, seems to know no bounds. The film makers, novelists, poets, playwrights and painters all give testimony to the frequent manifestation of a restless, angry unhappiness. So do alarming social statistics. Violent crime and vandalism have increased dramatically, as well as the senseless mass violence of sports fans. Too many well-off people drink too much, take too many prescribed and unprescribed drugs, and become depressed or bored. That ultimate act of despair, suicide, has also reached new statistical heights.

It is almost impossible to ascribe simple causes to such grim phenomena. Socially conservative people blame permissiveness in education and child rearing; religious people blame the decline of faith; those who are philosophically inclined lament the triumph of materialism over a faith in the ever expanding realm of liberal rationalism.

Yet who knows how much of the best of British life continues? There are countless millions of British people who still cherish the ideas and the ideals that made this country one of the most civilized places on earth in which to live, and they pass this heritage on to their youngsters. Otherwise Britain would not be such a gentle, neighborly country, one in which individuality, freedom, and liberty still prevail.

Index

abbey ruins, 111 *see also* specific abbeys
Aberdeen, Scotland, 126
accommodations, 16-23
  bathroom arrangements, 18-19, 71-72
  booking (making reservations), 21-22
  breakfast, 20-21
  vocabulary of accommodation, 22-23
Air travel to Britain, 14-16
"A Levels", 187
American Revolution, 241-244, 277
Americans and America,
  characteristics of, 11, 67-73
  class and, 162-164, 245-246
  crime and violence and, 66-67, 248-249
  gun control and, 246-248
  history, British, and, 251-253
  language and, 63-64, 167-170
  and politics, 207-208, 208-217, 219-220, 227, 229-232
  and race, 244-246
  relations with Britain, 11, 240-244
  see also Texas
Anglo-American Alliance, 11, 240-242
Anglo-Saxons, 138, 252, 254-258, 260,
appeasement, 297-298
art galleries, 97
Arthur, King, 78, 255-256
Attlee, Clement, 230, 302

austerity, age of, 302
Balmoral Castle, 102, 107
Bannockburn, battle of, 134
Bath, 127
bathrooms, 18-19, 71-72
B.B.C., *see* British Broadcasting Corporation
Baldwin, Stanley, 295
battlefields, 132-134
  Bannockburn, 134
  Bosworth, 132-134, 264
  Culloden, 134
  Hastings, 133-134, 260-261
Bannockburn Heritage Center, 134
Battle of Britain, 280, 298-300
bed and breakfast, *see* accommodations
Bill of Rights, 274
Birmingham, 40, 82,140,
black (industrial) England, 81-82
blacks, in Britain, 244-246
Blenheim Palace, 120-121, 122-123
blitz, the, 300
Boleyn, Anne, 265, 266
Bolton Castle, 107
Bosworth, battlefield, 132-134, 264
breakfast, 20-21,
Brighton, 127
Bristol, 127
British,
  climate and weather, 144-147
  defined, 137-138, 246
  Empire, 286-287, 303-304, *see also* food, imperial
  geography, 137-147

Isles, 137-138
population, 142-144
topography, 144-145
characteristics of the, 58-67
British Broadcasting Corporation, 100-101, 168, 195-196
British Museum, 95
Britrail, *see* trains
bureaucrats, *see* civil servants
busses, 55-56, 90, 95
 London tour busses, 95

Caernarvon (sometimes Caernarfon) Castle, 107-108
Cambridge, 127
Cambridge University, 127, 191, 259
Canterbury, 126-127
Canterbury Cathedral, 117
Carnaby Street, 305
Castles, 82-83, 105-110, 258, 267
 short list of, 107-110
 vocabulary of, 107
Cathedrals, 110-120
 diagram, 114
 short list of, 117-120
 vocabulary for, 114-117
Celts, 138, 254, 256
Charles I, 227, 242, 268-270
Charles II, 268, 272-273
Charles, Prince of Wales, 217, 222, 224, 227
Chartwell, 123
Chatsworth, 123
Chester, 127-128
Chipping Campden, 128
churches, *see* religion
Churchill, Winston, 123, 146, 222, 243, 247, 250, 252, 120-121, 123, 274, 294, 297-298, 300, 302, 307
Church of England, *see* religion
City of London, *see* London

cities (towns with Cathedrals) *see* towns
civil servants, 232-233
civil war, English, 268-272
class and class consciousness, 61, 157-164, 226, 245-246
 Americans and, 162-164, 245-246
 language and, 64, 161
climate, 144-147
clothes, 23-24, 68-70
Commonwealth, the, 303-304 *see also* British Empire
Conservative Party, 229-230, 240, 302, 308, 309-310
Conway Castle, 108
Cornwall, 49, 79, 80, 140
Cotswold region, 79, 128, 140
Coventry Cathedral, 117
crime, 66-67, 248-249
 see also gun control
Cromwell, Oliver, 205, 268, 270-272
Culloden, battlefield of, 134
culture shock, 12-14
currency, 13-14, 52

Deal Castle, 108
depression era, 295-298
Disraeli, Benjamin, 124, 229-230, 286
Dissenters, *see* religion
drink, 36
driving in Britain, 38-52
 on the opposite side, 45-46
 parking, 44-45
 petrol (gas) prices, 52
 road signs, 49-50
 roundabouts, 46-48
 vocabulary for, 40-42
Dunkirk, 299
Dunnottar Castle, 108
Durham, 128
Durham Cathedral, 117

Easter Rising, 1916, 235, 296
East Anglia, 138
economy, the, 148-157
  capitalism, 156-157
  E.C. (European Community) 306-307
  farming, 148
  mixed economy, 150-151
  National Health Service, 152-156
  nationalization, 151
  petroleum, 149
  socialism in, 150-151, 290, 302-303
  trade unions, 231
  welfare state, 151-152, 302-303, 305
Edinburgh, 99, 128-129, 141
  Castle, 108
education, 186-195
  comprehensive schools, 190, 191
  elementary, 188
  grammar schools, 190
  junior high and high school, 189-191
  open university, 191-192
  polytechnics, 191
  public "private" schools, 187-190
  secondary modern schools, 190
  tutors and tutorials, 192
  university, 191-194
  vocabulary for, 194-195
Edward VI, 265
Edward VII, 221-222, 291
Edward VIII, 222, 296
Edwardian era, 289-291
Elizabeth I, 96, 99, 123, 165, 252, 266, 269, 307
Elizabeth II, 222, 224, 226, 296
England and the English, 138, 140
  regions of:
    black, 81-82

East Anglia, 138
  Midlands, 138, 140
  northern, 81-82, 140
  southern, 81-82
  west country, 140
Episcopal Church (in America), 199-200, 264
Established Church, *see* religion
European Community (E.C.), *see* economy

Falkland Islands War, 239-240, 249, 308
feudalism, 259, 260
firths, 142
fish and chips, 28-29
food, 20-21, 26-36,
  British, 20-21, 26-30
  Chinese, 31, 90
  "Indian," 31-33
  vocabulary for, 30, 33-36
Fountains Abbey, 117-118
French Revolution, 275, 279-280

gender, 164-166, 286, 290
gentry, 269-270, 273, 276
geography, 137-147
George III, 242-243, 274
Georgian era, 275-279
  heritage of, in architecture, 122, 127
Germany, 225, 233, 292-294
Glasgow, 66, 82, 99, 141-142
Glorious Revolution, 227, 252, 273-274
gun control, 246-248

Hampton Court Palace, 123, 265
Hanoverian dynasty, *see* Georgian era
Harlech Castle, 108-109
Harrogate, 129
Hastings, battlefield of, 133-134, 260-261

Hatfield House, 123
health care, see National Health Service
Henry II, 261-262
Henry V, 262
Henry VII, 96, 104, 133, 263-264
Henry VIII, 96, 123, 201, 252, 264-265
heroic retreats, 66
Hever Castle, 109
Highlands, see Scotland
historic preservation, 253
historic towns and cities, see towns
Holyrood Palace, 124-125, 129
Home Rule, 235, 290-291, see also Ireland and the Irish
Hotels, see accommodations
House of Commons, 95-96, 209-213, 216, 259-260, 269-270, 276
House of Lords, 95-96, 214-216, 271, 276
housing, see accommodations
Hughenden Manor, 124
Hundred Years' War, 262-263

Imperial War Museum, 97-98
  food, 31-33
Industrial Revolution, 134, 203, 275, 278, 280
interwar era (1918-1939), 295-298
Ireland and the Irish, 137, 234-239, 290-291, 295-296
  Anglo-Irish Relations, 234-239, 290-291, 295-296
  Easter Rising, 235, 296
  Home Rule, 235, 290-291
  Irish in Britain, 237-238
  Irish Republican Army, 238, 249
  see also Northern Ireland
Irish Republican Army, 238, 249
Ironbridge, Coalbrookdale complex, 134

Jacobean, 269
James I, 99, 268-269
James II, 227, 268, 273
Jews, 205-206
John, King, 227, 262

Kenilworth Castle, 109
Kennedy Memorial, 134
King's Lynn, 129
Knole House, 124

Labour Party, 228-229, 230-231, 240, 303
Lake District, 79,
Lancashire, 82, 140
language, 63-64, 166, 167-186
  American use, 63-64, 167-170
  and class, 64, 161
  see also vocabulary
Lavenham, 129
Leicester Square, 87, 89, 94
Lewes, 129
Liberal Democrats, 231-232
Liberal Party, 228, 231-232
Lincoln Cathedral, 118
Liverpool, 66, 78, 82,
Lloyd George, David, 104, 216, 294, 296
London, 66, 75, 83-98
  bus tours of, 95
  City of, 86, 91, 157, 172
  Dungeon, 98
  East End, 86-87
  museums, 90, 95, 97-98
  West End, 87-90
  map, 88
  see also buses, taxis, underground
Longleat House, 124
Lyme Regis, 78-79, 129
luggage, 23-24

Madame Tussaud's, 98
Magna Carta, 134, 227, 252

maps, of Britain, 74
  of the West End of London, 88
Mary I (Bloody Mary), 264-266, 266
Mary, Queen of Scots, 266, 269
Marx, Karl, 78, 90
medieval Britain, 256-263
Methodists, *see* religion
Midlands, 138, 140
monarchy, 212, 216-228,
monasteries, dissolution of, 111,
money, *see currency*
Montgomery, Field Marshall Bernard, 301
Motels, *see accommodations*
Museum of London, 98
Museum of Mankind, 97
Museum of Natural History, 97
museums, *see also* by name, London museums

National Gallery, 89, 97
National Health Service, 152-156
national parks, 80
National Portrait Gallery, 89, 97
Natural History Museum, 97
Nelson, Horatio, 78, 135, 280
Newby Hall and Gardens, 124
Nonconformists, *see* religion
Normans, 133-134, 256, 260-261
  conquest of England, 133-134, 260-261
  style, 261
northern England, 81-82, 140
Northern Ireland, 235-237
Norwich, 129

"O Levels", 187
Oxbridge, 191
Oxford, 130, 259
Oxford University, 130, 191

Palace of the Holyrood House, *see* Holyrood Palace

Parliament, and the Parliamentary system, 208-216, 223-224, 233, 259-260, 276-277, 283-284
  history of, 259-260, 276-277, 283-284
  reform bills for, 283-284
  see also House of Commons, House of Lords
parking, 44-45
pedestrians, 37-38
Pembroke Castle, 109
Penshurse Place, 125
Philip, Prince Consort, 224-225
Piccadilly Circus, 89-90, 91, 95
political parties, 228-232
  Conservative Party, 229-230, 240, 302, 308, 309-310
  Labour Party, 228-231, 240, 302-303
  Liberal Democrats, 231-232
  Liberal Party, 228, 231-232
  Tories, 228, 230
  in the American Revolution, 243-244
  two party system, 228-229
  Whigs, 228
politics and government, 207-250
  American system compared, 208-217, 219-220, 227, 229-232
  cabinet, *see* Parliamentary system
  House of Commons, 95-96, 209-213, 216, 259-260, 269-270, 276
  House of Lords, 95-96, 214-216, 271, 276
  loyal opposition, 212-213
  monarchy, 212, 216-228
  Parliament and the Parliamentary system, 208-216, 223-224, 233, 259-260, 276-277, 283-284

prime minister, 209, 211-213,
219, 223-224, 276-277
see also political parties
population, of Britain, 142-144
post-war era (1945 to the present), 301-310
prehistoric Britain, 254
Prime Minister, 209, 211-213,
219, 223-224, 276-277
public safety, 66-67, 248-249
public schools, 187-190, see also education
puritanism, 202-204, 268-269, 271-272

quiet revolution, 230, 302-303
queues, 59-60

race, racisim and racial disturbances, 244-246
radio, 195-196
railroads, see trains
Reformation, 110-111, 112-113, 199, 200-201, 264-265
Regency era, 283
religion, 197-206
  catholic and Protestant labels, 199
  Church of England, 199-201, 223, 264, 271
  Church of Ireland, 199
  Church of Scotland, 201-202
  Church of Wales, 199
  Congregatonalists, 202-204
  Dissenters and Nonconformists, 202-204, 271-272
  Episcopal Church (in America), 199-200, 264
  established church, see Church of England
  high and low church, 200
  Jews, 205-206
  Methodists, 202-204, 279
  Presbyterians, 201-204

puritans, 202-204, 268-269, 271-272
Roman Catholics, 204-205, 235-238, 273
vocabulary for, 197-199
restaurants see food
Restoration, (1660), 272-273
Richard I, 262
Richard III, 132-133, 262, 264
Rievaulx Abbey, 118
Roman Catholics, 204-205, 235-238, 273
romanticism, 259, 280-283, 288
Rome, ancient, 254-256, 278
roundabouts, 46-48
Royal Pavilion, 125
royalty, see monarchy
Runnymeade, 134
Rye, 130

St. Andrews, 130
St. David's Cathedral, 118
St. Giles Cathedral, 119, 129, 201-202
St. Paul's Cathedral, 119
Salisbury Cathedral, 112, 118
scenery, in general, 79-80, 99, 140
Science Museum, 97
Scotland and the Scots, 98-103, 138, 141-142
  battlefields in, 134
  castles in, see individual castles
  cathderals in, see individual cathedrals
  Church of Scotland, 201-202
  cities and towns of, 99, see also individual cities and towns
  currency, 101
  geography of, 99, 100, 141-142
  highlands, 99, 102-103, 141-142
  museums of, 128
  nationalism, 98-102
  Scotch, a misnomer, 101, 174
  speech, 98-99, 100-101

Index

stereotypes, 99-102
seafood, 27-29
  fish and chips, 28-29
sexes, relations of the, 164-166, 286, 290
  see also gender, suffragettes
Shakespeare, 78, 263-264
shopping, 56-58, 86-87
smoking, 62-63
socialism, 150-151, 290, 302-303
  see also economy, National Health Service, welfare state
socialized medicine, *see* National Health Service
southern England, 81-82
stately homes, 120-125
  short list of, 122-125
Stonehenge, 78
Stratford-upon-Avon, 78
Sterling, 130-131
Sterling Castle, 109
Stratford-upon-Avon, 131
Stonehenge, 135, 254
Stuart era, 268-275
subways, pedestrian, 37-38
  see underground for what Americans call subways
Suez Crisis, 240
Suffragettes, 164, 290

Tate Gallery, 97
taxis, 16, 42, 93
telephone, use of, 25
  vocabulary for, 26
television, 195-196
Texas and Texans, 73, 140, 143, 147, 169
Thatcher, Margaret, 150-151, 166, 230, 238, 307-310
theater 93-95, 306
Tintern Abbey, 119
toilets, 18-19
topography, 144-145
Tories, *see* political parties

Tower of London, 89, 96
towns and villages, historic 125-132
  short list, 126-132
trade unions, 231,
Trafalgar Square, 89-90
trains, 53-55
transportation, 14-16, 55-56, 90, 38-55, 90-93
  air travel to Britain, 14-16
  buses, 55-56, 90
  driving, 38-52
  taxis, London, 16
  trains, 53-55
  underground, 90-93
  tube, *see* underground
Tudor age, 263-268
  architecture, 266-267

underground (the tube), 90-93
unions, *see* trade unions
universities, 191-194
  see also Cambridge, Oxford

Value Added Tax, 16, 57
Victoria, Queen, 102, 220-221, 224-225
Victoria and Albert Museum, 97
Victorian era, 241-242, 285-288
Victory (Nelson's flagship), 78, 135
Vikings, 132, 257
villages and towns, 125-132
  short list, 126-132
violence, 66-67, 248-249
vocabulary, British, for accommodations, 22-23
  for cars, *see* for driving
  for castles, 107
  for cathedrals, 114-117
  class and, 161
  cultural terms, 171-175
  for driving, 40-42
  educational terms, 194-195

ethnic and national designations, 138
for food and drink, 33-36
potentially embarrassing terms, 181-186
practical terms, 175-181
for religion, 197-199
for the telephone, 26

Wales and the Welsh 76, 79, 82, 103-105, 138, 140-141
abbeys and cathedrals in, *see* individual abbeys and cathedrals
castles in, 106-107 *see also* individual castles by name
cities and towns in, *see* individual cities and towns
geography of, 140-141
nationalism of, 103-104
Prince of, 217, 222, 224, 227
War of 1812, 241-243
Wars of the Roses, 263
Warwick, 131
Warwick Castle, 109-110
weather, 144-147

welfare state, 151-152, 302-303, 305
Wells Cathedral, 119
Welsh, *see* Wales
west country, 140
Westminster Abbey, 96-97
William the Conqueror, 260-261
Winchester, 131
Winchester Cathedral, 119-120
Windsor Castle, 110
Wolsey, Cardinal, 123, 265
World War I, 289-294
World War II, 91, 292, 297-302
    Appeasement, 297-298
    Battle of Britain, 280, 298-300
    Blitz, 300
    Dunkirk, 299
    North Africa, 301
Wren, Christopher, 119, 225

York, 131-132, 205
York Minster, 120, 132
Yorkshire, 78, 79, 80, 140

Zebra crossings, 37

COMPANION GUIDES FROM HIPPOCRENE BOOKS

COMPANION GUIDE TO AUSTRALIA, *by Graeme and Tamsin Newman*
With helpful tips on preparing for your trip, this cheerful guide outlines the distinctive characters and main attractions of cities, describes picturesque countryside, and links the things tourists like to do with the history and character of the Australian people.
_____294 pages • b/w photos and 4 maps • 0-87052-034-2 • $16.95

COMPANION GUIDE TO SOUTHERN INDIA, *by Jack Adler*
Travel with Jack Adler, writer for the *L.A. Times*, as he takes you on a journey that encompasses the exotic spices and intricate fabric of life on this continent.
_____301 pages • b/w photos • 0-87052-030-X • $14.95

COMPANION GUIDE TO MEXICO, *by Michael Burke*
Along with the usual tips on sites, this guide outlines contemporary realities of Mexican society, religion and politics.
_____320 pages • b/w photos • 0-7818-0039-0 • $14.95

COMPANION GUIDE TO POLAND (Revised), *by Jill Stephenson and Alfred Bloch*
"This quaint and refreshing guide is an appealing amalgam of practical information, historical curiosities, and romantic forays into Polish culture."—*Library Journal*
_____179 pages • b/w photos, maps • 0-7818-0077-3 • $14.95

COMPANION GUIDE TO PORTUGAL, *by T.J. Kubiak*
Learn about the land, the people, their heritage and much more with this guide to the unexpected bounty of Portugal.
_____260 pages • maps • 0-87052-739-8 • $14.95

COMPANION GUIDE TO ROMANIA, *by Lydle Brinkle*
Written by a specialist in Eastern European geography, this modern guide offers comprehensive historical, topographical, and cultural overviews.
_____220 pages • 0-87052-634-0 • $14.95

COMPANION GUIDE TO SAUDI ARABIA, *by Gene Lindsey*
Gene Lindsey, an American who has spent much of the last decade in Saudi Arabia, traces the history of the region, religion, development, harsh environment, foreign policy, laws, language, education, technology, and underlying it all, its mindset.
_____368 pages • maps • 0-7818-0023-4 • $11.95

(Prices subject to change.)

TO PURCHASE HIPPOCRENE BOOKS contact your local bookstore, or write to: HIPPOCRENE BOOKS, 171 Madison Avenue, New York, NY 10016. Please enclose check or money order, adding $4.00 shipping (UPS) for the first book and .50 for each additional book.

HIPPOCRENE INSIDER'S GUIDES

Hippocrene Insider's Guides provide you with tips on traveling to not-too-familiar lands. You'll be guided to the most interesting sights, learn about culture and be assured of an eventful stay when you visit with the Insider's Guide.

INSIDER'S GUIDE TO THE DOMINICAN REPUBLIC, by Jack Tucker and Ursula Eberhard
212 pages • b/w photos, maps • 0-7818-0075-7 • $14.95

INSIDER'S GUIDE TO HUNGARY, by Nicholas Parsons
366 pages • b/w photos, 20 maps • 0-87052-976-5 • $16.95

INSIDER'S GUIDE TO JAVA AND BALI, by Jerry LeBlanc
222 pages • b/w photos, maps • 0-7818-0037-4 • $14.95

INSIDER'S GUIDE TO ROME, by Frances D'Emilio
376 pages • b/w photos, map • 0-7818-0036-6 • $14.95

INSIDER'S GUIDE TO NEPAL, by Prakash Raj
136 pages • illustrated, maps • 0-87052-026-1 • $9.95

INSIDER'S GUIDE TO POLAND, 2nd revised edition, by Alexander Jordan
233 pages • 0-87052-880-7 • $9.95

INSIDER'S GUIDE TO TAHITI, by Vicki Poggioli
142 pages • 0-87052-794-0 • $9.95

(Prices subject to change.)

TO PURCHASE HIPPOCRENE BOOKS contact your local bookstore, or write to: HIPPOCRENE BOOKS, 171 Madison Avenue, New York, NY 10016. Please enclose check or money order, adding $4.00 shipping (UPS) for the first book and .50 for each additional book.